Health Policy Reform in America

Innovations from the States

SECOND EDITION

Health Policy Reform in America
Innovations from the States

Howard M. Leichter
EDITOR

M.E. Sharpe
Armonk, New York
London, England

Copyright © 1997 by M. E. Sharpe, Inc.

All rights reserved. No part of this book may be reproduced in any form
without written permission from the publisher, M. E. Sharpe, Inc.,
80 Business Park Drive, Armonk, New York 10504.

First edition published 1992 by M. E. Sharpe, Inc.
This second edition is entirely new. Chapter 4 previously appeared in
the fall 1996 issue of the *Journal of Health Politics, Policy and Law.*

Library of Congress Cataloging-in-Publication Data

Health care policy reform in America: innovations from the states/
edited by Howard M. Leichter.—2nd ed.
p.   cm.
Includes bibliographical references and index.
ISBN 1-56324-899-9 (c: alk. paper).
ISBN 1-56324-900-6 (p: alk. paper)
1. Medical policy—United States. 2. Health care reform—United States.
3. Medical policy—United States—States.
4. Health care reform—United States—States.
I. Leichter, Howard M.
RA395.A3H42564   1997
362.1′0973—dc20
96-43276
CIP

Printed in the United States of America

The paper used in this publication meets the minimum requirements of the
American National Standard for Information Sciences—
Permanence of Paper for Printed Library Materials,
ANSI Z 39.48-1984.

BM (c)   10   9   8   7   6   5   4   3   2   1
BM (p)   10   9   8   7   6   5   4   3   2   1

To Elisabeth, Laurel, and Alexandra,
the three most important people in my world

Contents

About the Editor and Contributors

Howard M. Leichter, Ph.D., is chairperson and professor of political science, Linfield College, McMinnville, Oregon. He is also a clinical professor of public health and preventive medicine, Oregon Health Sciences University, and a member of the board of editors of the *Journal of Health Politics, Policy and Law.*

Raymond G. Davis, Ph.D., is associate professor and chair, Department of Health Services Administration, University of Kansas. He has served on a number of health-related boards and groups for the state of Kansas.

Robert M. Fielder, J.D., is a doctoral student and research assistant in the Policy Sciences Graduate Program at the University of Maryland Baltimore County. From 1990 to 1994 he practiced law for a Michigan firm representing hospitals and other health care organizations on legal and regulatory issues.

Daniel M. Fox, Ph.D., is president of the Milbank Memorial Fund. His most recent book is *Power and Illness: The Failure and Future of American Health Policy* (Berkeley: University of California Press, 1995).

Barbara E. Langner, R.N., Ph.D., is associate professor and associate dean, School of Nursing, University of Kansas. She is a health policy consultant to the Kansas Department of Social and Rehabilitation Services, and a member of the Kansas Insurance Department Health Care Advisory Board. She served as the executive director of the Kansas Commission on the Future of Health Care, Inc.

Deane Neubauer, Ph.D., is professor of political science at the University of Hawaii, Manoa. For the past ten years his work has concentrated on health care policy and health care reform, areas in which he has published extensively. In 1992 he was facilitator of Hawaii's Governor's Blue Ribbon Committee on Health Care Costs.

Thomas R. Oliver, Ph.D., is assistant professor in the Policy Sciences Graduate Program at the University of Maryland Baltimore County. He was a postdoctoral fellow in the Pew Health Policy Program at the University of California, San Francisco, and currently holds an Investigator Award in Health Policy Research from the Robert Wood Johnson Foundation for a study entitled "Public Entrepreneurship and Health Policy Innovation."

Michael S. Sparer, Ph.D., is an assistant professor in the Division of Health Policy and Management in the School of Public Health at Columbia University. He spent seven years as litigator for the New York City Law Department, specializing in intergovernmental social welfare litigation. He is the author of *Medicaid and the Limits of State Health Reform* (Philadelphia: Temple University Press, 1996).

Jean I. Thorne, M.A., is currently the federal policy coordinator for Oregon Governor John Kitzhaber. For the past eight years she served as the state's Medicaid director. In that capacity, she oversaw the planning and implementation of that state's Medicaid reform under the Oregon Health Plan.

List of Tables and Figures

Tables

Figures

Preface

In the Preface to the first edition of this book, published just before the 1992 presidential election, I wrote that the 1990s might prove to be one of those rare decades in political astronomy in which the constellations of public and elite opinion will be in perfect alignment. It seemed, at that time, that both the public and the nation's political leaders were in agreement that the nation's health care system was in a state of crisis and that some fundamental change was needed to rein in costs and expand access to 37.4 million Americans (in 1992) who had no health insurance. The election of Bill Clinton, who had made health care reform a central feature of his presidential campaign, appeared to secure a prominent role for health reform in the nation's political firmament.

In the intervening five years Americans have witnessed the defeat of the Clinton Health Security Bill ("health care that can never be taken away"), the continuing and crippling climb, albeit somewhat more slowly, of health care costs (between 1990 and 1996 national health expenditures increased from $697.5 billion or 12.1 percent of the gross domestic product to $1 trillion or 14 percent of GDP), and an increase from 36 million uninsured people in 1992 to 42 million in 1996. It is politically noteworthy that one-third of the uninsured live in families with incomes that are more than $30,000, double the federal poverty level for a family of four.

In a sense, then, little has changed in terms of the problems that catapulted health care to the top of the nation's public policy agenda in the early 1990s. What has changed is that the focus—and hope—of reforming the American health care system has shifted back to where it was prior to the abortive national effort, namely the states (and the private sector). Reviewing the Clinton record on the eve of the 1996 presidential campaign, two *New York Times* reporters assessed the impact of Clinton's health reform failure and concluded: "Some three years later, 40 million Americans are without health insurance. And the Administration's principal legacy in health-care policy has been to get out of the way while states and big corporations swiftly remake the system."[1]

Not only has the locus of health care reform policy switched but the political realities of reform have also changed. Simply stated, the task of fixing the health care system is a good deal more formidable than it was in the late 1980s and early 1990s when the states first put health care reform on the policy agenda. As a number of the selections in this book demonstrate, the failure of the Clinton plan, and all the political fallout attending that event, poisoned the well of reform by exacerbating the already high level of disillusionment many Americans feel about the capacity of government to solve the country's problems. This, in turn, has made state policy makers more timid about embarking on changing the health care system and opponents of reform more bold in their resistance to change.

Despite these obstacles, doing nothing is not an option. States, for example, are staggering under the burden of paying for Medicaid, the state and federal program that provides health care for over 35 million children, low-income adults and elderly persons, as well as blind and disabled persons. In addition, hospitals, doctors, and other health care providers are shifting uncompensated care costs onto private insurers and individuals, and tens of millions of Americans are either postponing getting necessary medical care or not getting it at all because they do not have health care insurance. As a result, what the states have done already and will do in the next several years is even more important to academics who study health care policy and citizens whose lives are affected by those policies than it was when the first edition of this book was published five years ago. The story of health care policy in America is now, for the most part, the story of state policy and politics.

Much of what I have learned about state health care politics and policy in recent years has been facilitated by the generosity of Daniel M. Fox and the Milbank Memorial Fund. This fine institution has provided me the opportunity to study firsthand the process and content of health care reform in Oregon, Minnesota, and Vermont. In addition to all that I have learned about health care policy in these states, I have also come to appreciate and admire the extraordinary dedication, diligence, and skill of state lawmakers and administrators who have tried to spread the safety net of health insurance to more of their citizens. Although these state officials are far too numerous to name, I wish to acknowledge my gratitude to them. Finally, I dedicate this book to Elisabeth, Laurel, and Alexandra, three very special women.

Note

1. Michael Wines and Robert Pear, "President Finds Benefits in Defeat on Health Care," *New York Times,* July 30, 1996, A1.

Health Policy Reform in America

Innovations from the States

1

Health Care Reform in America: Back to the Laboratories

Howard M. Leichter

> *For the first time in this century leaders of both political parties have joined together around the principle of providing universal, comprehensive health care. It is a magic moment, and we must seize it.*
> President Clinton, speech before a joint session of Congress, September 22, 1993

> *I have no doubts that a bill will become law.*
> John Dingell, House Commerce Committee chairman, October 1993

> *The President has . . . set the [health policy] agenda. And only the most dedicated critics of his proposal are questioning the assumption that some kind of proposal will be enacted this year.*
> Jack W. Germond and Jules Witcover, *National Journal*, February 19, 1994

Missing the "Magic Moment"

It seemed to most media mavens, political operatives, and health policy cognoscenti that at long last the federal government was poised to enact significant national health care reform in 1994. Since Harris Wofford's upset victory in the 1991 Pennsylvania special U.S. Senate election, the conventional wisdom in Washington had been that health care reform was an issue whose time had come. Bill Clinton's election and the trajectory of public opinion in the run-up to his 1993 health care reform address to Congress seemed to validate this impression. In May 1993, for example, 90 percent of those Americans surveyed believed that there was a crisis in the nation's health care system.[1] Thus, anyone reading the entrails of American national politics in the fall of 1993 could be forgiven if they concluded that reforming one of the nation's largest industries—11 million workers, providing services valued at nearly $1 trillion and one-seventh of the entire economy—was no longer a matter of "if," but "how." Yet almost one year to the day after his speech to Congress, in which he asked its members to join him in writing "a new chapter to the American story," Bill Clinton's plan for fixing the nation's health care system lay in ruins, unable to garner enough support even to be brought to the floor for a vote in either chamber.

The story of what went wrong in 1994—or what went right depending on one's political perspective—is the thing of which legends are made and scholarly works written. And, indeed, there are already nearly as many separate explanations for the failure of reform as there are commentators.[2] The suspects in the political demise of national reform include biased, inaccurate, or inept newspaper and media coverage; the enormous structural and bureaucratic complexity of the plan itself; an extraordinarily expensive, and some would charge misleading and malevolent, media and lobbying campaign by the insurance industry; a failure of policy organization, salesmanship, statesmanship, and timing by the Clintons; the intrinsic organizational fragmentation and current intense partisanship of Congress; and a strong antistatist disposition in American politics that permeates virtually every debate over expanding the role of government, particularly the federal government.[3] All of these factors conspired to fuel the fears of an initially sympathetic but increasingly anxious and skeptical general public about the content and implications of national health care reform. By the time the Clinton plan was finally declared dead in September 1994, after nearly sixteen months of unrelenting political pressure and media attention, there was an almost audible sigh of relief that the plan had been put out of its misery.

But while the debate over national reform left its participants exhausted and the public confused, it also left intact the problems reform was intended to address. First, 42 million Americans in 1996 were without health insurance and, in fact, in the four years since the debate began an additional one million Americans, *per year,* have lost employer-based health insurance. Between 1988 and 1994 the percentage of nonelderly Americans receiving employer-based health insurance declined from 67 percent to 61 percent, while the number of uninsured rose from 32.7 million people to 39.3 million. Second, health care costs are continuing to climb, relentlessly and at a rate faster than overall inflation. In fact, health care cost inflation has exceeded overall inflation rates in thirty-one of the thirty-five years from 1960 to 1994.

In effect, the failure of national health reform changed nothing with regard to the problems of health care in America. What has changed is that the focus, and hope, of reforming the American health care system has shifted back to where it was prior to the abortive national effort, namely the states. What also has changed is that the task of fixing the health care system is a good deal more formidable than it was in the late 1980s and early 1990s when the states first put health care reform on the policy agenda.

The purpose of this chapter is to examine the nature of this task, the political context in which health policy reform takes place, and the conditions that have fostered increased state policy innovation and reform in general, and those that relate specifically to the health field. The story that will unfold is one of fundamental political and ideological reorientation toward the roles and responsibilities of the national and state governments in health care reform, unprecedented demands on the health care system, and a fundamental reorientation in the way both medical professionals and the general public have come to think about the problem of illness. Political, philosophical, epidemiological, and lifestyle changes have been joined to relocate the locus of health policymaking in this country to the state capitals. All of this is not to suggest that the federal government has meekly abandoned the field to the states. The chapters in this book tell a story of continued active federal involvement—some would say obstructionism—in the health policy arena. Yet that involvement, following on the heels of the federal failure to reform health care, will continue to take the form of piecemeal responses to chronic health policy problems rather than attempts at fundamental policy change. Either as models upon which federal policy is crafted, or as innovative providers and regulators of first instance, the states will play a major role in the shaping of health policy into the next century.

The Laboratories of Democracy

There was a time, not all that long ago, when the states were routinely maligned, derided, and denigrated by politicians and academicians as politically corrupt, administratively inept, or both. As two students of state politics observed in the mid-1970s, "the sorry fact is that most state and local governments—with some notable exceptions—are poorly structured and poorly staffed to carry out new and innovative tasks. They have a hard time even meeting their routine commitments."[4] Indeed another scholar predicted "the extinction of states and localities as meaningful political entities. Rather than remain viable political units, they have become extensions of a national society."[5] Yet by the late 1980s the states were reemerging, "reformed, reinvigorated, [and] resourceful."[6] Pundits, policymakers, and political scientists found "a burst of innovation at the state level."[7] The perception that domestic political power is gravitating toward, and policy creativity emerging from, the states is acknowledged, and even endorsed, by many within the Washington Beltway. "The fact is that there are few champions in Washington, outside the interest groups, of the notion that policy should flow toward and not away from Washington," according to one knowledgeable observer.[8] Suddenly national political leaders, including President Clinton, former senator Robert Dole, and House Speaker Newt Gingrich, were competing to lavish praise on the states and urging greater federal modesty.

Why, then, after nearly sixty years of subservience to the national government in most areas of domestic policy, have the states reemerged as vital actors in conducting the nation's business? In this regard I will emphasize two major points. The first relates to the shift in national politics to the right that began during the 1970s and continues today. Among other things, this shift has continued a centuries-old debate about the balance of power in our federal system between the national and the state governments. Conservatives have long argued that state governments are politically and administratively better situated than the national government to gauge popular sentiment, and to resist the temptations of prolific spending and social nannyism. This conservative affection for "leaving it up to the states" was articulated by George Bush in his 1991 State of the Union address when, explaining a proposal to turn over $20 billion in programs to the states, he said: "It moves power and decision making closer to the people. And it reinforces a theme of this administration: appreciation and encouragement of the innovative power of 'states as laboratories.'" In 1995, Senate majority leader and presidential candidate Robert Dole began carrying a copy of the Tenth Amendment, the sacred text of advocates of a more vigorous state role—"The powers not delegated to the United States by the Constitution, nor prohibited by it to the States, are reserved to the States respectively, or to the people."

The relationship between the political swing to the right and the policy assertiveness of the states is consistent with previous national cycles of federalism. According to Richard Nathan: "Typically the national government has been the source of innovations and policy initiatives in liberal (prospending and expansive) periods of our history; the states (not all states, but many of them) have been the centers of activism and innovation in conservative (retrenchment and contractive) periods."[9] Thus, as the "conservative" 1980s and 1990s replaced the "liberal" 1960s and early 1970s there has been a readjustment in the respective roles of the national and state governments.

The second explanation for the reemergence of the states as vital social policy players is that while the nation was becoming more conservative, the states were becoming more competent to handle the tasks of governing. This has meant that the states are politically and administratively better equipped than ever before to both initiate and implement social policy innovations. I will expand on each of these points below.

From Out of the Shadows: The Reemergence of the States

The states have emerged from the shadow of federal domestic policy dominance in part because that shadow has shrunk. The retreat from federal social policy hyperactivism began during the Nixon administration (1969–74) and its "new federalism," in which there was to be a rearrangement or rationalization of national and state/local responsibilities with the purpose of "strengthen[ing] the capacity of States and localities to make decisions which reflect their own priorities and needs."[10] The main tools in accomplishing this rationalization were block grants and revenue sharing, both of which were intended to give subnational governments greater autonomy and flexibility.

Whatever Nixon's intentions, the immediate results were quite different. Federal aid to states and localities increased appreciably during the Nixon–Ford years, as did categorical grants. But perhaps most significantly, says one analysis of the period, "the Nixon administration also presided over and contributed to the greatest expansion of federal regulation of state and local government in American history."[11] Nevertheless a case can be made that Nixon (and later Ford) was responsible for initiating the shift from national to state leadership in domestic policy innovation. Ironically this occurred not by design but as a by-product of the virtual federal government paralysis in the wake of Watergate, the 1973 Arab oil embargo, and the fall, under Gerald Ford, of Vietnam. One result of these events was a dramatic decline in citizen support for national institutions.[12] The national malaise and citizen disenchantment with the national government following the troubled Nixon–Ford administrations continued during the Carter years (1977–80) and was epitomized by the energy and the Iran hostage crises. By the early 1980s opinion polls were reporting significant popular disenchantment with the federal government and considerably more faith in state government. For example, Gallup found that in 1981, by a margin of 67 percent to 18 percent, the American people believed that state governments were more likely to run social programs efficiently than the federal government, while by a margin of 67 percent to 15 percent they believed the states were more understanding of their needs than the federal government.[13]

It was in the context, then, of both real and perceived national government impotence that Ronald Reagan, former governor of California, reached the White House, promising to restore America's greatness at home and abroad, and to reduce the role of the federal government in our lives. He adumbrated his view on the relative responsibilities of the federal and state governments in his first Inaugural Address by proclaiming a need "to curb the size and influence of the Federal establishment and to demand recognition of the distinction between the powers granted to the Federal Government and those reserved to the states or to the people."

Reagan officially launched his own "new federalism" in his 1982 State of the Union address when he announced his intention "to make our system of federalism work again," and "to strengthen the discretion and flexibility of State and local governments." In practical terms this would be accomplished in three ways: reduce federal aid to the states and localities, consolidate remaining specific (i.e., categorical) programs into block grants, and permanently transfer various federal programs, worth $47 billion in 1982, to the state and local governments. In terms of the latter approach, the administration proposed a transitional period during which the federal government would help state and local governments pay for these programs through a trust fund financed by federal excise taxes that would be phased out in ten years. The centerpiece of the proposal was a so-called great swap in which the federal government would assume full responsibility for Medicaid, while the states would take over the Aid to Families with Dependent Children (AFDC) and food stamp programs.

The results of the new federalism were, however, mixed. First, the great swap never took place. State officials declined the offer because they claimed that the trust fund would not cover the costs of the programs for which the states would be responsible. Second, the consolidation of scores of categorical grants into nine block grants actually involved only $7.5 billion of the total $88 billion of federal aid to states and localities.[14] Subsequent Reagan proposals for further consolidation and transfer of responsibility met with opposition and were ultimately rejected. Despite these setbacks, however, federal aid to the states and localities was reduced dramatically in the Reagan years. Federal aid as a percentage of state and local outlays declined from a high in 1978 of over 26 percent to just under 17 percent in 1988, although it climbed steadily again in both the Bush and Clinton years, reaching 23 percent by 1994.

In addition, along with the decline in the flow of money, there was a reduction in the onerous regulations and administrative oversight imposed by the federal government on the states and localities. Reagan boasted in his 1982 State of the Union address that there were twenty-three thousand fewer pages in the *Federal Register* in 1981 than there had been in the previous year. Furthermore, "the Reagan administration also eliminated or modified forty-seven of eighty federal regulations identified by the National Governors' Association as being burdensome to states."[15]

But perhaps the most lasting legacy of the Reagan (and really the Nixon and Bush) years with regard to the devolution of power to the states, and the concomitant trimming of federal power, rests in the transformation of the Supreme Court into a more conservative institution that is more solicitous of state power than any Court in sixty years. From a constitutional law perspective the critical Court decision in this regard was *United States v. Lopez,* (1995) in which five conservative Republican appointees—Chief Justice William Rehnquist (appointed as associate justice by President Nixon and elevated to chief justice under President Reagan), Reagan appointees Sandra Day O'Connor, Antonin Scalia, and Anthony Kennedy, and Bush appointee Clarence Thomas—invalidated the 1990 federal Gun-Free School Zones Act. The 5-to-4 majority ruled that Congress had exceeded the authority of the national government under the Commerce Clause. Writing for the majority, Chief Justice Rehnquist worried that, should the Court accept the government's reasoning in support of the gun law, "it is difficult to perceive any limitation on federal power, even in areas such as criminal law enforcement or education where States historically have been sovereign." Noting that earlier Courts have been expansive in their interpretation of the Commerce Clause, the chief justice made it clear where he and the majority stood on this point: "Admittedly, some of our prior cases have taken long steps down that road, giving great deference to congressional action. The broad language in these opinions has suggested the possibility of additional expansion, but we decline to proceed any further."[16]

Although the Court's personnel and perspective on federalism may change under a second Clinton administration, the current Court has made an important contribution toward Ronald Reagan's goal, announced in Executive Order 12612 (October 1987), "to restore the division of governmental responsibilities between the national government and the States that was intended by the Framers of the Constitution and to ensure that the principles of federalism established by the Framers guide Executive departments and agencies in the formulation and implementation of policies." In effect, the order required executive departments and agencies to routinely consider the implications of federal action on the states in terms of limiting state power or impinging on state jurisdiction. Among the fundamental principles that should guide executive departments in this effort were two that go to the very heart of the conservatives' philosophy of federalism: (1) "Federalism is rooted in the knowledge that our political liberties are best assured by limiting the size and scope of the national government"; (2) "In most areas of governmental concern, the States uniquely possess the constitutional authority, the resources, and the competence to discern the sentiments of the people and to govern accordingly."[17]

Other forces were at work propelling the redirection of domestic policy responsibility in the American system. Foremost among these were the mammoth budget deficits that emerged during the Reagan years and continued to influence policy in the Bush and Clinton administrations. In fact, these deficits may have had as much to do with the current devolutionary inclination in American politics and policy as any ideological concern, executive order, or legislative initiative.[18] Ronald Reagan inherited a federal deficit of $78.9 billion in 1981 and passed on to his successor a deficit almost twice that sum ($155.2 billion), who in turn bequeathed to his successor a deficit of $290.4 billion. Although the Clinton administration has reduced the federal deficit substantially—down to a predicted $116.8 billion in 1996—the problem continues to be a driving force in defining federal-state relations and the distribution of power between the two levels of government.[19]

Bill Clinton may not be as ideologically committed to devolution as his Republican predecessors, but twelve years as governor of Arkansas, the conservative mood of the nation and Republican control of Congress, along with the continuing federal deficit, make him mindful of the limitations of the national government and the new assertiveness and competence of the states.[20] Recalling his own years as governor, Clinton noted at a gathering of the Advisory Commission on Intergovernmental Relations (ACIR) in December 1993, "I haven't forgotten what it was like to be on the other [i.e., state] end of this [federal] relationship," and pledged to work with the ACIR to better define the nature of that relationship.[21] In sum, ideological, political, and practical forces have created a more sympathetic environment for the states in Washington and throughout the country.

The States Advance

In addition to forces at work in Washington, circumstances in the states helped inspire and facilitate a rejuvenation of state policy activity.[22] At first blush state governments may appear structurally and politically ill equipped to manage complex policy problems such as health care reform, particularly when compared to their national counterpart. States often face a number of what Giandomenico Majone calls "objective constraints" limiting their capacity to perform highly complex and technical policy tasks.[23] Such constraints may include balanced-budget requirements (all states but Vermont have such a requirement), inadequate technical support services, and relatively brief legislative sessions. For example, thirty-eight states have either constitutional or practical limitations (e.g., state law limits the number of days legislators may collect per diem) on the number of days legislatures may meet, with nearly half having annual sessions of no longer than 90 days, compared with about 150 days for the U.S. Congress. Seven states, in addition, meet only biennially. Furthermore, state legislatures, with an average size of 150 members, are a good deal smaller than Congress and generally draw from a shallower pool of expertise than their larger national counterpart. Institutional expertise is also apparently compromised by a higher turnover rate in state legislatures than in Congress. Average annual turnover in state legislatures is about 25 percent, compared with less than 5 percent (until recently) for the U.S. Congress. This apparent impediment will become institutionalized now that over twenty states have adopted state legislative term limits.

In addition, state governments, especially in the South, have long had a reputation as obstructionist and recalcitrant troops in the war on the various social evils identified by liberals. In the 1960s James Sundquist dubbed this the "Alabama syndrome" and illustrates it as follows: "In the drafting of the Economic Opportunity Act, an 'Alabama syndrome' developed. Any suggestion within the poverty task force that the states be given a role in the administration of the act was met with the question, 'Do you want to give that kind of power to [Alabama governor] George Wallace?'"[24]

The perception of the states as political yahoos, administratively inept and ethically wanting, is now for the most part misguided. In the last several years almost all the states have revised or rewritten their constitutions. In some instances these changes were imposed by the national government, as in the case of U.S. Supreme Court reapportionment decisions and national civil rights legislation, while in others, such as education and tax reform, political change grew out of problems and pressures from within the states themselves.

These reforms have been facilitated, or prompted, by the modernization of state governments, and particularly state legislatures. It is, of course, difficult to generalize about fifty state legislatures. Some, like New York, Wisconsin, and California, meet in annual sessions, include large numbers of professional legislators (77 percent of Pennsylvania state legislators, 64 percent in Wisconsin, and 37 percent in California identified themselves as full-time legislators in 1993), have large, sophisticated technical and staff support systems, and embody political cultures that support progressive policy innovation. Others exhibit few, if any, of these characteristics. Yet some general trends are apparent. The majority of state legislatures (forty-three) now have annual sessions, strengthened committee systems, recorded roll-call votes, open meeting laws, larger and more professional staffs, and computerized data analysis capability.[25] In addition, in order to improve the efficiency and effectiveness of the legislative process, many states now place limits on the number of bills that can be introduced in a session and set deadlines for their introduction.[26] Similarly, the power of many chief executives has been strengthened through either constitutional revision or statute, so that governors today are more likely to be able to succeed themselves, serve four-year rather than two-year terms, have larger professional staffs, and wield broader appointive and budgetary powers than their recent predecessors. In addition, as a measure of the recent increase in both the activity and capacity of state executive branches of government, state bureaucracies have grown substantially. Between 1980 and 1993 while the number of full-time federal employees increased only from 2.9 million to 3.0 million, the number of state employees increased from 3.7 million to 4.6 million.[27]

State courts, too, have emerged as important actors in many critical policy areas, including civil rights and environmental protection. Specifically with regard to the rights of individuals, one former chief judge of the Court of Appeals of New York State noted, "We are now experiencing a renaissance with respect to state constitutional rights. As the U.S. Supreme Court retreats from the field, or holds the line on individual rights, state courts and litigants seeking solutions to new problems are turning with greater frequency to the state constitutions, which for many years lay dormant in the shadow of the federal Bill of Rights."[28]

Whatever the scope, focus, or impulse of these reforms, the results have been the same. "The cumulative effects of these independent reforms have been stronger, more capable governmental institutions and a desire on the part of state government officials to expand the scope of their responsibility even further," concludes a recent survey on the states.[29] In fact, there are many in state government today who believe that in some areas of domestic policy the states are now more knowledgeable, competent, and innovative than their national counterparts. At the 1994 National Governors Association annual conference, Governor Arne Carlson of Minnesota expressed his frustration at the failure of Congress to move forward on health care reform: "We know more about [health] than Congress does. Minnesota already has its plan."[30]

In addition to structural changes, there have been a number of important behavioral changes involving state government and politics. The last three decades have witnessed dramatic changes in the composition of state legislatures that are likely to increase the effectiveness and vitality of state government. In recent years, for example, improved salaries and benefits have resulted in lower turnover rates (although, again, this will be affected by term limits), and more members, about 15 percent in 1993, who consider themselves full-time legislators (up from 2.7 percent in 1976 and 11.5 percent in 1986). But most important, state lawmakers are beginning to look more like the people they represent, thereby enhancing their credibility, legitimacy, and responsiveness. In 1995, for example, 20.6 percent of all state legislators were women, up from 8 percent in 1975 and 14.8 percent in 1985. In fact, in some states, women comprise one-third or more of the state legislators.[31] By way of comparison, only 12.6 percent of the members of the 104th Congress (1995–96) were women. In addition, black state legislators have increased from 5.4 percent of the total in 1988 to 7.1 percent in 1995, while Hispanic legislators have increased from 1.6 percent to 2.4 percent of all state legislators.[32]

The increased role of women in state politics is particularly relevant to health care reform. First, public opinion surveys during the national debate over health care reform found that women were more likely than men (16 percent versus 11 percent) to believe that health care was "the most important problem" facing the country.[33] This generally more sympathetic attitude toward health care, and other social issues, is apparently reflected in the behavior of female elected officials. According to one scholar, "Women [state officials] are more active on women's rights legislation and more likely to target public policies that affect children and families," while another adds that women "are perceived by voters as being more compassionate."[34] Indeed, there are already indications that women have made a difference in such health-related state policies as mandating that health insurance companies cover breast cancer screening and midwife services. Finally, it should be noted that some of the states that have adopted ambitious health care reform legislation are also among those with the highest percentages of female legislators (e.g., Washington, 39.5 percent; Colorado, 31 percent, Vermont, 30 percent; Oregon, 28.9 percent, and Maryland, 28.7 percent).

Limits to State Reform Activity

In sum, for reasons that were both internal and external to their own political environments, the structure and processes of state politics have changed significantly in the past two decades. All this is not to suggest, however, that the states can or will necessarily fill the void left by the national government or fulfill the promise expected of them by some observers. Indeed, there is an entire academic cottage industry devoted to the question of state competence and capacity, especially in the field of health care reform. (See Daniel M. Fox's chapter in this volume on this very question.) Foremost among the problems facing reform-minded states are the fiscal constraints that periodically and seemingly inevitably visit themselves on state governments, and the statutory restrictions imposed by the federal government on the states. One particular recurring nightmare for state policymakers who wish to pursue state health care reform is the 1974 federal Employee Retirement Income Security Act (ERISA). Initially intended to protect the pensions of retired workers from fraud and mismanagement, ERISA has been interpreted by the courts to prohibit states from regulating the health benefits of self-insured companies. Since about 65 percent of all companies, and about one-half of all companies with more than fifty employees, choose to self-insure, ERISA has severely crimped the capacity of states to adopt comprehensive reforms. States may seek a federal waiver or exemption from ERISA, but thus far only one state, Hawaii in 1983, has received such a waiver. Several of the authors in this volume will return to the state health policy albatross of ERISA.

In addition, there are many, even among state officials, who while conceding the point about the modernization of state government, still question the competence and appropriateness of state leadership. This question is particularly and persistently asked in relation to health care reform. A common rendition of the question during the recent national debate was "Can states take the lead in health care reform?"[35] and a common response was that health care reform is "simply too big a problem to be handled at the state level."[36]

It is, of course, difficult to generalize about fifty states. "In terms of administrative capacity, the states are all over the lot," a recent *New York Times* article observes. "Some are on the level with the Federal Government. Some are innovative and exciting. But some are a long way from that kind of competence."[37] Although this point is well taken, the existential reality in this country is that over the last decade or so innovative social policy—in education, welfare, criminal justice, and most notably health care—has come from the states, not the federal government. Many scholars, including myself, would prefer a health care policy in which the federal government sets certain national standards and then allows the states flexibility to craft specific programs consistent with those standards and the diverse needs of their populations. However, the inability of the federal government to act on health care reform in any meaningful way renders the debate over whether the states or the national government should take the lead purely academic. The states have no choice but to take the lead and they are, for the most part, quite capable of this undertaking. It is, in fact, to the specific role of the states in health care policy that I now turn.

The Growing Health Policy Role of the States

Although it would be misleading to suggest that the states have shown greater inventiveness in one particular area of public concern than in others, few have stimulated as much creativity, activity, and interest as that of health policy. Faced with problems involving access, cost containment, the quality of health care, and the promotion of responsible lifestyles, virtually every state government has assumed new health policy roles and obligations. The reasons why health care reform in particular has demanded the attention of state lawmakers are readily apparent.

To begin, the states traditionally have maintained a high level of interest and activity in health policy. They are, after all, one of the largest purchasers and providers of health care services in the country, and the astronomical increase in total health care costs over the past decade—$949.4 billion in 1994 compared with $396 billion in 1984—alone would have warranted increased state concern and activity in this area. Beyond this, however, the states are the primary regulators of the health care industry. States license physicians, nurses, pharmacists, and other health professionals, regulate the insurance, nursing home, and hospital industries, set rules governing workers' compensation, and establish standards for environmental pollution. Finally, state and local governments have historically played a major public health role. In this capacity they are responsible for laws and standards governing immunizations and inoculations, school health programs (including sexuality and reproductive counseling), public sanitation, waste disposal, and protection of food and water supplies. The regulatory, administrative, and provider roles of the states have all come at a high cost— "when the expense of all areas of state involvement in health care are considered, state governments now finance approximately one-third of all public health care services being provided to Americans."[38]

Medicaid: The Monster That Ate the States

This investment would have warranted a high profile for state governments in health policy under normal circumstances. But the failure of the federal government to act, combined with the continued growth in the number of Americans without health insurance—31 million people in 1987, 34.7 million in 1990, and 39.7 million in 1994—and the escalating costs of health care have placed the problem at the forefront of state budget and social policy considerations. And at the very epicenter of these considerations is Medicaid, the program that former governor of Oregon Neil Goldschmidt called "the monster that ate the states." Medicaid has been the engine that has powered state health care reform.

Medicaid, enacted in 1965, is jointly funded by the federal and state governments—the national government, on average, pays about 60 percent of the costs—and is administered by the states within general national guidelines concerning eligibility and services. Medicaid provides access to health care for over 35 million low-income Americans, 60 percent of whom are women, and covers one of every eight adults and one-fourth of all the children in the country. The program pays for over one-third of all births and more than one-half of all nursing home care.[39]

Medicaid presents a seemingly intractable problem for state governments: the number of recipients and the costs are climbing faster than the states can afford. As indicated in Figure 1.1, the number of people covered by Medicaid has increased substantially over the years, from 14.5 million in 1970 to 35.1 million in 1994, although only recently has the rate of increase become a significant policy problem. For example, whereas between 1981 and 1989 the Medicaid population grew by only 7.3 percent (from 21.9 million to 23.5 million), between 1990 and 1994 it increased by nearly 40 percent (from 25.3 million to 35.1 million). The reasons for this growth are not hard to find. First, the recession of the late 1980s drove an increasing number of Americans into poverty, and therefore on to the Medicaid rolls. More important, however, was the expansion of Medicaid eligibility beginning in the mid-1980s and continuing through the rest of the decade. Ironically, the genesis of this expansion was an effort by the Reagan administration to rein in Medicaid costs.

When Ronald Reagan took office in 1981 he argued that the double-digit annual percentage cost increases in Medicaid (see Table 1.1) both fueled and reflected the double-digit overall inflation rate of the late 1970s and early 1980s, and were unsustainable given federal budget deficits. Reagan proposed significant reductions in federal domestic spending, including Medicaid, to reduce the deficit and rein in inflation. To help accomplish this goal, Congress approved a reduction in eligibility and benefit levels in Medicaid, most dramatically in the 1981 Omnibus Budget Reconciliation Act (OBRA), in which the Medicaid budget was cut by nearly $1 billion. As a result, the overall annual Medicaid inflation rate plummeted from 17.8 percent in 1981 to 6.8 percent in 1982—but so did the number of children and single parents, mostly women, eligible for Medicaid. By the mid-1980s

Figure 1.1 Growth in Medicaid Recipients, 1970–94 (in millions)

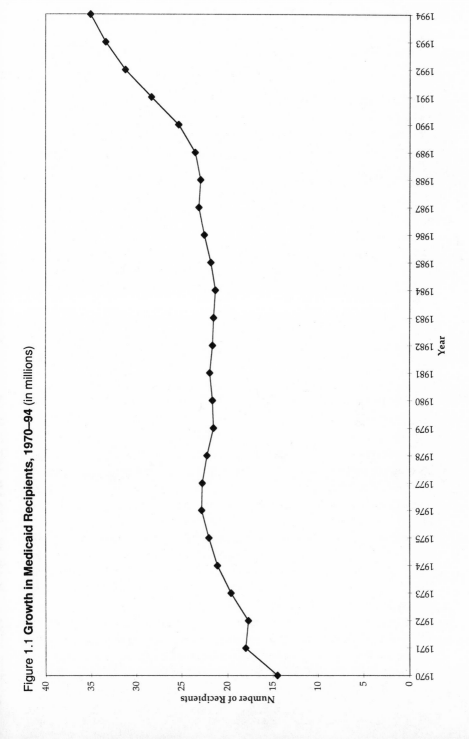

Table 1.1

Government Medicaid Spending, 1975–94

Year	Annual Percentage Increase			Total spending (in millions of dollars)
	Total	Federal	State	
1975	23.5	21.0	26.9	12,637
1976	15.9	17.7	13.5	14,644
1977	16.8	16.9	16.7	17,103
1978	10.8	10.0	11.9	18,949
1979	14.8	14.9	14.8	21,755
1980	18.5	18.6	18.4	25,781
1981	17.8	17.3	18.4	30,377
1982	6.8	2.6	12.2	32,446
1983	7.7	8.4	7.0	34,956
1984	7.7	5.8	9.8	37,569
1985	8.7	12.7	4.1	40,917
1986	9.6	10.3	8.7	44,851
1987	10.0	9.8	10.3	49,344
1988	9.7	11.0	8.0	54,116
1989	13.2	13.6	12.7	61,246
1990	18.4	18.8	17.8	72,492
1991	30.1	30.5	29.6	94,310
1992	25.2	n.a.	n.a.	118,067
1993	6.0	n.a.	n.a.	125,153
1994	9.5	n.a.	n.a.	137,600

Sources: Data from *Statistical Abstract of the United States*, various years, and Congressional Research Service, "Medicaid: An Overview" (October 1992).

the consequences of the Reagan-inspired Medicaid (and AFDC) cuts were becoming evident. "By 1983, 22 percent of all children were living in poverty—the highest rate in two decades,"[40] and Medicaid was now covering only 70 percent of the nation's poor children, compared with 90 percent in 1979.

Congress responded to the growing evidence and criticism of adverse health consequences of limiting Medicaid eligibility by increasing appropriations for the program and once again expanding eligibility and benefits. Beginning in the mid-1980s, new Medicaid rules made it easier for pregnant women and young children, and people who were making the transition from welfare to work, to qualify for the program, as well as increasing the health services available to these groups. For example, in the 1984 Deficit Reduction Act Congress detached Medicaid eligibility from cash assistance program participation, thus extending Medicaid coverage to such groups as women who were pregnant for the first time or who lived in two-parent homes in which the primary wage earner was unemployed. In 1988 Congress mandated that the states extend Medicaid coverage to all pregnant women and children in households with incomes below the federal poverty level. This mandate was expanded again in 1989 to cover all children up to age six if their family's income was less than 133 percent of the poverty level. In 1990 the federal government instructed the states to start phasing in coverage for poor families' children up to age eighteen. As noted above, the result was a steep climb in the number of Medicaid recipients.[41] In effect, Medicaid has become the last resort insurer for many Americans.

Expansion of the Medicaid population is the central, but not the sole, factor in the program's soaring costs. Policy analysts have identified three basic factors influencing the level of Medicaid costs: "changes in the number of people eligible for the program; changes in the prices of the services that Medicaid purchases on their behalf; and changes in the use of services by those eligible."[42] One example of a service-related cost increase was the Omnibus Budget Reconciliation Act of 1989, which provided for certain mandatory benefits to children on Medicaid, including dental examinations, orthodontics, services for disabled children, and (very costly) organ transplants.

Yet in recent years the main factor driving costs upward has been the expanded population. In an analysis of recent (circa 1990s) cost increases, the Urban Institute reported that two-thirds of the rise can be attributed to enrollment growth.[43] The magnitude of that growth and the essence of the problem facing state lawmakers is documented in Table 1.1. State general-fund spending on Medicaid, the largest and costliest health program run by the states, is one of the fastest growing items in every state budget. Annual increases, for state and federal governments, have been in the double digit range in fifteen of the last twenty years and during much of that time have been climbing at more than double the overall inflation rate. Medicaid now consumes 20 percent of most state general-fund budgets, compared with about 5 percent in 1967 and 11 percent in 1990. (By way of comparison, Medicaid accounted for 5.5 percent of the federal budget in 1995.) Today Medicaid is second only to elementary and secondary education in consuming state dollars, and is a major obstacle to the ability of state lawmakers to serve state needs and citizen demands in other areas, such as criminal justice, education, mass transit, and environmental protection.[44]

In response to the growth in Medicaid spending the states have adopted one or more of three strategies. First, they have eliminated optional benefits. Oregon, for example, did this in 1987 when it ended state funding of organ transplants, a decision that set in motion the state's much ballyhooed and criticized rationing plan. Second, states have redefined eligibility and, consequently, thrown people off the Medicaid rolls. The Children's Defense Fund, for example, estimated that there were 200,000 fewer children served by Medicaid in 1986 than there were in 1978, despite lower poverty rates in that earlier year.

Third, states have reduced reimbursements to providers, a strategy that has exacerbated an already existing problem of low provider reimbursement. For example, a study done in the early 1990s by the nonpartisan Physician Payment Review Commission found that Medicaid pays physicians only about 69 percent of what Medicare pays and even a smaller proportion of private insurance rates. The consequences of this are twofold. First, the study found that forty-four states have had difficulty getting physicians to accept Medicaid clients.[45] Second, when health care providers do accept Medicaid patients they often shift costs associated with underreimbursement onto their private patients, or insurance companies, to cover expenses. This cost shifting in turn contributes to an increase in private insurance costs and is yet another Medicaid-related concern of state governments. All of this has placed an enormous burden on state policymakers, requiring of them, as selections in this book demonstrate, considerable imagination and innovation as they try to balance budgets, provide non-health-related services, and satisfy the seemingly insatiable demand for more and better health care.

A New Perspective on Health

Yet another factor that explains the emerging dominance of the states in health policy can be traced to a fundamental shift in the field from an emphasis on access to one that placed considerable importance on the role of prevention. This shift, which began in the early 1970s, reinforced the trend toward increased state responsibility in health policy. This point needs some elaboration.

For much of the last century or so the prevailing wisdom has been that people can best maximize their prospects for good health through access to adequate health care. As a result, the emphasis in national debates on health policy has been on health care delivery. In this context, one major issue has been whether or not the government should help people secure access through a national health insurance system. Ultimately this nation decided, yet again in 1994, that only certain vulnerable populations (e.g., the needy and the aged, blind, and disabled) or special groups (e.g., veterans and members of Congress) should receive direct assistance from the state in getting health care. Many more, of course, receive indirect assistance through tax deductions on private health insurance.

In the past two decades there has been an important shift in the debate over how people can maximize their chances of staying healthy. Since the mid-1970s greater rhetorical and material emphasis has been placed on reducing environmental health hazards and encouraging more prudent life-styles. The "new perspective" on health, as it came to be known, heralded an era in which health care professionals, public policymakers, academics, and the general public have come to believe that greater progress toward our becoming a healthy people can be made through reducing both environmental hazards and self-indulgent, health-endangering personal behavior, than in expanding access to health care.

Because health promotion and disease prevention have traditionally been the primary responsibility of state and local governments, adoption of the "new perspective" on health has meant that the locus of health policy activity, and opportunities for innovative programs, have shifted to these arenas. The health policy agenda beginning in the late 1970s became crowded with such issues as mandatory seat belt and minimum drinking age laws, restrictions on the sale, promotion, and advertisement of tobacco and alcohol products, distribution of free condoms and clean hypodermic needles, as well as various environmental health problems. Health politics became, to a considerable extent, the politics of health promotion and disease prevention. And, state governments have been at the very epicenter of the action, often providing models of or impetus for subsequent federal action.

In the last decade the states have also been at the center of another relatively recent health phenomenon, namely the battle against AIDS, considered by some a lifestyle-related disease. Rarely, if ever, in this century has any disease so captured popular fears, frustrations, and prejudices as AIDS. Rarely, indeed, has any disease emerged so rapidly and embedded itself so firmly in the health policy landscape. While recent public health problems such as Legionnaires' disease and toxic shock syndrome enjoyed similarly rapid infamy, their impact was much more circumscribed in terms of numbers affected and duration of the etiological mystery surrounding them. AIDS has placed an enormous burden on the state and local governments, including state Medicaid programs—estimates range from 20 to 60 percent of these costs being absorbed by Medicaid—but the cost will also be borne by public hospitals run by state and local governments. Although it is unclear exactly how the bill will be distributed, it is certain that the states will continue to play a major role not only in the financing of care for AIDS victims but in other AIDS-related policy efforts, including health education, protection of civil rights, and even research.

State policymakers will confront other major health problems that will stretch both their resources and their ingenuity. These include care and treatment of the mentally ill, the aged, and people with chemical dependencies. Unlike many of the public health problems that faced the states at the turn of the last century, such as tuberculosis, influenza, measles, and other infectious or contagious diseases, these problems will neither be episodic, as epidemics historically have been, nor lend themselves to a "magic bullet" solution. Instead, state governments can expect to find pressing health issues high on the policy agenda for decades to come, even if a cure for AIDS is found tomorrow.

Conclusion

Short of the adoption of a federally run national health insurance system, something that is unlikely to occur any time soon, the states will play an increasingly prominent role in the provision, regulation, and financing of health care in this country. Beyond the important question of whether or not the states will have the financial ability to handle this challenge lie other, more fundamental, ones: What are the potential consequences and significance of this increased state responsibility in health policy? Are the states likely to do a good job in guaranteeing the quality of care or in the equitable distribution of resources? What about the commitment of state governments to insuring access to quality health care for all who need it? Proponents of state activism argue that the states will be more responsive to local needs, and are in a better position to experiment and find innovative solutions to difficult health problems. The selections in this book would lend credence to this perspective.

In states as geographically, economically, and demographically diverse as Hawaii, Vermont, Oregon, and Minnesota, policymakers have shown extraordinary inventiveness and sensitivity in dealing with some of our most intractable health-related problems. But the chapters in this book are also cautionary tales of the political and fiscal constraints under which states must operate and the limits to state health reform activity. Nonetheless, the inability and/or unwillingness of the federal government to address some of the more pressing health problems of our times will leave a policy void that the states have no choice but to fill.

Plan of This Book

The selections in this book are intended to illustrate the theme that the states are now, and will remain for the foreseeable future, the main arenas of health policy change in America. The book begins with a discussion by Daniel M. Fox of the competence of the states to handle the task of reform—he concludes that they are indeed effective units of government—and what he calls the "federalism of mutual dependence." The latter concept is a reminder that health policy, as it has evolved over the last several decades, is an interdependent enterprise involving both the federal and state governments. Fox suggests, however, that a modification of this relationship may well be under way as employers and state government begin to recognize common goals (e.g., contain costs and maintain a healthy and productive workforce). According to Fox, "[if] state officials and business executives become allies rather than adversaries in purchasing health care and overseeing providers, they could collaborate on broader health policy." This, in turn, would enhance the role of the states as the focus of health policy change, and reconfigure the interrelationship between the states and the national government.

One potential area of collaboration between the private sector and the states is private health insurance. In 1993, 51 million Americans had no health insurance during some part of the year. And, the majority of these people were employed in small firms with fewer than fifty employees. In the absence of a national policy of comprehensive, universal health insurance, much of the policy activity in the states—and Congress—in the immediate future will involve making private health insurance more accessible and affordable to this group. In chapter 3, Thomas Oliver and Robert Fiedler discuss the pattern of insurance market reforms initiated by the states over the last several years dealing with such issues as portability, preexisting condition clauses, benefit packages, and underwriting practices. Although of a seemingly technical nature, these private practices raise a fundamental political and ideological question, namely: How far should state government intervene in private insurance market practices to facilitate access to health care for working Americans?

Managed care has become the holy grail of health care reform. State and federal officials, as well as private employers, believe managed care is the most promising approach to reining in the galloping costs of health care. Of particular importance to state governments is the impact that managed care will have on the costs of Medicaid, the second most costly program in most state budgets. In chapter 4 Michael Sparer examines the managed care public policy initiatives of our two largest states, California and New York. He finds that, contrary to received wisdom among health policy observers, "New York's Medicaid program is less regulatory than its reputation suggests, whereas California's program is hardly a model of free-market competition." Sparer concludes that the expansion of managed care has both positive (e.g., encouraging more primary care and less emergency room use) and negative (e.g., encouraging underserving of patients) consequences for the health care system and those who pay for and consume its services. As a result, he urges a "strong federal role" to prevent the possible abuses of this rapidly expanding health care delivery model.

In chapter 5 the reader gets a very different perspective on state health care reform than that presented in any of the other chapters in this volume. For the past eight years Jean Thorne has worked for the state of Oregon, first as its chief Medicaid officer and currently as Governor John Kitzhaber's adviser on federalism. Thorne was present at the birth of Oregon's controversial health rationing plan and describes the political obstacles states face in trying to reform health care within a federal system. This "view from the trenches" reveals the remarkable frustration state officials often experience in trying to do what they believe to be the right thing for their citizens only to find that national partisan and bureaucratic politics take precedence over goodwill within Washington's Beltway.

Each of the next five chapters deals with specific state efforts to extend the protection of health insurance to all citizens and to control health care costs. In chapter 6, Oregon again comes under scrutiny when Howard Leichter examines that state's "bold experiment" in health care rationing in an attempt to provide access to health care for all poor Oregonians. Few policy reforms have generated as much interest and controversy in recent years as the Oregon Health Plan. Oregon has extended a basic level of health services to all people whose incomes fall below the federal poverty level. The state solicited citizen as well as expert opinion on what constitutes a "basic level of services," and now funds only those procedures and no more to its Medicaid population. Although widely applauded for its effort, it is a measure of the controversial nature of this experiment that no other state has chosen to follow Oregon's lead in prioritizing health services and funding only those that popular consensus and professional opinion deem essential.

The state of Hawaii was the first in the nation to systematically address the problem of access to health care for the uninsured. In fact, Deane Neubauer in chapter 7 argues that Hawaii state officials see physical well-being as a critical ingredient in the economic vitality of their state. Hence, the promotion of Hawaii as a place of healthy living has become part of the state's tourism and economic development efforts. Indeed, so important is this goal that state officials have taken to calling Hawaii "The Health State." Neubauer describes the series of policy steps Hawaii has taken to enhance its image as a place concerned with the good health of its population. Neubauer's account of the Hawaiian "health culture" is a reminder of the central role that good health plays in the American value system, and the potential political and economic advantages that go along with promoting this value. Yet this chapter also demonstrates that even in a health care paradise, reform can fall on hard political and economic times.

Vermont too was among the early reforming states. In 1992 this small and in many ways unique state took the first step down a road state officials and national policy observers predicted would end with universal access to health care and effective cost containment. This optimism was fueled by Vermont's history of health insurance reform and expanded coverage for its uninsured children. Many even speculated that Vermont might go the route of its neighbor to the north and become a laboratory for a Canadian-style single-payer system, since single-payer enthusiasts were one of the best organized and most visible lobbies in the state. In chapter 8, Leichter shows just how many things can go wrong even when health reform begins with such widespread support and under such committed and talented public and private leadership. In the end Vermont has had to settle for far more modest change than it imagined for itself just a few years ago.

The importance of experience with incremental changes in health care policy in the run-up to comprehensive reform is well illustrated by the case of Minnesota. As Leichter describes in chapter 9, as early as 1987 Minnesotans enacted a Children's Health Plan that provided non-Medicaid-eligible, low-income pregnant women, and children under six years of age with health insurance for a modest annual fee. In 1992 and 1993 the state built on this experience and enacted one of the most far reaching reforms of any state in the nation, promising to expand access to all Minnesotans, contain health care costs, revitalize rural health care, systematically collect health care data, and restructure the very way people receive and providers deliver health care. Yet, much like the other states described in this volume, Minnesota's lawmakers too had to retreat from their ambitious goals in the face of the demise of the Clinton plan, Republican control of Congress, and the complexity of the task itself.

Although Hawaii, Oregon, Vermont, and Minnesota can all be described as having achieved varying degrees of health care reform success—or, for those less generous, failure—Raymond Davis and Barbara Langner describe, in chapter 10, the case of Kansas, in which two years of reform effort resulted in the state doing absolutely nothing. In many respects, the Kansas experience mirrors that of the failed federal effort. Despite endless hearings, strong citizen involvement, and the efforts of a highly visible health reform commission, the end product did not even have enough legislative or popular support to be voted on by the state legislature. Partisanship within the state and the changing national political climate were obstacles simply too imposing to overcome.

Notes

1. David W. Moore and Lydia Saad, "Most People Are Satisfied with Own Health Insurance but Still Feel There Is a National Crisis," *Gallup Poll Monthly,* May 1993, 14.

2. Just some of the analyses that have appeared thus far are: Haynes Johnson and David S. Broder, *The System: The American Way of Politics at the Breaking Point* (Boston: Little, Brown and Company, 1996); Columbia Institute, *What Shapes Lawmakers' Views: A Survey of Members of Congress and Key Staff on Health Care Reform* (Menlo Park, Calif.: Kaiser Foundation, May 1995); James Fallows, "A Triumph of Misinformation," *Atlantic Monthly,* January 1995, 26–37; James Mongan, "Anatomy and Physiology of Health Reform," *Health Affairs* 14 (spring 1995): 99–101; Theda Skocpol, "The Rise and Resounding Demise of the Clinton Plan," *Health Affairs* 14 (spring 1995): 66–85; Hugh Heclo, "The Clinton Health Plan: Historical Perspective," *Health Affairs* 14 (spring 1995): 86–98; Sven Steinmo and Jon Watts, "It's the Institutions, Stupid! Why Comprehensive National Health Insurance Always Fails in America," *Journal of Health Politics, Policy and Law* 20 (summer 1995): 329–72; and various contributors to the "Roundtable on the Defeat of Reform," *Journal of Health Politics, Policy and Law* 20 (summer 1995): 391–494.

3. A September 1994 ABC News/*Washington Post* survey asked respondents which word best described how they felt about the way the federal government works. Nearly three-fourths of the respondents described themselves as either "dissatisfied" (53 percent) or "angry" (20 percent). "Opinion Outlook," *National Journal,* June 11, 1994, 1378.

4. E. Ginsberg and R. Solow, "Some Lessons of the 1960s," *Public Interest* 34 (winter 1974): 217.

5. James A. Stever, *Diversity and Order in State and Local Politics* (Columbia: University of South Carolina Press, 1980), xv.

6. Mavis Mann Reeves, "The States as Polities: Reformed, Reinvigorated, Resourceful," *Annals of the American Academy of Political and Social Sciences* (hereafter *The Annals*) 509 (May 1990): 83–93. See also Ira Sharkansky, *The Maligned States* (New York: McGraw-Hill, 1978); Malcolm E. Jewell, "The Neglected World of State Politics," *Journal of Politics* 44 (August 1982): 638–57.

7. David Osborne, *Laboratories of Democracy* (Boston: Harvard Business School Press, 1990), 1. See also Ann O'M. Bowman and Richard C. Kearney, *The Resurgence of the States* (Englewood Cliffs, N.J.: Prentice-Hall, 1986), 2.

8. R. W. Apple, Jr., "Washington, 1995: Echoes of a 200-Year Debate," *New York Times,* December 24, 1995, sec. 4, p. 1.

9. Richard P. Nathan, "Federalism—The Great 'Composition,' " in *The New American Political System,* ed. Anthony King, 2d version (Washington, D.C.: American Enterprise Institute, 1990), 241.

10. Richard M. Nixon, "White House Memorandum," June 1970, quoted in Nathan, "Federalism," 251.

11. Timothy Conlan, *New Federalism: Intergovernmental Reform from Nixon to Reagan* (Washington, D.C.: The Brookings Institution, 1988), 84.

12. See Daniel Elazar, "Opening the Third Century of American Federalism: Issues and Prospects," *The Annals* 509 (May 1990): 14.

13. Dick Pawelek, "State vs. Federal Government: Which Is Most Trusted?" *Senior Scholastic,* March 19, 1982, 13.

14. Bowman and Kearney, *Resurgence of the States,* 8.

15. John Kincaid, "The State of American Federalism—1987," *Publius* 18 (summer 1988): 1.

16. *U.S. v. Lopez*, 115 Sup. Ct. 1624 (1995).

17. *Public Papers of the Presidents of the United States: Ronald Reagan, 1987,* Book II (Washington, D.C.: Government Printing Office, 1989), 1235.

18. For such a view, see "A Good—and Bad—Time to Be a Governor," *The Economist,* March 3, 1990, 28.

19. United States Department of Commerce, *Statistical Abstract of the United States, 1995* (Washington, D.C.: Government Printing Office, 1995), 333.

20. In 1995, 38 of the 100 senators and 215 of the 435 representatives had served in state legislatures, and 17 senators were former governors, reinforcing a strong state orientation in Congress as well. See Robert Pear, "Source of State Power Is Pulled from Ashes," *New York Times,* April 16, 1995, A16.

21. *Public Papers of the Presidents of the United States: William J. Clinton, 1993,* "Remarks to the Advisory Commission on Intergovernmental Relations," December 1, 1993 (Washington, D.C.: Government Printing Office, 1994), 2: 2084.

22. For the distinction between "external" (i.e., Washington) and "internal" (i.e., the states) factors stimulating state vitality, see Reeves, "The States as Polities." This section draws heavily upon this work and Bowman and Kearney, *Resurgence of the States,* 10–31.

23. Giandomenico Majone, *Evidence, Argument, and Persuasion in the Policy Process* (New Haven: Yale University Press, 1989), 83.

24. James Sundquist, *Making Federalism Work* (Washington, D.C.: The Brookings Institution, 1969), 271.

25. In 1940 only four states had annual legislative sessions. This number grew to nineteen in the 1960s, thirty-five in 1975, and forty-three today. William Pound, "State Legislative Careers: Twenty-Five Years of Reform," in *Changing Patterns in State Legislative Careers,* ed. Gary F. Moncrief and Joel A. Thompson (Ann Arbor: University of Michigan Press, 1992), 10.

26. For a discussion of the modernization and professionalization of state legislatures, see Rich Jones, "State Legislatures," in *The Book of the States, 1994–95* (Lexington, Ky.: The Council of State Governments, 1995), 98–107.

27. *Statistical Abstract of the United States 1995* (Washington, D.C.: Government Printing Office, 1995), 351; and *The Book of the States 1994–95* (Lexington, Ky.: Council of State Governments, 1995), 439.

28. Sol Wachtler, "Constitutional Rights: Resuming the States' Role," *Intergovernmental Perspective* 15 (summer 1989): 23.

29. Carl E. Van Horn, "The Quiet Revolution," in *The State of the States,* ed. Carl E. Van Horn (Washington, D.C.: CQ Press, 1989), 2.

30. Ceci Connolly, "Governors Agree System Ailing, Disagree with Clinton on Cure," *Congressional Quarterly Weekly Report* 52, February 5, 1994, 249.

31. Center for the American Women and Politics, "Women in State Legislatures, 1995—Fact Sheet," (New Brunswick, N.J.: Eagleton Institute of Politics, 1995).

32. Harold W. Stanley and Richard G. Niemi, *Vital Statistics on American Politics* 2d ed., p. 368, and 5th ed., p. 373 (Washington, D.C.: CQ Press, 1990, 1995).

33. Times Mirror Center for the People and the Press, "The New American Electorate and Health Care Reform," July 1994, 4.

34. Rita Thaemert, "Twenty Percent and Climbing," *State Legislatures* 20 (January 1994): 28–29.

35. Marilyn Moon and John Holahan, "Can States Take the Lead in Health Care Reform? *Journal of the American Medical Association* 268 (September 23/30, 1992): 1588–94. Moon and Holahan's response to their own question is the dominant position in the literature: "state efforts on their own are unlikely to be successful."

36. Deborah A. Stone, "Why the States Can't Solve the Health Care Crisis," *American Prospect*, no. 9 (spring 1992): 51.

37. David E. Rosenbaum, "Governors' Frustration Fuels Effort on Welfare Financing," *New York Times*, March 21, 1995, A1.

38. Saundra K. Schneider, "Governors and Health Care Policy in the American States," *Policy Studies Journal* 17 (summer 1989): 911; emphasis supplied.

39. Kaiser Commission of the Future of Medicaid, *Medicaid in Transition* (Washington, D.C.: Kaiser Family Foundation, October 1995).

40. Sally S. Cohen, "The Politics of Medicaid: 1980–1989," *Nursing Outlook* 38, no. 5 (September/October 1990): 230.

41. See Marilyn Werber Serafina, "No Strings Attached," *National Journal*, May 20, 1995, 1231. Even with this expansion, however, less than one-half of all adults and children who fall below the federal poverty level are covered by Medicaid.

42. Kaiser Commission on the Future of Medicaid, "Policy Brief," March 1995, 3.

43. Ibid.

44. In 1995–96 Congressional Republicans proposed significant changes in Medicaid that were intended, in part, to bring costs under control. Among the proposals in the Republican plan, which was rejected by the Clinton administration, were to cap federal contributions to Medicaid and reduce projected federal expenditures from 1996 to 2002 by $182 billion. The feature of the plan most objectionable to President Clinton was the proposal to end Medicaid as an entitlement and leave it up to the states to determine eligibility. Although the plan was never approved, it seems probable that some reductions in Medicaid spending are likely as both Democrats and Republicans are committed to balancing the federal budget by the early part of the next century. For a list of the proposals and their fiscal implications, see Kaiser Commission, *Medicaid in Transition*.

45. For a discussion of the commission's findings, see Robert Pear, "Low Medicaid Fees Seen as Depriving the Poor of Care," *New York Times*, April 2, 1991, A1.

2

The Competence of States and the Health of the Public

Daniel M. Fox

Government in the states has become more effective since the 1960s than at any time in the history of this country. During the same years, however, the authority of state government has been diminished by all three federal branches and its competence disparaged by interest groups and academic experts.

Nationally and in the states influential persons in the public and private sectors have exploited this contradiction, transposing conflict about particular policies to debates about democratic theory, constitutional law, and managerial capacity. These debates about fundamental issues serve the interests of ideologues of all persuasions and leaders of interest groups eager to prevent policy they oppose from being made.

The politics of health care in the 1990s offer many examples of the effects of the contradiction. Large employers who self-insure for their employees' health services have exploited it in lobbying Congress to continue preempting state laws that would regulate their health plans and require them to participate in paying for care for uninsured persons. At the same time they lobby state government for subsidies to promote economic growth and development. Liberal reformers praise state health care initiatives, but usually as examples of what the federal government should do to create universal access. Some academic liberals even blamed the failure of the Clinton administration's health program on "structural" problems, which prominently include the powers that the states still have in our federal system. Many conservatives advocate devolving federal funds and authority to the states. But many Republican congressmen and policy intellectuals at conservative research organizations also advocate limiting state regulation of policies they favor, for example networks organized by physicians and hospitals, and medical savings accounts.

This essay explores the persistence of the contradiction between the increasing competence of state government and ongoing disparagement of it, emphasizing the implications of the contradiction for health policy. The contemporary history of federalism began during the New Deal. By the 1960s centralizers disparaged the strongest advocates of state government, not always inaccurately, as racists or right-wing enemies of the inevitability of centralization in government and the economy.

However, state government was changing in the 1930s. The unprecedented transfer of federal money to the states through New Deal programs required their leaders to improve the management of finances and personnel. After World War II, Americans expected the states to meet increased demand for education at all levels and infrastructure. From the 1960s to the 1980s, while the competence of states increased, mainly as a result of political reform responsive to both suburbanization and Supreme Court decisions on reapportionment, so did disparagement of their competence and an intrusive federalism.

The persistence of the contradiction has inhibited health reform in the 1990s. Promising state reform efforts have slowed, stalled, or been reversed because of the inability of state leaders to obtain regulatory relief from the federal government. Promising federal efforts to assist the reforming states have been frustrated by interest groups and by ideologues of both the left and the right.

The Origins of the Contradiction

The national government asserted greater authority over the states in the 1960s than at any time since the Civil War. Assessing federalism in the 1960s, political scientist Martha Derthick described in 1996 how "holders of national power who were trying to reconstruct American society and politics" made policy on the assumption that the states were "dependent, subordinate and inferior." They did this by expanding the "definition of constitutional rights," enlarging the "jurisdiction staked out by Congress under Article I of the Constitution," revising the "infrastructure of citizen participation to make it more inclusive and egalitarian," and increasing the "leverage of the national government and the depth of its intervention in programs shared with subnational governments."[1] Another scholar counted twenty-three of thirty-eight federal grant-in-aid programs enacted in the 1960s bypassing the states; the Economic Opportunity Act of 1964 invited nonprofit organizations to bypass local government as well.[2]

This assertion of national power was the culmination of three decades of erosion of the assumption, written into the Constitution, that the states were separate, sovereign, and equal governments. According to Derthick, most historians and political scientists, before and since the 1960s, have regarded the "centralization of governmental power within the American federal system" as a "secular trend of long standing."[3]

Most scholars locate the origins of this inexorable centralization in the Progressive period. A recent article synthesizing this research concluded that states retarded the development of the welfare state because their leaders "felt enormous pressure to maintain an attractive business climate characterized by low taxes, balanced budgets and limited social expenditure."[4] Another scholar claims that the Progressive Era reinforced "our inability to resolve our greatest national problem, the conflict between centralization and decentralization."[5] Yet another says that state policy experiments only became national policy, in pensions and child welfare for example, when state officials feared that people from other states would migrate to take "free rides" on their benefits.[6]

Many contemporaries believed that only economic and social policy that was centralized would relieve the destitution created by the Great Depression of the 1930s. In subsequent years, many scholars and advocates of national policies quoted with approval this 1933 remark by an expert on public administration: "I do not predict that the states will go but affirm that they have gone . . . because they were unable to deal . . . with the . . . life and death tasks of the new national economy."[7]

Although leaders of the three branches of the federal government asserted ever increasing authority over economic affairs and broad areas of social policy after 1932, until the 1960s they did not make rules about who should govern the states and how their governments should behave. Historian Robert Wiebe recently described federalism from the New Deal through the 1950s as the "compromise of the 1930s." Under the terms of the compromise, national and local leaders "traded support." National leaders, working through the federal government, "would set broad economic policy." Members of the "local middle class" would "set the rules in their own localities, including . . . how federal monies would be spent." Wiebe believes that this compromise began to break down in the 1960s, as the result of two forces: the "outpouring of national rules" described by Derthick and others, and the countercultural challenge symbolized by "hippies."[8]

Whether or not Wiebe is exaggerating the sociopolitical effects of the counterculture, the proliferation of national rules generated irritation and outrage among state officials and leaders of many interest groups. The polemical phrase "unfunded mandates" describes a generation of policy-making by all three branches of the federal government. Between 1789 and 1993, Congress enacted 439 statutes that significantly preempted action by the states. Seventy percent of these statutes were enacted after 1930; fifty-three after 1969.[9]

Preemption takes both partial and total forms. Federal statutes that partially preempt permit state law to supersede federal law if the state sets standards that equal or exceed national standards, or combine federal and state regulation, or allow the federal government to transfer regulatory authority to a state that has a law consistent with federal standards. Under total preemption, the federal government assumes complete regulatory authority. The U.S. Advisory Commission on Intergovernmental Relations identified ten types of total preemption in 1992, from "no need for state or local assistance" to "contingent total preemption."[10]

The federal courts have sustained the preemptive powers of Congress and "often imp[lied] federal preemption where there is no explicit statutory statement." In a series of cases in the 1980s, for example, the Supreme Court reinterpreted the Tenth Amendment to the Constitution to mean, as one legal scholar wrote, that "federalism is a political structure in which states' interests are . . . represented in the national political process."[11]

Recent Supreme Court decisions upholding the prerogatives of the states under the Commerce Clause and the Eleventh Amendment may signal that the consensus is changing. But it would take many court decisions and statutory changes to reverse more than three decades of regulatory federalism, through which the federal government commands the states to take as well as desist from particular action.

In the mid-1980s, political scientist Donald Kettl observed that federalism had changed, permanently. "In functional terms," he wrote, "nearly everything has become intergovernmental" rather than either federal or state. The new intergovernmentalism has "broadened participation in the crafting of federal policy" by creating a specialized politics that operates at all levels of government.[12] But the contradiction between the competence of states and their persistent disparagement has continually unsettled this specialized politics.

The Persistence of the States

Most commentators have exaggerated both the incompetence of the states and the extent of the centralization imposed on them in the twentieth century. State spending increased during the Progressive Era, especially for infrastructure and education, as a result of the close relationship between state government and business. At the height of the New Deal, in 1938, states still accounted for 81 percent of public spending for health care and hospitals (down only slightly from 82 percent in 1927), 87 percent of welfare costs (down from 94 percent in 1927), and 94 percent of educational costs (99 percent in 1927).[13] Even in 1985, states outspent the federal government by 71 percent to 29 percent for health care, and 56 percent to 14 percent for education; only for welfare did federal spending exceed state, and then only since the mid-1970s. Federal grants-in-aid were a higher percentage of state and local spending in 1955 (31.7 percent) than they were in 1988 (18.2 percent), even after a quarter century of the most systematic nationalization of government functions in American history. Between 1978 and 1983 alone the real value of federal grants to the states fell by 25 percent.[14]

Throughout the century, moreover, the standard career path to Congress and, often, to appointive posts in the federal executive and judicial branches has included service in state government. Nationalization has never been as extreme in the United States as, for example, in the United Kingdom, where none of the cabinet or subcabinet members or even civil servants who crafted the changes in local taxes that helped bring down Margaret Thatcher had served in local government.[15]

More important, the centralizing policies and court decisions of the 1960s accelerated changes that had already begun in the executive and legislative branches of state government. Political scientist V. O. Key described this transformation in 1955. The "growth of federal power," he wrote, "has served to liberate the states by making practicable state legislative action earlier estopped by fear of loss of competitive position among the states."[16]

Moreover, the collapse of local government revenue in the 1930s had increased citizens' reliance on subsidies from the states, most of which introduced income and sales taxes in that decade. States were hardly "vestigial remnants." If their legislatures became more professional and executive management more efficient, states would become increasingly important, Key concluded, refusing to leave American "nationhood" to the persons he described, with irony, as the "finished professionals who operate[d] in Washington."[17]

Reforming State Government

The gradual reform in state government that Key described in the 1950s accelerated in the 1960s. The Supreme Court's reapportionment decisions and federal grants that bypassed the states were only part of the stimulus for change. Prosperity and the demographic dominance of the suburbs created effective constituencies for highway and mass transit subsidies and for school aid. Rising expectations among persons from all classes and races fueled the expansion of public higher education. For example, states established forty medical schools after 1960; the private and public sectors combined had organized only sixteen during the preceding half century.[18]

Expansion and reorganization transformed the executive branch of state government after the 1950s. The number of state employees has tripled since the late 1950s. Each state reorganized its executive branch; in the two decades before 1965, twenty-eight had replaced agencies headed by boards, commissions, and elected officials with a cabinet, in which agency heads are responsible to a governor; between 1965 and 1992, twenty-two states undertook comprehensive administrative reorganization.[19] Several states created public benefit corporations to manage more flexibly hospitals and universities, just as, a century earlier, they had created such corporations to construct roads and bridges. Every state reorganized its procurement and personnel management policies and improved its management of local government debt.

In 1971, John Gardner, former secretary of health, education, and welfare, called on states to modernize their management in order to carry out their "vast residual responsibility" in a centralized society.[20] Two decades later states were using the latest management techniques, and centralization no longer seemed either inevitable or benign.[21]

Legislative reform was even more substantial. Between 1967 and 1971 alone, the number of legislatures meeting in annual sessions increased from twenty to thirty-six; and then to forty-three by 1990. Some legislatures became full time. Part-time legislatures, many of which demanded significant commitments of time from their members, began to offer better salaries and reimbursement for expenses. Surveying a quarter century of reform in 1992, William Pound, the executive director of the National Conference of State Legislatures, documented the elimination of constitutional limitations on sessions and salary, the increase of professional staff and hence the improvement of information and analysis, more time spent in sessions and related to them, improved legislative facilities, and increased regulation of campaign finance and conflicts of interest.[22]

The demography of legislatures also changed. The percentage of women members increased from 4 percent to 20 percent in the three decades after 1960. The percentage of attorneys and farmers fell; that of teachers and persons in business increased.[23]

By the 1990s, however, the results of legislative reform became evidence for advocates of term limits. The "careerist state legislature" that was "laudable government" in the 1960s, say the editors of a recent book, was "suspect" to antigovernment activists three decades later.[24] By 1996, twenty-one states had adopted term limits in response to referenda or by legislation; in only one, Mississippi, had voters rejected them.[25]

Evidence of State Government Competence

Centralizers and advocates of term limits share the opinion that reforms in state government do not necessarily benefit the public. Many people of both liberal pro-government and conservative antigovernment convictions interpret evidence of reform in the states as proof of their failure. State government expanded, they argue, often in response to federal initiatives. But it may have done so at the expense of their citizens' earnings (conservatives and liberals say), equality (liberals insist), or liberty (conservatives complain).[26] There are many examples of these charges, which include, from the right, allegations that state regulations intrude in business and, from the left, that states compete at each other's expense for industry to relocate; from the left, that citizens' entitlements to welfare and Medicaid vary among states and, from the right, that the expansion of state government itself has diminished their citizens' self-reliance.

Consider, however, assessing how states perform the tasks they set for themselves rather than grading them by standards derived from ideology. Do states achieve their objectives? Are they responsive to citizens' opinions and complaints? Do they perform services that have positive results?

A few political scientists have used statistics to assess the competence of states in acting on behalf of their citizens. Two recent studies offer quantitative evidence that the states are effective units of government. Kim Quaile Hill concluded, for example, that "gloomy . . . generalizations about the sad state of US democracy are inaccurate" because many states have "mov[ed] beyond their formerly oligarchic regimes."[27]

A more sophisticated statistical study found that "state political structures appear to do a good job of delivering more liberal policies to more liberal states and more conservative policies to more conservative states." Robert S. Erikson and his colleagues concluded that "state politics—elections, legislatures, and executives in all their variations—do matter." Moreover, "even under adverse conditions such as the limited interest and information that the average voter has regarding state politics, public opinion can be observed to influence state policy."[28]

For many years Daniel J. Elazar has argued that states serve their citizens because their policies reflect legitimate differences in political culture. States differ in mutually reinforcing ways, which he calls "cultural distinctiveness," "self conscious public attachment," a "sense of a common historical experience," "distinctiveness in policy matters," and "substantial geographic isolation or distinctiveness." As a result of these differences, "every state has certain dominant traditions about what constitutes proper government action." Competent state officials act on these traditions; incompetent officials are fired or defeated for reelection. Because states require different policies to satisfy their citizens, federalism properly makes it impossible to achieve equality of results among them.[29]

Moreover, the states have in recent years been extraordinarily successful in stimulating economic change. As economist Robert Wilson summarized in 1993, the states have created "new economic development initiatives, substantial adaptation in educational systems, new approaches to telecommunications policy," and increased state financing for economic activities. They did this, according to Wilson, as a result of local politics and economic issues and in response to "responsibilities thrust on them by a fiscally stressed federal government."[30]

Many states became entrepreneurial in the 1980s, adopting what political scientist Peter Eisinger called "demand side" policies. States generated venture capital, encouraged high-technology research and product development, and promoted "export goods" produced by local businesses. Moreover, states "embrace[d] the notion that economic development involves a qualitative increase in collective well-being." According to Eisinger, thirty-seven states adopted such policies in response to shifts in the distribution of jobs and people to the Southwest and West, the decline in the purchasing power of federal aid to the states, and the transformation of the American economy from manufacturing to service-based industry.[31] In an article for an international audience, Eisinger claimed that the industrial policies of American states compared favorably in effectiveness with those of central governments in Japan and the countries of Western Europe. As a result of these policies state government had a "more intimate form of involvement in the private market than anything to which Americans have been accustomed."[32]

A 1993 analysis of published research on how the states have influenced economic performance concluded that those with "government capacity, economic development policies and higher levels of investment expenditures appear better suited to sustain economic growth." The author found that party control was "largely irrelevant in shaping economic performance," but that states with the highest per capita income growth had similar policies for taxation, spending, higher education, and collective bargaining.[33]

Public pension funds have been an important source of venture capital to carry out the entrepreneurial policies of state government. From the early nineteenth century to the 1970s, the courts enforced a "prudent man" rule under which trustees of pension funds and charitable trusts were required to avoid risk in each of their decisions about investments. In 1979, however, the U.S. Department of Labor, which administers the Employee Retirement Income Security Act of 1974 (ERISA), changed this rule. Trustees of pension funds could now contemplate increased risk in some of their investments because they were permitted to act prudently only in managing their entire portfolio.[34]

Public pension funds, which by 1996 were investing around $500 billion in stocks, gradually accommodated to their new opportunities. Michigan, in 1982, had been the first state to enact a statute earmarking a proportion of public retirement funds for investment as local venture capital. Within a few years, these investments had created thirty-two hundred new jobs and leveraged $200 million in private investment in Michigan. Other states took similar action with similar results.[35]

Public pension funds also became more aggressive in using their holdings to influence the management of large corporations. In the late 1980s, the Washington state fund was the "second biggest investor in leveraged buyouts organized by Kohlberg Kravis Roberts & Company."[36] In 1995, the State of Wisconsin Investment Board forced the reorganization of one of the largest advertising firms in the world, Saatchi and Saatchi PLC.[37] An article in the *New York Times* in 1996 described the California Public Retirement System as the "leader of the decade-old shareholders' campaign to hold poorly performing chief executives' feet to the fire."[38] A few months later a columnist for the *Wall Street Journal* evaluated the economics and politics of such investing. He concluded that "state pension administrators have emerged to shlep most of the burden of fixing American capitalism."[39]

There is, in sum, considerable evidence that states are effective units of government. State governments are alert to the dominant preferences of their citizens. They are particularly successful in economic development, and in such areas as education and infrastructure that contribute to the economy. These are also areas of policy that have been subject to fewer federal mandates and received less federal subsidy than, for example, health, welfare, and the environment.

Health Policy: The Federalism of Mutual Dependence

The states and the federal government are mutually dependent in health policy as a result of half a century of decisions about financing acute and long-term care. Federal social insurance, Medicare, pays for acute services to the elderly and persons with disabilities. Federal subsidy on behalf of persons with low incomes, Medicaid, pays acute care costs for many children and adults of working age and long-term care costs for many persons who are elderly or have disabilities. State and local governments pay much of the cost of care for low-income children and adults, persons with severe and chronic mental illness, adults with other disabilities, and the frail elderly. Federal taxpayers (through the exclusion of benefits from income tax), employers, and employees pay most of the costs of acute care for most persons in the workforce and their dependents. Almost everyone pays for some health care out of his or her own pocket. Together, these funding streams comprise America's almost universal health care financing policy, criticized by some as inadequately comprehensive in whom and what it covers, by others as wasteful, and by nearly everyone as inefficient.[40]

These intertwined policies have accumulated during six decades of intense negotiations. Any change in national policy affects state government and most employers and employees, their dependents, health care providers, and the poor. Any change in state policy, especially if emulated by other states, affects the federal government and a multitude of persons with other interests. Because of the profound implications of any change in health care financing policies, prudent leaders in the public and private sectors are suspicious of any proposed solutions to the well-known problems of financing health care, and particularly to increasing access to care by physicians and hospitals for persons who lack social or private insurance and are not eligible for Medicaid.

Nevertheless, significant change has occurred in health care financing policy during the past half century. Some experts say that change occurred despite the politics of federalism; others insist that it occurred as a result of those politics.

Because the stakes are high in the federalism of mutual dependence in health affairs, its politics attracts persons of considerable competence on all sides of any issue that merits serious attention in state capitals or Washington, D.C. For many of these people competence includes access to cash for advertising their views and contributions of "soft" and "hard" money to political campaigns. For others, it requires the ability to mobilize substantial blocs of voters. As a result, significant changes in financing policy occur infrequently and often because they are linked to other issues.

Three events have transformed national health financing policy during the past half century. During World War II, the federal government, in order to prevent inflation and profiteering, permitted employees and employers to substitute "fringe" benefits for wages and excluded their value from the taxable income of individuals and corporations. Then in 1965 the federal government enacted Medicare and, secondary to it, Medicaid, federal participation in state programs of health care to the poor and persons with disabilities. Finally, in 1974, ERISA preempted the states from regulating employee benefit plans that paid directly for services instead of purchasing insurance.

All three policy changes had important results for federalism. The tax exclusion freed the states from being the payers of last resort for millions of workers who could bargain collectively for health benefits. Any subsequent policy that eliminated or reduced the exclusion would require substantial changes in the tax policies of both the federal government and the states. Reducing or eliminating the exclusion would, moreover, increase the taxable wage base for federal and state income tax and increase the risk of catastrophic health care costs, and hence reliance on state and local subsidy, for most individuals and families.

Medicare and Medicaid transformed federalism in health care financing. Medicare, like federal Old Age Survivors and Disability Insurance (OASDI) before it, eliminated a whole category of dependent persons from state and local responsibility. Medicaid became a dependable source of financing for care for persons with low incomes and created an open-ended obligation for the states to match federal contributions, even when they were the result of federal changes in benefits. Moreover, Medicaid gave the states a financial incentive to medicalize (or, as it was often called, "Medicaidize") and thus make more costly, programs for the frail elderly, the mentally ill, and the disabled.

The profound significance of ERISA preemption for federalism emerged gradually. Enacted as a minor amendment proposed in the conference committee on a bill that substantially reformed pension policy, the preemption of state regulation of self-insured benefit plans did not attract attention as health policy for several years. ERISA preempted the states from regulating self-insured health plans. But many federal lawmakers, as well as lobbyists for business and labor, assumed that the federal government would soon regulate health benefits under a national health insurance statute just as, under ERISA, it now regulated pensions.[41]

By the late 1970s, however, many large employers and craft unions discovered economic advantages in the persistence of a regulatory vacuum for their self-insured health plans. They lobbied hard to remain free of any regulation of the coverage and solvency of these plans by either the federal government or the states, or both. The subsequent success of the defenders of ERISA preemption, in both Congress and the federal courts, prevented the states from mandating minimum health benefits or using taxes on employee health plans to help finance care for the uninsured. By the end of the 1980s, the health benefits of a majority of employees in most states were outside the jurisdiction of state government. By the mid-1990s, the health plans of 40 percent of employees nationally, and 60 percent of those in the largest firms, escaped regulation by the federal government and the states.[42]

In the 1990s, ERISA preemption became both a treasured regulatory precedent and a model for proponents of massive changes in the organization and financing of acute health services under the broad slogan of managed care. Employers, including government itself in more than half the states, used their unregulated buying power to force medical specialists and hospitals to perform more efficiently or at least to discount their prices and ration the use of expensive services.

Although the techniques and motives of the persons creating managed care varied widely among sectors of the health industry and regions of the country, its proponents everywhere shared an interest in a regulatory vacuum. ERISA preemption permitted self-insured employers to hire any providers they chose, for whatever price they negotiated, to provide any benefits they could persuade their employees to tolerate. Moreover, it permitted employers to escape the cost of paying for indigent care, either because providers shifted costs to public or private employee health plans or because the states taxed those plans on behalf of persons without health insurance. State subsidies from prior years, for example to build hospitals or train health professionals as a means to serving persons with low incomes, had become sunk costs.

The vacuum created by ERISA preemption was just as important as a model for the removal of regulations that powerful groups perceived as onerous. When managed care plans excluded some physicians and pharmacists, their professional associations petitioned the states to prohibit plans from making such regulations. When states required physicians and hospitals seeking to do business as health plans to have financial reserves because they assumed risk, their leaders asked state legislatures and then the U.S. Congress to relieve them of such regulations. When state regulations penalized insurance companies that profited by dropping or refusing to insure poor risks or offered medical savings accounts with dubious catastrophic coverage, their executives demanded that governors and members of Congress create a regulatory vacuum.

Because ERISA preemption was a model for powerful groups promoting profound changes in the health industry, Congress refused to set it aside for states that had enacted health reform. In Florida, Maryland, Massachusetts, Minnesota, Oregon, Vermont, and Washington, for example, major self-insured employers agreed that contributing to care for the poor and offering minimum coverage would benefit their communities without significantly increasing their costs. In national politics, however, defenders of preemption, fearing a precedent that would lead other states to request exemption, prevented state-by-state relief from ERISA. More than a decade earlier, Hawaii had paid a high political price for Congress to grant it a limited exemption; at the time Congress had warned other states that it did not intend to create a precedent.

In the summer of 1994, however, state, industry, and congressional leaders considered modifying the regulatory vacuum created by ERISA preemption. While the Clinton administration's health plan was expiring in Congress, representatives of about thirty of the largest employers in the nation and leaders in the legislative and executive branches of nine states negotiated a limited compromise on preemption. Under the compromise, self-insured employers would pay a federal tax to subsidize care for the uninsured in states that chose to enact universal coverage that met certain minimal standards. The proceeds of this tax would then be returned to those states. As a result, states would be able to finance insurance programs that would limit cost shifting from hospitals to employer plans while self-insured firms would remain exempt from state regulation and direct taxes on their payments for health care. This compromise was incorporated in a general health reform bill offered, unsuccessfully, by then majority leader George Mitchell, and was reported in the national press.[43]

Since 1994, a substantial number of states have continued to broaden and make more efficient their Medicaid programs and to improve the subsidized insurance policies they offer to persons with low incomes. But the near universal coverage that is now available only in Hawaii cannot occur without federal health reform or, failing that, regulatory relief to other states.[44]

Federal insurance reform enacted in 1996, named Kassebaum-Kennedy after its authors in the U.S. Senate, modifies ERISA preemption substantially by requiring self-insured plans, as well as insurance companies, to meet minimum standards for portability and coverage of preexisting conditions. Industry opposition to the bill was muted for at least two reasons. Many large self-insured companies already met such standards. More important, however, is an emerging employer strategy to shift the risk of managed care to health plans and providers by abandoning self-insurance. This strategy, now in its early stages of development, would end the ERISA vacuum and make federal government, states, and employers allies in the regulation of health services.

Health Policy and the Competence of States: Next Steps

The frustration created by the federalism of mutual dependence in health policy could be reduced in the late 1990s as a result of the competence that states have acquired in the past generation combined with the shared interests of state government and private employers as purchasers of health care. States are major purchasers of managed health care. Public employees and their dependents are the largest insured group in most states. The number of persons on Medicaid whose care is managed under contracts supervised by the states is increasing everywhere.

States and private employers, whether they insure or self-insure to pay for care (most employers in fact do both), share interests in the financing and oversight of managed care just as they do in economic development, education, and infrastructure. Shared interests may become more compelling as the states recede as regulators of rates charged by hospitals; by the end of 1996 only Maryland regulated such rates. Moreover, many private employers welcome state oversight of the solvency and quality of health plans and providers, particularly when they participate in setting the standards and processes for state action.

State officials and executives of leading employers increasingly describe themselves as having the same goals for health policy. Both want to contain costs. Both want to purchase care of sufficient quality to maintain or improve the productivity of employees. Both are eager to reduce costly complications from inappropriate treatment and complaints from consumers. In a few states, public officials and business executives have begun to act on their shared goals—to discuss, for example, what standards for accountability and performance they might jointly demand of plans and providers.[45]

This collaboration between employers and state government could gradually modify the politics of the federalism of mutual dependence. If state officials and business executives become allies rather than adversaries in purchasing health care and overseeing its providers, they could collaborate on broader health policy: for example, to prevent and treat illness among persons without insurance, a problem that, if neglected, could increase the burden of health care costs on a community and hence state and local taxes.

This observation is more than conjecture. I have participated in meetings of state and business leaders to discuss collaboration in purchasing and oversight in, at this writing, seven states, and know of similar activities in half a dozen others. The discussion at these meetings exemplifies the contradiction between the disparagement of the states and their effectiveness. Business leaders are initially wary about regarding state officials as colleagues rather than as regulators to be lobbied or avoided. They assume that legislative leaders and heads of executive branch agencies have lower standards than they do for quality and efficiency in health care. But business leaders are gradually impressed by the enormous purchasing power of state government in health care and by the sophistication of state officials in using it on behalf of government employees, Medicaid recipients, and taxpayers. Each of the meetings I attended has led to plans for collaboration to hold health plans and providers more accountable.

A self-study by state leaders of the oversight of large integrated health systems in the fifty states, completed in 1996, concluded that many states are expanding public scrutiny of the health care industry on behalf of purchasers and consumers. This study was conducted by the Reforming States Group, a voluntary association of senior state officials from more than thirty states, in collaboration with leaders of the national associations of state health officers, insurance commissioners, and Medicaid directors.[46] As the study neared completion, the Reforming States Group and the federal Health Care Financing Administration began a joint project to assist the states in sharing with each other what they are learning from the oversight of integrated health systems about how best to set and implement standards for Medicaid managed care.

The states have not withered away. Instead they have become increasingly competent and essential to the well-being of the public. Moreover, their importance in health policy is increasing. The federalism of mutual dependence in health policy is likely to persist precisely because it is mutual rather than hierarchical.

Notes

1. Martha Derthick, "Crossing Thresholds: Federalism in the 1960s," *Journal of Policy History* 8, no. 1 (1996): 64–80.

2. Joseph Zimmerman, *Federal Preemption: The Silent Revolution* (Ames: Iowa State University Press, 1991), 48.

3. Derthick, "Crossing Thresholds," 78.

4. David Brian Robertson, "The Bias of American Federalism: The Limits of Welfare State Development in the Progressive Era," *Journal of Policy History* 1, no. 3 (1989): 261–91.

5. Barry D. Karl, *The Uneasy State: The United States from 1915 to 1945* (Chicago: University of Chicago Press, 1983), 5–6.

6. Keith Boeckelman, "The Influence of States on Federal Policy Adoption," *Policy Studies Journal* 20, no. 3 (1992): 365–75.

7. Luther H. Gulick, who made this remark, was a well-known pioneering scholar and consultant in public administration. The remark has frequently been quoted in the literature, usually with approval. The fullest modern text is in Robert H. Wilson, *States*

and the Economy: Policymaking and Decentralization (Westport, Conn.: Praeger Publishers, 1993), 4.

8. Robert H. Wiebe, *Self-Rule: A Cultural History of American Democracy* (Chicago: University of Chicago Press, 1995), especially 211–62.

9. U.S. Advisory Commission on Intergovernmental Relations, *Federal Statutory Preemption of State and Local Authority: History, Inventory, and Issues* (Washington, D.C.: Government Printing Office, September 1992), iii, 7.

10. Ibid., iii–iv.

11. David M. O'Brien, "The Rehnquist Court and Federal Preemption: In Search of a Theory," *Publius: The Journal of Federalism* 23 (fall 1993): 17. See also David M. O'Brien, "Federalism as a Metaphor in the Constitutional Politics of Public Administration," *Public Administration Review* 49 (May 1989): 411–19; Charles Wise and Rosemary O'Leary, "Is Federalism Dead or Alive in the Supreme Court?" *Public Administration Review* 52 (November–December 1992): 559–72; and U.S. Advisory Commission on Intergovernmental Relations, *Federal Regulation of State and Local Governments: The Mixed Record of the 1980s* (Washington, D.C.: Government Printing Office, July 1993).

12. Donald F. Kettl, "The Maturing of American Federalism," in *The Costs of Federalism,* ed. R. T. Golembrewsky and A. Wildavsky (New Brunswick, N.J.: Transaction Publishers, 1984), 73–88.

13. Thomas Dye, *Politics in States and Communities,* 7th ed. (Englewood Cliffs, N.J.: Prentice Hall, 1991), 71.

14. David McKay, *Domestic Policy and Ideology: Presidents and the American State, 1964–1987* (New York: Cambridge University Press, 1989), 28. See also Joseph F. Zimmerman, *Contemporary American Federalism: The Growth of National Power* (Westport, Conn.: Praeger Publishers, 1992), 117.

15. David Butler, Andrew Adonis, and Tony Travers, *Failure in British Government: The Politics of the Poll Tax* (Oxford, U.K.: Oxford University Press, 1994), 221.

16. V. O. Key, *American State Government: An Introduction* (New York: Alfred A. Knopf, 1956, reprinted 1963), 4. For another contemporary view of the reciprocal growth of the federal government and the states in these years see Jane Perry Clark, *The Rise of a New Federalism: Federal–State Cooperation in the United States* (New York, Columbia University Press, 1938; reprinted, New York: Russell and Russell, 1966).

17. Key, *American State Government,* 3.

18. Daniel M. Fox, "From Piety to Platitudes to Pork: The Changing Politics of Health Workforce Policy," *Journal of Health Politics, Policy and Law* 21, no. 4 (1996): 826.

19. Keon S. Chi, "Trends in Executive Reorganization," *Journal of State Government* 65 (April–June 1992): 33–40.

20. John Gardner, introduction to *The Sometime Governments: A Critical Study of the Fifty American Legislatures,* Citizens Conference on State Legislatures (New York: Bantam Books, 1971), viii. Gardner's essay was a model of condescension: for instance, a "mere handful" of states were "able to fulfill the . . . responsibilities inherent in the concept of federalism."

21. The best study of state managerial competence is U.S. Advisory Commission on Intergovernmental Relations, *The Question of State Government Capability* (Washington, D.C.: Government Printing Office, January 1985). See also Richard C. Elling, *Public Management in the States: A Comparative Study of Administrative Reform and Politics* (Westport, Conn.: Praeger Publishers, 1992). Elling conducted his research a decade earlier. In the 1990s the states actively employed the technology of Continuous Quality Improvement in managing their Medicaid and other health care programs.

22. William Pound, "State Legislative Careers: Twenty-Five Years of Reform," in *Changing Patterns in State Legislative Careers,* ed. Gary F. Moncrieff and Joel A. Thompson (Ann Arbor: University of Michigan Press, 1992), 9–21.

23. Moncrieff and Thompson, *Changing Patterns,* 23 ff.

24. Ibid., 2.

25. Karen Hansen, *Living with Term Limits* (Denver and New York: Milbank Memorial Fund and National Council of State Legislatures, in press 1996).

26. Much is compressed in this sentence. There are numerous sources for conservative complaints about state incursions against citizens' earnings and liberty. See particularly the publications of the various state "research centers" financed by philanthropic foundations that promote conservative doctrine. A sharp analysis of the liberal position on equality is Aaron Wildavsky, "Federalism Means Inequality: Political Geometry, Political Sociology, and Political Culture," in Golembrewsky and Wildavsky, *Costs of Federalism,* 35–69. A recent liberal view of the complicity of the states in thwarting national health reform in the 1990s (blaming "structural" rather than political problems for the disaster that occurred to the Clinton administration) is Jerry L. Mashaw and Theodore R. Marmor, "Can the American State Guarantee Access to Health Care?" in *The State, Politics, and Health: Essays for Rudolf Klein,* ed. P. Day, D. M. Fox, R. Maxwell, and E. Scrivens (Cambridge, Mass.: Blackwell Publishers, 1996), 61–76. For an alternative view, see Daniel M. Fox, "Negotiating Health Problems," 95–106 in the same volume.

27. Kim Quaile Hill, *Democracy in the Fifty States* (Lincoln: University of Nebraska Press, 1994), 108, 131.

28. Robert S. Erikson, Gerald C. Wright, and John P. McIver, *Statehouse Democracy: Public Opinion and Policy in the American States* (New York: Cambridge University Press, 1993), 95, 253.

29. Daniel J. Elazar, *The American Mosaic: The Impact of Space, Time, and Culture on American Politics* (Boulder, Colo.: Westview Press, 1994); 281, 288.

30. Robert H. Wilson, *States and Economy,* 272–73.

31. Peter K. Eisinger, *The Rise of the Entrepreneurial State: State and Local Economic Development Policy in the United States* (Madison: University of Wisconsin Press, 1988), 9–10, 30, 39, and passim.

32. Peter Eisinger, "Do the American States Do Industrial Policy?" *British Journal of Political Science* 20 (October 1990): 509–11, 530.

33. Paul Brace, *State Government and Economic Performance* (Baltimore: Johns Hopkins University Press, 1993), 111, 114, 120.

34. Eisinger, *Entrepreneurial State,* 255.

35. Ibid., 256.

36. Holman W. Jenkins, Jr., "The Rise of Public Pension Funds," *Wall Street Journal,* April 16, 1996, A15.

37. Patricia Lipton, executive director, State of Wisconsin Investment Board, General Letter for Public Distribution, June 30, 1995; enclosed in Ken Johnson, State of Wisconsin Investment Board, letter to D. M. Fox, January 9, 1996.

38. Judith H. Dobrzynski, "Small Companies, Big Problems: But Calpers Finds Shareholders Can Still Be Ignored," *New York Times,* February 6, 1996, D1.

39. Jenkins, "Public Pension Funds."

40. For an extended discussion of the history of health financing policy summarized here, see Daniel M. Fox, *Power and Illness: The Failure and Future of American Health Policy* (Berkeley: University of California Press, paperback edition 1995), 56–84.

41. For the history of ERISA preemption, see Daniel M. Fox and D. C. Schaffer, "Health Policy and ERISA: Interest Groups and Semi-Preemption," *Journal of Health Politics, Policy and Law* 14 (summer 1989): 239–60.

42. Current numbers are from Gregory Acs, Stephen H. Long, M. Susan Marquis, and Pamela Farley Short, "Self-Insured Employer Health Plans: Prevalence, Profile, Provisions, and Premiums," *Health Affairs* 15, no. 2 (1996): 266–78. These authors also conclude, more optimistically than most state officials would, that "ERISA may not present significant obstacles to effective implementation of many of the current state initiatives that focus on insurance rating, underwriting, and purchasing reforms for small businesses," 277.

43. For example, (no byline) "State Officials Strive to Bring the Health Care Debate Home," *New York Times,* September 25, 1994, 16. The Mitchell bill was printed but never introduced, so it lacks a number. See also Harry Nelson, *Federalism in Health Reform: Views from the States That Could Not Wait* (New York: Milbank Memorial Fund, 1994).

44. A useful survey is Dana Milbank and Laurie McGinley, "While Washington Fiddles, Many States Devise Solutions to Problems of Welfare and Health Care," *Wall Street Journal,* May 31, 1996, A12.

45. Reforming States Group, *Information for Accountability in Health Care Purchasing: A Report on Collaboration between the Private and Public Sectors* (New York: Milbank Memorial Fund and the Reforming States Group, 1996).

46. Reforming States Group, *State Oversight of Integrated Health Systems* (New York: Milbank Memorial Fund and the Reforming States Group, forthcoming).

3

State Government and Health Insurance Market Reform

Thomas R. Oliver and Robert M. Fiedler

Introduction

In the first half of this decade, concerns about the nation's health care system moved into the mainstream of political consciousness and debate. The early movement occurred in the statehouses, where recognition of urgent problems generated widespread study and a variety of legislative responses. Then came the battle royal in Washington. In the wake of an election that, to many, promised to end deadlock and drift on domestic policies, President Bill Clinton sought to erase a century of failure by giving Americans "health care that can never be taken away." The contest matched the seemingly irresistible forces of popular opinion, expert analysis, and presidential commitment against the immovable objects of fragmented governmental power and short-term self-interest. The results mirrored those of earlier generations, as defenders of the status quo emerged victorious and relatively unscathed.[1] The battle ended with a whimper in the fall of 1994, leaving the president and the Democratic Party badly wounded from the outcome. The bedrock goal of universal coverage appears to be, in retrospect, the most quixotic of dreams.

The experience of those seeking national reform reminds us that many barriers to action have little to do with health care per se, but rather are endemic features of American politics:

> Social policy reformers must struggle in an institutional system that tilts the survival odds in favor of incremental action or inaction and against big new expressions of public authority. More recent developments in our informal, unwritten constitution—declining attachments to political parties, reforms in Congress, proliferating interest groups, widening access to policy litigation in the courts, and so on—have only added to the formal constitutional fragmentation of power. The result, spread across the historical record, is that major social reform efforts rarely succeed. It is the weaselly, piecemeal adjustments to social policy that make up the bulk of successful reform efforts.[2]

Perhaps "piecemeal adjustments" understate what came out of this unprecedented surge of political activity—or perhaps not. While national efforts hit a dead end, several states adopted plans that authorized a substantial reconfiguration of health care financing and organization.[3] But the failure of national reform poisoned the atmosphere in the states, not only in those that waited for federal action but also in those that took major steps on their own to expand insurance coverage and control health care costs. In one state after another—Florida, Massachusetts, Oregon, Minnesota, Vermont, and Washington—the original plans have been slowed or reversed.[4] Where only a short time ago there was local pride among those in the vanguard, there is now retrenchment and retreat. Many legislators and other leaders of major state reforms have moved on and been replaced with officials who are not steeped in health care problems or solutions, and who believe that governmental action of any kind is questionable.

It is too soon to tell whether these are temporary setbacks in a gestation period that will ultimately yield broad state or national reforms;[5] or whether the political fallout may create even higher hurdles for major reform in the future.[6]

What are we left with, then? Amid the ruins of bolder initiatives are some lesser, incremental actions that will nonetheless shape how and how well a substantial segment of the American population is served by the health care system. While national policymakers have contemplated public and private insurance reforms since the Bush administration,[7] the states have instituted many changes and are at work on many more. Indeed, the failure of the Clinton plan has not pushed health care reform entirely off the governmental agenda and, in certain areas, it appears to have accelerated discussion and action.

One set of reforms aims to control the explosive cost of state Medicaid programs, primarily by moving beneficiaries from fee-for-service medicine into managed care organizations. Some states are also using managed care "research and demonstration" waivers, which are allowed under Section 1115 or Section 1915 of the Social Security Act, to expand Medicaid eligibility or benefits. Altogether, forty-eight states had adopted or applied for such a waiver program by 1995.[8]

The focus of this chapter is on a second set of reforms, those that aim to make private health insurance more accessible and more affordable, especially to individuals and workers in small firms. Our purpose is to describe and analyze the pattern of insurance market reforms adopted by state governments in the past several years.

Why is reform of the private health insurance system worthy of examination? From a practical standpoint, it can help us understand whether governmental action is in fact helping to solve problems and improve conditions in the real world. It is true that the policy changes considered here are essentially incremental—they do very little to expand insurance coverage for close to 40 million uninsured Americans and do not reach far enough to provoke systemwide cost containment.[9] For example, official estimates accompanying the 1992 California legislation predicted that only about one hundred thousand additional individuals would receive employer-based insurance coverage, less than 2 percent of the estimated six million state residents currently uninsured.[10]

Nonetheless, insurance reforms that have only a marginal impact on the system affect the income and security of millions of individuals. A built-in feature of our patchwork insurance system is a "revolving door" through which a substantial proportion of the population regularly changes insurance coverage because individuals switch or lose jobs, enter adulthood, have a child, leave a marriage, or suffer an illness. In 1993, more than 51 million Americans were without health insurance at some time during the year.[11] It follows that individuals (and their families or firms) who pose a financial risk to an insurer because of an existing or new medical condition may find it difficult to get back through the revolving door and obtain coverage because they either face large premium increases or are denied any coverage at all.

Insurance regulations such as guaranteed access and renewal, community rating, and limits on preexisting condition clauses are small but important steps, therefore, toward a health insurance system based on social solidarity rather than actuarial fairness. If, as Deborah Stone argues, the ultimate question for our society is whether medical care will be distributed as a right of citizenship or as a market commodity, these reforms represent attempts to reverse the trend toward commodification of health insurance. In an important way, they promote a different vision of distributive justice and community than the vision intrinsic to the unregulated marketplace.[12]

Insurance reforms may also promote efficiency in the administration of insurance and delivery of health services. Some provisions aim to reduce competition among insurers based on avoiding sick or potentially sick patients, and to increase competition based on efficiently delivering needed services to patients regardless of their health status and actuarial risk. Other provisions such as purchasing cooperatives offer greater economies of scale to employers and insurers in the small-group market. In addition, they enhance the information, choices, and bargaining power of consumers vis-à-vis insurers in the marketplace.[13]

It may be argued that the state insurance reforms undertaken in the last few years serve as institutional and political infrastructure for broader changes in the future. Since the problems that generated several seasons of political attention have not gone away,[14] stronger regulation of insurance practices may establish a new practical and political baseline for governmental intervention. Of course, these reforms may prove in many cases to be primarily symbolic and not lead anywhere; or, where they are effective, incremental reforms may come to be viewed as sufficient in and of themselves and may dilute the pressure for serious structural reforms.[15]

This exploratory analysis of state insurance reforms can also sharpen our understanding of the connection between policy analysis and policy choice. We start from the proposition that policy design is substantially a political, not technical, process,[16] and see this as an opportunity to observe varied influences on policy design. Judith Feder and Larry Levitt assert that even though insurance reforms are regarded as the "motherhood and apple pie" issues of health care reform, the perception that everyone agrees on what to do reflects limited debate (at the national level) instead of genuine consensus.[17] Some of the specific provisions are highly controversial, and there are substantial disagreements on what insurance practices to regulate and what populations they should apply to. In addition, there is as yet little empirical evidence with which to estimate the effects of proposed reforms;[18] this appears to be true of incremental insurance reforms in the states as well as the major reforms debated in Washington in 1995.

For these reasons, we expect to find that, even in this relatively consensual area of health care reform, there are few, if any, "rational" design features that will be universally accepted from a strictly technical point of view. Even these "piecemeal adjustments" rest on a foundation of knowledge so limited that there is likely to be substantial variation in the policies adopted across the states—and the pattern of change is likely to reveal that policy prescription is shaped as much by power and existing practice as by the findings of rational analysis. If so, then we will find that, amid a historic political opportunity where incremental insurance reforms were viewed as barely minimum achievements, the policy choices made were still more a matter of mutual partisan adjustment—"muddling through"—than sure-footed social engineering.[19]

We begin by setting forth the ideas for reforming the private health insurance system—the *assumptions* and *prescriptions* that reflect problems in the system and generate specific alternatives to improve its performance. We then examine the pattern of selected state *actions* to reform insurance practices. How closely do these actions conform to the ideas advanced by rational analysis, and how might policy design be shaped by other ideas, institutions, and interests that policymakers have to concern themselves with? Finally, we consider the consequences of this pattern of actions for policy performance. Throughout the analysis, we employ arguments and evidence from a study of insurance reforms adopted by the state of California in 1992.[20]

Assumptions and Value Choices in Health Insurance Market Reforms

Why and how should government regulate private health insurance—what are the main options for intervention? This section outlines the key arguments made by analysts to justify reforms in the health insurance system and the options and trade-offs that must be considered in their design.

The state reforms we examine below are primarily aimed at what is referred to as the small-group health insurance market. This typically includes business firms or associations covering fifty or fewer persons, although some reforms apply to individuals and others extend to groups of up to one hundred. These actions reflect the fact that the greatest barriers to insurance coverage originate in that market. It surprises many casual observers of the health care reform debate to learn that over three-quarters of Americans without insurance are gainfully employed or are dependents of employees. Two-thirds of these "working uninsured" are associated with firms with one hundred or fewer employees, and one-half are in firms with twenty-five or fewer employees.[21]

The prevalence of small-group market reforms also reflects the fact that states have been barred from regulating the health plans of employers who elect to self-insure by the federal Employee Retirement Income Security Act of 1974. Nationally, ERISA exempts between one-third and one-half of the private insurance market from state regulation, making effective marketwide reform at the state level difficult, if not impossible.[22] So states have chosen a path of lesser resistance, regulating a part of the health care system that is clearly within their jurisdiction.

Important Elements in the Design of Insurance Reforms

The reforms we examine are broadly directed at: (1) creating greater access to health insurance for higher-risk groups, (2) restricting the ability of insurers to compete based upon subscriber risks, (3) restructuring the marketplace to encourage price and quality competition among insurers, and (4) increasing the efficiency of administering health insurance to these populations.

The states have attempted to achieve these goals by regulating insurance underwriting and marketing practices, by controlling variation in premiums, and by establishing or enabling the formation of health plan purchasing cooperatives (HPPCs, also referred to as purchasing pools or alliances). Below, we describe the main elements of small-group insurance reforms and some of the choices required in policy design.

Guaranteed Issue and Renewal of Health Plans

Under traditional state policies, an insurer may decline to offer coverage to groups or individuals that it deems too risky. For example, it is not unusual for insurers to "redline" certain employers such as construction firms or ski resorts.[23] Similarly, if an insurer has unprofitable experience with a group, it may deny that group an opportunity to renew its coverage.

A state mandate requiring insurers to guarantee the issuance and renewal of health insurance policies improves access for these risky populations. At the same time, it is likely to increase the costs to the insurer if these populations do in fact utilize more medical services. Consequently, insurers faced with such a mandate can be expected to increase their premiums.

In addition, where the insurance coverage is voluntary, guaranteed issue may encourage individuals and groups not to purchase insurance until it is actually needed. This form of adverse selection may reduce the overall rate of insurance coverage in the market and raise the average premiums for those who do purchase coverage.[24]

Where insurers are mandated to guarantee the issue and renewal of state-certified "standard" plans but not all plans, there is also a risk of adverse selection because those plans are likely to attract groups that would be denied coverage for other plans. This creates an incentive for insurers to avoid offering the standard plans unless they are required to do so—and even then they can limit marketing efforts for those plans.

Provisions for guaranteed issue and renewal help ensure access to health insurance, but they clearly create concerns about adverse selection and cost containment that must be addressed through other elements of reform proposals.

Preexisting Condition Clauses

Under a preexisting condition clause, an employee's medical condition that manifested itself prior to the effective date of the policy will not be covered by the insurer for a specified period of time.

This saves the insurer from paying for treatment that individuals have postponed and sought only after obtaining insurance coverage. But such clauses are particularly onerous for millions of individuals for whom a change in employment means a change in insurance. Reforms to limit preexisting condition clauses help increase the "portability" of insurance and reduce "job lock," where individuals are unable to accept a preferred job or start a new business because doing so would jeopardize existing insurance coverage for themselves or members of their family.

In the absence of universally mandated health insurance, preexisting condition clauses discourage currently healthy individuals from going uninsured and reduce the amount of adverse selection that might otherwise occur.[25] Establishing rules for such clauses requires policymakers to balance the need for access and fairness to individuals with chronic conditions against the costs of adverse selection and free riding.[26] A logical way to maintain incentives to carry insurance coverage and also enhance fairness is to prohibit insurers from applying preexisting clauses to individuals who are merely switching from one source of insurance coverage to another.

Community Rating of Insurance Premiums

Most insurers use rating categories such as age, gender, geographic location, business or industry, occupation, claims experience, and health status to predict risk and set premiums in the small-group market. The resulting variation in premiums—if these factors accurately predict beneficiaries' use of services and expenses—conforms to the principle of actuarial fairness under which individuals with the highest health risks pay the highest premiums.[27] This is consistent with industry practices in other areas such as life, auto, and property insurance.

There are several objections to these practices in health insurance, however. First, the actuarial methods used by insurers to predict risk are often not particularly accurate. A recent study indicates that prospective medical screening does not do a good job of predicting use of services in the small-group market.[28] Another study argues that experience-rating techniques are only able to predict about 10 percent of the observed variation in the individual use of services.[29] Second, many methods of risk classification reflect cultural biases rather than firmly established financial experience.[30] Thus, certain kinds of groups—for example, those having members with chronic illness or disability—may be charged higher premiums than their actual use of services warrants.[31] Third, since a perfectly fair market requires *individual* premiums, no classification scheme results in actuarially fair premiums as long as insurance is provided through employers or other social groups. Within an arbitrary group (the firm), there will always be individuals with substantially higher risks than others, yet all members pay the same rate for coverage. In small firms, an illness that strikes one or more employee may cause a large increase in premiums for their colleagues. So workers with identical risks in two different firms may pay substantially different insurance premiums—a violation of the principle of horizontal equity in social policy.[32]

In an actuarial sense, horizontal equity is possible only if companies abandon health plans altogether and force their employees to obtain insurance in the individual market. What the current insurance system really does is substitute certain bases of social solidarity and cross-subsidy (membership in a company and other risk categories) for other bases of social solidarity used in the past or in other places (membership in a community or nation).

The rationale for limiting variation in insurance premiums extends well beyond these criticisms. The key argument is that medical care is not a commodity but an object of mutual aid. It should therefore be distributed according to one's medical need, not one's ability to pay.[33] Indeed, the onset of sickness and disability often means that those in greatest need are least able to pay for medical services. So the main issue for policymakers to resolve is defining what conditions are deserving of mutual aid—and implicitly, what cross-subsidies are acceptable to members of society.[34]

Under pure community rating, everyone in a specified geographic area would pay the same premium for health insurance, regardless of their current age, employment, or health status. This policy would result in lower-risk individuals subsidizing the cost of health insurance for higher-risk individuals. Even if this is politically feasible, there are potential trade-offs to consider.

One concern is that community rating will cause further erosion of insurance coverage and undermine the goals of greater risk pooling and mutual aid. Where insurance coverage is not compulsory, community rating will increase premiums for lower-risk groups and cause them to seek self-insurance or withdraw from the insurance market entirely.[35] New York's adoption of community rating in 1993 demonstrates this undesirable side effect, at least in the short term, as the overall insured population dropped by an estimated twenty-five thousand during the first year following the reforms.[36]

Another concern is that pure community rating might reduce price competition in the market by eliminating the opportunity for employers to negotiate lower premiums and for insured individuals to benefit from health-promoting behaviors.[37] The latter argument assumes that current rating practices are accurate risk predictors and that individuals are substantially rewarded or penalized for their health-related behaviors under the current system. Since neither of these assumptions are true, the potential effect of rating regulations on individual incentives should be a minor concern.[38]

These concerns may lead policymakers to reject pure community rating and instead accept "rate bands" that allow a range of premiums for a given health plan based on a limited set of rating categories. Under a rate band, premiums offered to groups or individuals are permitted to vary by a certain percentage compared with the average premium in that class of subscribers.

Employee Choice of Health Plans

Most of the insurance reforms discussed above modify market practices to increase social equity and reduce the economic penalties for becoming sick. In contrast, other reforms attempt to improve the efficiency of the health care system by strengthening the market tendency to force those who use more health services to pay higher costs. Here, the assumption is not that the market works too well, but that it does not work well enough.

Part of the reason for high costs in the small-group insurance market is that price competition among health plans is often quite limited. Some analysts, therefore, advocate increasing price elasticity by requiring employers to offer a number of competing health plans and allowing individual employees to choose their individual plan.[39] In addition, employees must pay some of the cost of a health plan as an incentive to limit their demand for services.[40] These provisions, it is argued, will lead to more prudent purchasing of insurance and result in plans better tailored to what consumers really need.

If policymakers decide to expand the choice of health plans, they must also decide whether and how to limit the number of choices. The main concern is that choices must be numerous enough and diverse enough to satisfy consumers, but not so large as to make a meaningful comparison of plans impossible.

Standard Benefit Plans

One way to enhance consumer choice of health plans is to make side-by-side comparisons easier. This can be done by requiring or encouraging insurers to offer one or more plans with standard benefits.

In theory, simplifying and standardizing contractual benefits forces insurers to compete on overall price and quality instead of using selective benefits to lure the best risks. Without this kind of market regulation, health plans can be designed to attract or discourage certain kinds of subscribers. The range of physician choice, the level of cost sharing, and particular benefits affect the potential number and actuarial risk of subscribers. Any attempt to reduce risk-based competition, therefore, requires some controls over plan design and benefit packages.[41]

Authorizing standard benefit plans is a way to broaden access as well as equalize competition among insurers. A fairly broad benefit package can help guarantee the availability of services that consumers might have difficulty obtaining in an unregulated market (e.g., AIDS therapy, mental health care).

An obvious problem for policymakers is that creating a standard benefit package becomes a political and ethical exercise as provider and patient advocates lobby for particular services. Clearly, any package will exclude benefits that would be of considerable value to some individuals. In addition, it creates an economic dilemma in that each added benefit can make the package less affordable to the small businesses and individuals that policymakers are trying to extend insurance to in the first place.[42]

The choice to adopt standard benefit plans is also complicated by the need to decide whether insurers will be allowed to offer nonstandard plans. If there are parallel systems, then adverse selection may follow as the standard plans become "dumping grounds" for the bad risks. This could cause access to the guaranteed benefit package to decline as the premiums become less affordable and as insurers restrict marketing efforts for the unprofitable standard plans.

Information on the Quality of Health Plans

Making consumers more cost-conscious in their choice of health plans requires better information about the quality of services as well as premiums.[43] The concept of "accountable health partnerships" advanced by the Jackson Hole Group suggests that market competition can be facilitated by indicators of patient satisfaction, clinical status, function, well-being, and other aspects of quality.[44]

While some information of this kind is helpful, the state of the art in clinical information systems and outcomes management is far from providing uniform measures of quality for insurers, providers, and purchasers of health plans.[45] Thus, policymakers interested in fostering a more efficient insurance market need to recognize that quality standards and data are a critical public good, and to work with private-sector providers, insurers, and purchasers to create an information infrastructure that will encourage greater health plan performance and consumer satisfaction.

Risk Adjustment Mechanisms

The stakes for insurers in accurately predicting or avoiding high-risk individuals are sizable, as about 5 percent of the population accounts for half of all annual health care spending, and 10 percent of the population accounts for 70 percent of expenditures.[46] Even if risk-based competition were totally eliminated however, high-risk individuals are unlikely to be evenly distributed among insurers. The chance of drawing a significant number of high-risk subscribers causes all insurers to raise their costs to protect against such an eventuality. It is also likely that reforms would not eliminate all ability to engage in risk selection strategies, in which case some insurers would be favorably advantaged in comparison to others.

The rational solution is to adopt a risk adjustment mechanism to transfer revenues from health plans with below-average risks to plans with above-average risks. Such a policy would act as a disincentive to risk-based competition by eliminating the fruits of such a strategy, and prevent some insurers being forced out of the market because they have ended up, by chance, serving a riskier population.[47]

A risk adjustment mechanism is also desirable to encourage health plans to develop specialty services for populations with demonstrably higher risks and costs. It is an important step, therefore, toward competition that rewards overall quality and efficiency instead of the lowest, unadjusted price.

The challenge, however, is that an accepted method of risk adjustment is one of the missing links on the path to fair market competition.[48] To work properly, a method must be constructed to adjust only for differences in risk, as nearly as possible. It must not become a means to subsidize inefficient health plans and thereby reduce incentives to improve the value of services for a given premium.[49]

Health Plan Purchasing Cooperatives

A relatively new and potentially powerful way to reshape the small-group insurance market is to create health plan purchasing cooperatives.[50] Allowing small employers to purchase insurance through a public or private cooperative reduces an insurer's risk for any given employer by increasing the size of the risk pool. In addition, purchasing cooperatives reduce the high administrative expenses that insurers incur in the small-group market for marketing, enrollment, collection of premiums, claims administration, and so forth.

These reductions in risk and administrative overhead should permit insurers to offer lower and more uniform premiums for a given plan through a purchasing cooperative than if they deal with individual employers.[51] The pooling of risk reduces the need for medical screening, making more firms and individual employees eligible for insurance coverage. The lower premiums should also expand access to insurance.

There are a number of key choices in the design of purchasing cooperatives. The first choice is sponsorship. Since most if not all the functions of a purchasing cooperative can be performed by either a public or private entity, a judgment must be made as to which offers the proper mix of flexibility and accountability. This choice is partly a matter of ideology as well: Alain Enthoven and Sara Singer promote private cooperatives based on a rhetorical assertion that public agencies are "often associated with waste, complexity, rigidity, and coercion."[52]

The second choice is whether to authorize a single purchasing cooperative in a state, a network of regional cooperatives, or multiple cooperatives in any jurisdiction.[53] This choice depends on whether competing cooperatives will have sufficient size to effectively pool risks, achieve economies of scale, and, if authorized to do so, negotiate premiums. A California policymaker captured the essence of the issue when he asked whether the state intended to place small employers in *pools* or in *puddles*.[54] In addition, a judgment is necessary as to whether the insurance system will perform better if dissatisfied employers can join other cooperatives or can only return to the conventional small-group market— what combination of "exit" and "voice" is best?[55] At what point do the advantages of redundancy and parallel systems give way to the need for hierarchy and authority?[56] Finally, the choice also depends on whether there is sufficient administrative expertise to organize and operate several cooperatives in the short and long term. This is a perennial problem for public agencies,[57] and presumably would limit the number of effective private cooperatives as well.

A third design choice is whether to allow purchasing cooperatives to select participating insurers and negotiate premiums. In a perfectly competitive market, there would be no advantage to negotiation and all purchasers would be price takers. But the recent experience of major health care purchasers such as state employee programs, Medicaid programs, and private large-employer purchasing cooperatives demonstrates that selective contracting or price negotiation results in lower premium increases than in the market as a whole.[58] Overall, the history of state health policy suggests that governmental agencies with central bargaining power are the common ingredient in effective cost containment.[59] A state may be obliged, however, to put purchasing cooperatives under the same rules as large employers in the self-insured market.

A fourth choice is whether purchasing cooperatives should market plans through insurance agents and brokers. Since employers can obtain insurance directly from the cooperative, rational analysis suggests that agents and brokers are superfluous to insurance administration and that their fees represent excess costs to subscribers. So substantial savings are possible—perhaps 10 to 12 percent of total premiums—if agents and brokers are cut out of the system.[60] On the other hand, agents and brokers may provide small-business owners and employees with valuable advice about the quality of health plans and additional concerns; in addition, the economic incentives of agents and brokers to sell insurance may translate into broader coverage among small groups than if health insurance was not marketed in the context of the company's other insurance needs. Ultimately, the judgment policymakers face is whether small employers will find their way to purchasing cooperatives without the guidance of agents and brokers. This judgment enters into the decision of how much to provide in compensation: the purchasing cooperative can pay agents and brokers who bring in business a percentage commission, or it can pay them a flat fee, or it can pay them nothing. The cooperative must also decide whether to include the fees in the premium, leaving the amount unstated to employers, or publish the fees showing the added cost to the employer. California, for example, has chosen to make the use of agents and brokers voluntary and allow the employer to decide whether to pay a fee on top of the premium. Given that employers are not mandated to use the purchasing cooperative, policymakers must consider whether agents and brokers might boycott the cooperative and the participating insurers if they can receive substantially greater compensation doing business with plans outside the pool.

Actions Taken to Reform State Health Insurance Markets

In the preceding section, we outlined the possible actions that states might take to reform the small-group insurance market, the rationale for those actions, and the possible consequences of various policy choices. We now turn to examine how states have actually designed their reforms. Our analysis is based on a review of statutes in forty-five states that have adopted small-group health insurance reforms in the 1990s, available reports on those reforms, and interviews with state officials and with executives of public and private health plan purchasing cooperatives.

We begin by discussing notable patterns across the states in this area of legislation. What does the timing of these reforms suggest about the relationship of these incremental reforms to the push for national health care

Table 3.1

Timing of Legislative Adoption of Access Reforms, 1990–95

State	1990	1991	1992	1993	1994	1995
Alabama	–	–	–	–	–	–
Alaska	–	–	–	X	–	–
Arizona	–	–	–	X	–	–
Arkansas	–	X	–	–	–	–
California	–	–	X	–	–	–
Colorado	–	X	–	–	X	–
Connecticut	X	–	–	X	–	–
Delaware	–	X	X	–	–	–
Florida	–	X	X	X	–	–
Georgia	–	–	–	–	–	–
Hawaii	–	–	–	–	–	–
Idaho	–	–	–	X	–	–
Illinois	–	–	–	X	–	–
Indiana	–	X	X	–	–	–
Iowa	–	X	X	X	–	–
Kansas	–	X	X	–	X	–
Kentucky	–	–	–	–	X	–
Louisiana	–	X	–	X	–	–
Maine	–	X	X	X	–	–
Maryland	–	–	–	X	–	–
Massachusetts	–	X	–	–	–	–
Michigan	–	–	–	–	–	–
Minnesota	–	–	X	–	–	–
Mississippi	–	–	–	X	X	–
Missouri	–	–	X	–	–	–
Montana	–	–	–	X	–	–
Nebraska	–	X	–	–	X	–
Nevada	–	–	–	–	–	X
New Hampshire	–	–	X	X	X	–
New Jersey	–	–	X	–	–	–

(continued)

reform? On what elements of policy design is there nearly universal acceptance and on what elements is there substantial variation? Then, we explore various explanations for the observed patterns in policy design.

Timing of Small-Group Insurance Reforms

The first notable pattern is the timing of the small-group reforms. The data in Table 3.1 indicate that twenty-two states had debated and enacted their initial small-group market reform measures prior to 1992, when the issue of health care reform became an important issue in the U.S. presidential campaign. Another twelve states enacted reforms in 1992.

Thus, thirty-four states acted before President Clinton formed his task

New Mexico	–	X	–	–	X	–
New York	–	–	X	–	–	–
North Carolina	–	X	–	X	–	–
North Dakota	–	X	–	X	–	X
Ohio	–	–	X	–	–	–
Oklahoma	–	–	X	–	X	X
Oregon	–	X	–	X	–	–
Pennsylvania	–	–	–	–	–	–
Rhode Island	–	X	X	–	–	–
South Carolina	–	X	–	–	X	–
South Dakota	–	X	–	–	–	–
Tennessee	–	–	X	X	–	–
Texas	–	–	–	X	–	–
Utah	–	–	–	–	X	–
Vermont	–	X	–	–	–	–
Virginia	–	–	X	X	–	–
Washington	–	–	X	X	–	–
West Virginia	–	X	–	X	–	–
Wisconsin	–	X	X	–	–	–
Wyoming	–	–	X	X	–	–
# Initial Reforms	1	21	12	8	2	1
# Additional or Revised Reforms	0	0	8	14	8	2
# Total Reforms	1	21	20	22	10	3

Sources: Data for this table were gathered from a variety of materials provided by the Institute for Health Policy Solutions (Washington, D.C.), supplemented by a review of state legislation on the LEXIS database.

As used here, "access reforms" include: legislatively mandated guaranteed issue and/or renewal of at least some insurance products in the small-group market, limitations on the use of preexisting condition exclusion clauses in insurance contracts, and requirements that insurers give credit for prior insurance coverage when imposing contract restrictions on new subscribers (enhanced portability).

force in 1993, while only eleven states initiated small-group reforms once the design of the Clinton plan and the national debate were under way. This timing strongly suggests that the states were leaders in this area of reform, at once sensing the importance of the health insurance issue yet also responding to inaction at the national level. Once there was a promise of action from the federal government, the state activity in small-group reforms slowed dramatically, as did state action on more comprehensive reforms.

Restricting Insurance Underwriting Practices

The comparative data on underwriting provisions are presented in Table 3.2. The vast majority of the state underwriting reforms are targeted at groups of fifty or fewer individuals. Eleven states apply their reforms to

Table 3.2

Restricting Insurance Underwriting Practices

State	Maximum Size of Small Groups (by 12/31/96)	Guaranteed Issue[a]	Guaranteed Renewal[b]	Enhanced Portability[c]	Limited Preexisting Condition Exclusions[d]
Alabama	—	—	—	—	—
Alaska	50	X	X	X	X
Arizona	40	X	X	X	X
Arkansas	25	—	X	—	—
California	50	X	X	X	X
Colorado	50	X	X	X	X
Connecticut	25	X	X	X	X
Delaware	50	X	X	X	X
Florida	50	X	X	X	X
Georgia	50	—	—	—	—
Hawaii	—	—	—	—	—
Idaho	49	X	X	X	X
Illinois	25	X	X	X	X
Indiana	50	X	X	X	X
Iowa	50	X	X	X	X
Kansas	50	X	X	X	X
Kentucky	100	X	X	X	X
Louisiana	35	X	X	X	—
Maine	25	X	X	X	X
Maryland	50	X	X	X	X
Massachusetts	25	X	X	X	X
Michigan	—	—	—	—	—
Minnesota	49	X	X	X	X
Mississippi	35	X	X	X	X
Missouri	25	X	X	X	X
Montana	25	X	X	X	X

(continued)

groups up to twenty-five members, while thirty states set the maximum size of groups between twenty-five and fifty members. Only Kentucky, New Hampshire, and Virginia include groups of up to one hundred. Some states have extended the upper and lower bounds of the small-group market. Approximately half of the states fold self-employed individuals into the reforms. Other states have applied some of the reform measures beyond the confines of small groups. Washington and Minnesota, for example, mandate that insurers guarantee the issuance and renewal of at least some health benefit plans regardless of group size, including individuals.

Nebraska	50	X	X	X	X
Nevada	–	X	X	X	X
New Hampshire	100	X	X	X	X
New Jersey	49	X	X	X	X
New Mexico	50	X	X	X	X
New York	50	X	X	X	X
North Carolina	49	X	X	X	X
North Dakota	25	X	X	X	X
Ohio	50	X	X	X	X
Oklahoma	50	X	X	X	X
Oregon	25	X	X	X	X
Pennsylvania	–	–	–	–	–
Rhode Island	50	X	X	X	X
South Carolina	50	X	X	X	X
South Dakota	50	–	X	–	–
Tennessee	25	X	X	X	X
Texas	50	X	X	X	X
Utah	50	–	X	X	X
Vermont	49	X	–	X	X
Virginia	99	X	X	X	X
Washington	50	X	X	X	X
West Virginia	60	–	X	X	X
Wisconsin	25	X	X	X	X
Wyoming	50	X	X	X	X

Sources: Data for this table were gathered from a search of state statutory codes addressing small–group market reforms using the LEXIS database.

Notes:

[a]*Guaranteed Issue*: Mandate that at least one health plan be available for purchase within the small–group market regardless of a group's health status or claim experience.

[b]Guaranteed Renewal: Mandate that insurers must offer to renew an existing health plan (or specific types of plans) within the small-group market, regardless of the claim experience or health status of the group.

[c]*Portability*: Limits are imposed on health plan waiting periods and/or exclusions for preexisting conditions within the small-group market when changing insurers and/or health plans.

[d]*Limited Preexisting Condition Exclusions*: Limits placed on how long preexisting medical conditions can be excluded from coverage.

Each of the forty-five states that adopted reforms of some kind require insurers to guarantee the issuance and renewal of at least some of their health benefit plans in the small-group market. These requirements often apply only to the "basic" or "standard" health benefit plans established by the state insurance department or some other designated body. Other states have gone further, requiring guaranteed issue and renewal for all health benefit plans offered in the small-group market.

Every state continues to permit some exclusions from coverage due to preexisting conditions. However, the reforms define what will constitute a preexisting condition (although these definitions are not narrowly drawn) and restrict the period of exclusion from coverage, usually to a maximum of six to twelve months.

To encourage a greater sense of personal security, all state reforms adopted provisions that enhance the portability or continuity of health insurance coverage by prohibiting preexisting condition exclusions for individuals who join a new plan within one or two months after their previous coverage ends. A few states have adopted special rules for persons whose involuntary unemployment interrupts their health benefit plan coverage.

Controlling Variation in Premiums

Historically, insurers have used a wide variety of factors as a basis for setting the premiums charged to a group. Some factors are discrete (age, gender, family size and composition) and others tend to be more ambiguous or subjective (occupation, perceived health status). Age and health status together have been found to account for a 500 percent or more variance in health insurance premiums.[61]

The data presented in Table 3.3 (on pages 66–73) indicate that the reforms impose some constraints on how insurers use certain personal characteristics or classes of business to assess group risk and set premiums. States often allow the use of certain discrete factors for establishing comparable groups, the most common being age, gender, geographic location, and family composition. A few states have specifically prohibited gender as a rating factor. The factors that states most frequently prohibit insurers from using to establish rates are claims experience, health status, and duration of insurance coverage.

In groups classified according to discrete factors, many states restrict the variance between the highest and lowest premium based on additional, more subjective factors. Most importantly, however, no state has restricted the variation in premiums between the highest and lowest risk groups in the entire small-group market.

Pure community rating, according to the American Academy of Actuaries, allows premiums to vary only according to family composition, geographic location, and the design of the health benefit plan.[62] Only the New York reforms meet those criteria. Thirteen other states have adopted legislation requiring a modified form of community rating (sometimes heavily modified). Of those states, only Connecticut and Vermont expressly exclude age as a basis of risk classification. Gender is excluded as a risk characteristic in Connecticut, Montana, New Hampshire, and Vermont. None of the states with modified community rating permit risk classification on the basis of health status, claims experience, or duration of coverage. Only two of the thirteen permit risk classification on the basis of industry or occupation.

The majority of states have not adopted even modified community rating as a part of their small-group reform initiatives. Actuarial rating in these markets is extraordinarily complicated. To begin with, insurers create many "classes" of business that involve distinct marketing strategies or administrative costs. Each small group within a business class is then rated by "case characteristics" such as age, gender, industry, and so forth.

In addition to this two-part risk classification, almost all states still allow rate variation within the permitted risk classes, often including consideration of the claims experience and health status of a group. However, the rating reforms do restrict the variation in premiums, so that an individual insurer cannot charge one group more than a set percentage (e.g., 200 percent) of the lowest premium that is charged to another group in the same risk class, regardless of the group's claims experience or health status.

Closer approximations to community rating are incorporated into some of the state purchasing cooperatives. California, for example, established very tight rate bands within its HPPC: as of 1996, potential subscribers must be offered premiums within 10 percent of an insurer's average premium for a given plan, with additional variation permitted only for specified age categories, geographic location, and family composition.

Regulating Insurance Marketing Practices and Products

Twenty-eight states have authorized the creation of one or more benefit packages for the small-group market, as shown in Table 3.4 (pages 74–75). The designs of such plans are delegated to regulatory bodies or independent commissions and vary between states. The "standard" plans are generally comparable to the health benefit plans of public and private employers in the market as a whole. The "basic" plans provide less comprehensive benefits, reflecting an effort to reduce premium costs and attract employers who do not presently offer a health plan for their workers.

Only Kentucky and Maryland require insurers to offer only state-authorized benefit packages. The halfway regulation in the rest of the states will continue to make it difficult for small-group sponsors and members to easily compare all available insurance plans, and makes it likely that insurers will continue to engage in risk selection strategies by promoting insurer-designed plans through insurance agents and brokers.

The data in Table 3.4 also indicate that eighteen of the twenty-eight states with standardized plans have adopted new rules of disclosure and fair marketing. These provisions suggest that legislators recognize that, where the state-authorized plans must compete with traditional insurer-designed plans, efforts must be made to prevent insurers from seeking out low-risk groups through their marketing practices.

Table 3.3

Constraints on Premiums and Premium Variation

States (CR/MCR)[a]	Maximum Difference in Premium between Groups with Similar Characteristics[b]			Group Characteristics as a Basis for Risk Comparisons		
	Within risk class (%)	Within class of business (%)	Limits on premium increase	Expressly permitted[c]	Expressly prohibited	Other with approval
Alabama	—	—	—	—	—	—
Alaska	—	208	Yes	Age, industry,[d] gender, geography, family composition	—	Yes
Arizona	—	267	Yes	Geography, family composition, and other objective characteristics as determined by carrier	Claims experience, health status, industry, duration of coverage	—
Arkansas	200	167	Yes	Demographic and other relevant characteristics as determined by carrier	—	—
California	—	122	—	Age, geography, family composition, health status	—	—
Colorado (MCR)	150	—	—	Age, geography	—	Yes
Connecticut (MCR)	125	—	—	Age, gender, geography, industry, family composition	Claims experience, medical history	—

State	*e	*f		Objective criteria	Claims/health criteria	
Delaware	—	—	Yes	Objective criteria as determined by carrier	Claims experience, health states, duration	—
Florida (MCR)	—	—	Yes[g]	Age, gender, family composition, tobacco usage, geography	—	—
Georgia	—	167	—	Age, gender, group size, geography, industry, occupation, avocation	—	Yes
Hawaii	—	—	—	—	—	—
Idaho	200	167	Yes	Age, gender, tobacco usage	Claims experience, health status, duration	Yes
Illinois	200	167	Yes	Demographic or other objective characteristics as determined by carrier	Claims experience, health status, duration	—
Indiana	—	208	Yes	Demographic or other objective characteristics as determined by carrier	Claims experience, health status, duration	Yes
Iowa	200	167	Yes	Age, geography, family composition, group size	Health Status or claims experience[h]	Yes
Kansas	200	167	Yes	Age, gender, industry, geography, family composition, group size	—	Yes
Kentucky (MCR)	—	—	—	Age,[i] geography, family composition	—	—

Table 3.3 (continued)

States (CR/MCR)[a]	Maximum Difference in Premium between Groups with Similar Characteristics[b]			Group Characteristics as a Basis for Risk Comparisons		
	Within risk class (%)	Within class of business (%)	Limits on premium increase	Expressly permitted[c]	Expressly prohibited	Other with approval
Louisiana	200	167	Yes	Age, gender, industry, geography, family composition, group size, tobacco usage	Claims experience, health status, duration	Yes
Maine (MCR)	150	—	—	Age, industry or occupation, family composition, tobacco usage, wellness programs, group size	Claims experience, health status, gender	—
Maryland (MCR)	138	—	—	Age, geography, family composition	Claims experience, health status, duration	Yes
Massachusetts	—	*[j]	—	Age, gender, industry, family composition, employee participation rate	—	—
Michigan	—	—	—	—	—	—
Minnesota	—	390	—	Health status, claims experience, industry, duration), age, geography[k]	Gender, marital status	—
Mississippi	200	167	Yes	Demographic or other objective characteristics as determined by carrier	Health status, claims experience, duration	—

Missouri	200	Yes	167	Demographic or other objective characteristics as determined by carrier, including Industry[l]	Health status, claims experience, duration	—
Montana	200	Yes	167	Demographic or other objective characteristics as determined by carrier	Gender, claims experience, health status, duration	—
Nebraska	200	Yes	167	Age, gender, industry,[d] geography, family composition, group size	—	Yes
Nevada	200	—	167	Age, gender, industry, geography, family composition, group size	—	Yes
New Hampshire (MCR)	300[m]	Yes[n]	—	Age, family composition	Gender, geography, occupation, health status, claims experience duration	—
New Jersey (MCR)	200	—	—	Age, gender, geography	—	—
New Mexico	180	Yes	120	Age, gender,[o] geography, family composition, tobbaco usage	Health status	—
New York (CR)	—	—	—	Family composition, geography	Age, gender, health status, occupation	—

(continued)

Table 3.3 (continued)

States (CR/MCR)[a]	Maximum Difference in Premium between Groups with Similar Characteristics[b]			Group Characteristics as a Basis for Risk Comparisons		
	Within risk class (%)	Within class of business (%)	Limits on premium increase	Expressly permitted[c]	Expressly prohibited	Other with approval
North Carolina (MCR)	150	–	Yes	Age, gender, geography, family composition	–	Yes
North Dakota	173	150	Yes	Age, gender, industry, geography, family composition, group size	Claims experience, health status, duration	Yes
Ohio	–	208	Yes	Age, gender, industry,[d] geography, group size, and other objective criteria as determined by carrier	Claims experience, health status, duration	–
Oklahoma	200	167	Yes	Demographic or other objective characteristics as determined by carrier	Claims experience, health status, duration	–
Oregon (MCR)	200	–	Yes[p]	Geography, family composition	–	–
Pennsylvania	–	–	–	–	–	–
Rhode Island	200	167	Yes	Age, gender, geography, family composition, tobacco usage, group size	–	Yes

State						
South Carolina	200	167	Yes	Demographic or other objective characteristics as determined by carrier	Claims experience, health status, duration	—
South Dakota	200	167	Yes	Demographic or other objective characteristics as determined by carrier	Claims experience, health status, duration	—
Tennessee	260	216	Yes	Demographic or other objective characteristics as determined by carrier	Claims experience, health status, duration	—
Texas	200	167	Yes	Age, gender, geography, industry, size, and other objective characteristics as determined by carrier	Claims experience, health status, duration	—
Utah	200	167	Yes	Demographic or other objective characteristics, including Industry,[d] as determined by the carrier	Claims experience, health status, duration	—
Vermont (MCR)	150[q]	—	—	—	Age, gender, geography, industry, claims experience, duration, tier	—
Virginia (MCR)	150[r]	—	—	Age, gender, geography	—	—
Washington (MCR)	425[s]	—	—	Age, geography, family composition, wellness activities	—	—

(continued)

Table 3.3 (continued)

States (CR/MCR)[a]	Maximum Difference in Premium between Groups with Similar Characteristics[b]			Group Characteristics as a Basis for Risk Comparisons		
	Within risk class (%)	Within class of business (%)	Limits on premium increase	Expressly permitted[c]	Expressly prohibited	Other with approval
West Virginia	—	150	Yes	Demographic or other objective characteristics, including Industry,[t] as determined by carrier	Claims experience, health status, duration	—
Wisconsin	—	208	Yes	Demographic actuarially based characteristics such as age, sex, geography, and occupation	Claims experience, health status, duration	—
Wyoming	200	167	Yes	Demographic and other objective characteristics as determined by carrier	Claims experience, health status, duration	—

Sources: Data for this table were gathered from a search of state statutory codes addressing small-group market reforms, using the LEXIS database.

Notes:

[a] Use of community rating (CR) or modified community rating (MCR) within small-group market.

[b] Maximum difference in premium is expressed as a percentage of the lowest premium for groups with similar characteristics (age, gender, etc.). Limits within a "risk class" refer to groups with similar characteristics regardless of their "class of business." Limits within a class of business refer to all groups within a "class of business" regardless of their group characteristics. Limits on premium increases are calculated by adding the percentage change in the new business premium rate, plus changes in health status, claim experience, and duration (capped at 15 percent, except for New Mexico at 10 percent), *plus* increases from changes in demographic characteristics.

cDifferences in health benefit plan design are a permissible basis for premium variance but are not listed as a group characteristic. We suspect that family composition is also universally recognized as a permissible characteristic. However, given the prominence that a number of states have given it (unlike plan design), where explicitly listed in the reform, we include it in our table.

dDifferences due to industry limited to 135 percent.

eIn addition to the limits specified in note e, an additional premium variance of 150 percent is permitted with respect to similar groups.

fDifference in premium for similar groups is limited to 208 percent based upon unspecified characteristics, with an *additional* 122 percent combined difference for gender and geography, with *no* limits on differences due to age and family characteristics.

gRenewal and new business rates must be identical.

hRestriction relevant only to the Standard and Basic Health Benefit Plans.

iPremium difference due to age limited to 300 percent.

jPremium variance restrictions are imposed, but are not convertible to the format presented here.

kDifferences due to characteristics limited to plus or minus: 25 percent of index rate for health status, claim experience, industry, and duration; 50 percent for age; and an additional 20 percent for geography.

lDifference due to industry limited to 122 percent.

mLimit applies only to differences due to age.

nPremium increases are capped at 25 percent plus increases attributable to cost and health care utilization trends.

oRate variation due to gender within an age grouping are limited to 150%.

pPremium increases are limited to changes in the geographic rate plus changes in family composition plus changes in benefit plan design, plus 15 percent cap on any other changes.

qLegislation provides that by regulation, the state may permit the use of risk classes so long as premium variation does not exceed 150 percent and does not include use of medical underwriting or medical screening.

rWithin a risk classification, premiums may not vary by more than 150 percent due to claim experience, health status, or duration of coverage.

sThis limitation pertains only to age.

tDifferences due to industry limited to 15 percent.

Table 3.4

Mandatory Marketwide Offerings and Marketing Practices Reforms

State	Mandatory Marketwide Offering of Standardized[a] Small-Group Plans			Marketing Practices Reforms	
	Basic plans[b]	Standard plans[c]	Exclusive of other plans[d]	Disclosure of rating practices[e]	"Fair" marketing rules[f]
Alabama	—	—	—	—	—
Alaska	Yes	Yes	—	Yes	Yes
Arizona	Yes	—	—	Yes	Yes
Arkansas	—	—	—	Yes	—
California	—	—	—	Yes	—
Colorado	Yes	Yes	—	Yes	—
Connecticut	Yes	—	—	—	—
Delaware	Yes	Yes	—	Yes	Yes
Florida	Yes	Yes	—	Yes	Yes
Georgia	—	—	—	—	—
Hawaii	—	—	—	—	—
Idaho	Yes	Yes	—	Yes	Yes
Illinois	—	—	—	Yes	—
Indiana	—	—	—	Yes	—
Iowa	Yes	Yes	—	Yes	—
Kansas	Yes	Yes	—	—	*g
Kentucky	Yes	Yes	Yes	Yes	Yes
Louisiana	—	—	—	Yes	—
Maine	—	—	—	Yes	Yes
Maryland	Yes	Yes	Yes	Yes	—
Massachusetts	—	—	—	Yes	—
Michigan	—	—	—	—	—
Minnesota	—	—	—	Yes	—
Mississippi	—	—	—	Yes	—
Missouri	Yes	Yes	—	Yes	Yes
Montana	Yes	Yes	—	Yes	Yes
Nebraska	Yes	Yes	—	Yes	Yes
Nevada[h]	—	—	—	Yes	—
New Hampshire	—	—	—	Yes	—
New Jersey	—	—	—	—	—
New Mexico	—	—	—	Yes	—
New York	—	—	—	—	—
North Carolina	Yes	Yes	—	—	—
North Dakota	Yes	Yes	—	Yes	Yes
Ohio	—	—	—	—	—
Oklahoma	Yes	Yes	—	Yes	Yes
Oregon	Yes	Yes	—	Yes	Yes
Pennsylvania	—	—	—	—	—
Rhode Island	Yes	Yes	—	Yes	Yes
South Carolina	Yes	Yes	—	Yes	Yes
South Dakota	Yes	Yes	—	Yes	Yes
Tennessee	Yes	Yes	—	—	—

(continued)

Table 3.4 *(continued)*

Texas[i]	Yes	Yes	–	Yes	–
Utah	Yes	–	–	Yes	–
Vermont[j]	–	–	–	–	–
Virginia[k]	Yes	Yes	–	Yes	–
Washington	Yes	–	–	–	–
West Virginia	–	–	–	Yes	Yes[l]
Wisconsin	Yes	–	–	Yes	Yes
Wyoming	Yes	Yes	–	–	–

Source: Data for this table were gathered from a search of state statutory codes addressing small-group market reforms, using the LEXIS database.

Notes:

[a]We expect that the degree of plan "standardization" varies between the states, as the legislation reviewed was rarely sufficiently precise to permit an interpretation that all such plans are truly identical as between carriers. These plans are, however, likely to be at least sufficiently similar as to greatly facilitate price/quality comparisons as opposed to the nonstandardized plans that the majority of states allow the carriers to continue to offer.

[b]A "basic" plan is typically one that does not contain all of the insurance coverage mandated for a "standard" plan in an effort to reduce premium costs, thereby increasing the number of small-groups offering health benefit plans.

[c]A "standard" plan is typically one that contains all of the insurance coverages thought to be necessary and appropriate for adequate, but not excessive, health insurance coverage.

[d]State designed basic and/or standard plans, together with approved supplemental policies, are the *only* small-group health benefit plans that may be marketed by insurance carriers.

[e]Legislatively mandated disclosure, in some form and instance, of the rating practices of the insurance carrier to the small-employer group being marketed to, and/or to the relevant state agency responsible for oversight of the small-group market.

[f]While specific requirements vary, such requirements often will mandate that basic and standard health benefit plans be actively marketed, that carriers neither directly nor indirectly discourage small groups from applying for coverage because of their collective health status, claim experience, industry, occupation, or geographic location. Carriers are also prohibited from suggesting the small group seek such coverage from another carrier, and must establish a compensation system for their agents and brokers that does not create a disincentive to the marketing of such plans.

[g]Rather than mandating specific market practices (or prohibiting them), Kansas has elected instead to mandate the inclusion of specific information in all marketing materials developed by the small-group insurance carriers.

[h]It is possible that Nevada also utilizes some form of basic/standard health plans, but the statutes reviewed left considerable doubt in that regard and therefore we declined to include it in the list of states using same.

[i]Texas provides a "catastrophic" plan and a basic plan.

[j]Vermont legislation refers to "common" plans that *may* be developed by regulation but does not appear to mandate their use across the small-group market.

[k]Virginia utilizes an "essential" plan and a standard plan.

[l]Small-group insurance carriers, and their agents or brokers, are prohibited from marketing health benefit plans to specific groups, legal occupations, geographic locales, zip codes, neighborhoods, races, religions, or any other discriminatory group.

Another policy to reduce risk-based competition is to mandate risk adjustment among health plans. The extent to which this policy has been adopted is unclear, because most of our data are limited to statutory provisions and risk adjustment mechanisms may be adopted by state officials in subsequent implementing regulations.

In many states that promote purchasing cooperatives, however, policymakers have chosen to include risk adjustment with other provisions for market restructuring. Of the nine states with HPPC enabling legislation, Kentucky, Maine, and North Carolina mandated the use of risk adjustment in their legislation. The remaining six states left it to the discretion of the purchasing cooperative or a regulatory body, or else failed to address the issue explicitly. The purchasing cooperatives in California, Kentucky, and Utah each report that risk adjustment mechanisms are in place and have been implemented. The Minnesota Employees Insurance Program also reports that it is using risk adjustment, though there is no enabling HPPC legislation. The remainder of the states have yet to fully develop their mechanisms or presently have no plans to do so.

Promoting Health Plan Purchasing Cooperatives

Nine states have enacted legislation to create small-group health plan purchasing cooperatives or to specifically enable their creation; a summary of the design choices these states have made appears in Table 3.5 (pages 78–82). The insurance reforms in some other states may permit the creation of HPPCs, but the legislation does not make explicit policy decisions regarding their structure and operations.

States have chosen three basic approaches for purchasing cooperatives: (a) the HPPC may be operated and controlled by a public agency, (b) the HPPC is operated privately but controlled by a publicly appointed board, or (c) the HPPC is operated and controlled by private organizations.

The data in Table 3.5 compare the operational design of individual HPPCs controlled by public agencies or public boards, based on legislation and implementing regulations. Five of the nine states that adopted HPPC legislation authorized operation by a public agency or public appointment of the HPPC boards. California and Kentucky HPPCs are operated by public agencies, while those in Florida, North Carolina, and Texas are private not-for-profit organizations whose boards are appointed by public officials. In addition to these five states with HPPCs devoted specifically to the small-group market, Minnesota and Washington offer small groups access to health insurance through state agencies that administer the health plan purchasing for public employees.

Thus, a total of seven states have opted for public-sector control of HPPCs. The current operational design (after implementing regulations) of individual HPPCs controlled by public agencies or public boards is presented in Table 3.5. For now, the publicly sponsored or publicly enabled cooperatives are statewide except for the regional organizations in Florida and South Carolina. Four states (Colorado, Maine, South Carolina, and Utah) have opted for wholly private control.[63] Only two private purchasing cooperatives operate on a statewide basis (in Connecticut and Utah), while all the others are regional entities.

Requirements for employer participation are generally not established by state legislatures. Most public and private HPPCs have established their own participation rules to protect against adverse selection, however. A minimum percentage of employees, most commonly 70 percent, must purchase coverage for the group to participate in the HPPC. The public HPPCs generally require employers to make a contribution of 50 percent of the lowest-cost plan available through the cooperative, while the private HPPCs generally do not impose such a requirement.

No legislature has mandated that insurers participate in HPPCs in order to do business in the state. On the other hand, insurers are typically not guaranteed participation, either. Almost all of the purchasing cooperatives are able to select participating insurers. Only Florida and North Carolina require the cooperatives to accept all certified plans. The public cooperatives are not typically very restrictive in the number of insurers and plans they offer, however. Several state programs offer plans from about twenty different insurers, and Minnesota is the only cooperative with fewer than ten participating insurers. In contrast, only one of the private cooperatives has more than four participating insurers.

Almost all HPPCs, both public and private, negotiate premiums with insurers in some fashion. Again, only Florida and North Carolina prohibit selective contracting and require HPPCs to act as price-takers. Because participation by insurers in the cooperatives is voluntary, however, price negotiation is not necessarily a hardball game. In California, for example, "negotiation" consists of providing insurers general feedback on where their proposed premiums fit in relation to those of all plans, and allowing them a week to adjust their price if they desire to do so. Insurers are not given any information about specific competitors, nor are they told the exact rankings of the proposed premiums.[64]

The publicly sponsored or publicly enabled cooperatives provide distinctly greater choice for employees than do the private cooperatives. Florida mandates that employees be able to choose from between a minimum of two insurers. California, Kentucky, and Washington provide for full em-

Table 3.5

Design Elements of Public Cooperatives or Cooperatives with Publicly Appointed Boards

Design Elements	California Health Insurance Plan of California[a]	Florida Community Health Purchasing Alliances[b]
Public or private cooperative	Public agency	Private, not-for-profit
Membership requirements[c]	70 percent employee participation requirement; 50 percent employer contribution requirement	70 percent employee participation requirement; 50 percent employer contribution requirement
Carrier participation	Open participation	Open participation
Employee choice	Employee choice from among plans and carriers	Employee choice from among at least two plans/carriers
Price negotiation	Request for proposal and negotiation	Request for proposal
Benefit plan design	Public design for use in cooperative	Public design for use in small-group market generally
Agent/broker participation	Use permitted, fees limited and separately stated from premium	Use mandatory, negotiated fees between agents and carriers
Geographic market	Statewide	Regional cooperatives (11)
Risk adjustment mechanism	Implemented and unique to cooperative	None
Comparative cost/quality info.	Comparative cost information, quality information under development	Comparative cost information, quality information under development
Marketing materials	By cooperative and carriers (after cooperative review)	By cooperative and carriers (after cooperative review)
Number of participating carriers	22	32
Number of standardized plans offered[d]	2	3
Number of persons insured	106,000	76,763
Number of participating groups	5,800	17,303

Design Elements	Kentucky Kentucky Health Purchasing Alliance[e]	Minnesota Minnesota Employer's Insurance Program[f]
Public or private cooperative	Public agency	Public agency
Membership requirements	80 percent employee participation requirement	75 percent employee participation requirement
Carrier participation	Open participation	Selective contracting
Employee choice	Employee choice from among plans and carriers	Employer selects benefit level (plan) and employee selects carrier
Price negotiation	Request for proposal and negotiation	Negotiation
Benefit plan design	Public design for use in small-group market generally	Public design for this program
Agent/broker participation	Use permitted, fees limited (5 percent) and separately stated from premium	Mandates use of local agents/broker or program's own "master" agent
Geographic market	Statewide	Statewide
Risk adjustment mechanism	Implemented and unique to cooperative	All claims in excess of $50,000 are pooled
Comparative cost/quality info.	Comparative cost information,– quality information under development	Comparative cost information only
Marketing materials	Developed by third-party administrator	All materials prepared by program
Number of participating carriers	10	3
Number of standardized plans offered	4	4
Number of persons insured	30,700	5,000
Number of participating groups	1,800	370

(continued)

Table 3.5 *(continued)*

Design Elements	North Carolina CareAlliance[g]	Texas Texas Insurance Purchasing Alliance[h]
Public or private cooperative	Private, not-for-profit	Private, not for profit
Membership requirements	100 percent employee participation requirement; 50 percent employer contribution requirement	75 percent employee participation requirement; 50 percent employer contribution requirement
Carrier participation	Open participation	Open participation
Employee choice	Employee choice, but with 70 percent + employer contribution, employer able to control all choices	Employer selects benefit level (plan) and employee selects carrier
Price negotiation	Request for proposal and negotiation	Request for proposal and negotiation
Benefit plan design	Public design for use in small-group market generally	Public design for use in small-group market generally
Agent/broker participation	Use mandatory, negotiated fees between agents and carriers	Use permitted, fees limited (7.5 percent)
Geographic market	Regional (6) operating similar to independent franchises of single statewide CareAlliance	Statewide
Risk adjustment mechanism	Under development	None
Comparative cost/quality info.	Comparative cost information only	Comparative cost information only
Marketing materials	Materials by all parties, but with alliance review	Materials primarily developed by alliance but included some carrier submitted material
Number of participating carriers	15	10
Number of standardized plans offered	3	4
Number of persons insured	650	8,086
Number of participating groups	200	659

Design Elements	Washington Basic Health Plan[i]
Public or private cooperative	Public agency
Membership requirements	Open to all groups without restriction
Carrier participation	Open participation
Employee choice	Employee choice from among plans and carriers
Price negotiation	Request for proposal
Benefit plan design	Public design unique to program
Agent/broker participation	Use permitted with some limitations on commission
Geographic market	Statewide
Risk adjustment mechanism	None
Comparative cost/quality info.	Comparative cost information only
Marketing materials	Materials developed by carriers and by program
Number of participating carriers	18
Number of standardized plans offered	1
Number of persons insured	400
Number of participating groups	100

(continued)

82

Table 3.5 *(continued)*

Notes:

[a]Data provided by the Health Insurance Plan of California and current for June 1, 1996.

[b]Data provided by State Health Purchasing Division of Florida Agency for Health Care and current for July 5, 1996.

[c]Unless otherwise specified, employer contributions are a given percentage of the lowest-cost health benefit plan available through the cooperative.

[d]Number of plans offered refers to the number of basic designs. For example, where four basic designs exist, and each is available through HMO or POS contracts, the number of plans listed is four rather than eight.

[e]Data provided by PlanSource and current for June 15, 1996. Number of persons insured estimated by PlanSource from the number of certificate holders (2:1).

[f]Data provided by Minnesota Department of Employee Relations, Minnesota Employers Insurance Program (MEIP), and current for July 1, 1996.

[g]Data provided by the North Carolina State Health Plan Purchasing Board and current for July 1, 1996.

[h]Data provided by Texas Insurance Purchasing Alliance and current for July 5, 1996.

[i]Data provided by Washington Health Care Policy Board and current for June 1, 1996. Sale of the current insurance product began only in April 1996 and represents a redesign of the program after it became apparent to the board that the previous product was "virtually unmarketable."

ployee choice of plan (basic or standard) and insurer. Minnesota and Texas permit the employer to select the plan, but the employees are free to select their preferred insurer. And North Carolina requires free employee choice unless the employer contributes 70 percent or more of the premium. In contrast, private HPPCs have varying degrees of employee choice, with some reserving all choice to employers and others providing employees full choice unless the participating employer objects.

With the exception of Kentucky, it appears that states are willing to risk adverse selection by permitting insurers to market their own small-group plans outside the HPPC in direct competition with the state-designed benefit plans within the HPPC.[65] When insurer-designed plans are marketed outside a purchasing cooperative, they may attract better risks and leave the HPPC and its standardized products as dumping grounds for the relatively poorer risks. The Independent Health Alliance of Iowa, now out of business, identified this form of risk selection and differences in rating methodologies as key factors in its failure.[66]

The desire to increase competition between insurers on the basis of cost and quality rather than risk was one of the driving forces behind the small-group reforms. The prevalence of employee choice and the use of state-designed benefit plans has aided progress toward this goal within the state HPPCs. The availability of another means to fair and efficient competition, comparative information on health plan quality, has yet to be realized. Every state with a publicly sponsored or publicly enabled HPPC has committed itself to develop quality measures and consumer information on plan performance in the future, but the systems to accomplish that are still being developed. Private HPPCs that offer subscribers a choice among competing insurers are even further behind in this crucial area of market regulation.

No purchasing cooperative in either the public or private sector has eliminated the use of agents and brokers for enrolling subscribers. Officials in various HPPCs acknowledge the importance of agents, arguing that health insurance is a product that must be *sold* in the small-group market because it is not actively *bought*. While every cooperative either mandates or permits the use of agents and brokers, however, most in the public sector have reduced the commissions or fees they receive for bringing business to the cooperative. This is consistent with the fact that much of the market information normally available only through agents is provided by the cooperatives themselves, thereby reducing the value of the service agents can provide. The evidence to date shows that cooperatives rely on agents and brokers for a majority of their enrollment, even where their use is not mandatory. In California, nearly 80 percent of subscribers used agents and brokers when the state purchasing cooperative first started up in 1993. Two years later, direct enrollment was slowly increasing but 65 percent of subscribers were still referred by agents and brokers.

The enrollment in recently created small-group HPPCs ranges from a few hundred to over one hundred thousand subscribers in California. It is readily apparent that the public HPPCs have been able to achieve a greater penetration of the small-group market than have their private-sector counterparts. It is not clear whether the early differences in enrollment are due to initial resources for staffing and marketing, perceptions of need for HPPC services across the states, leadership skills of HPPC staff, or other factors.

Sources of Explanation for the Pattern of State Actions

What are the foremost influences on the design of state insurance reforms? We approach this question by reiterating the perspective that policy debates are political contests with material and ideological winners and losers. There is inevitable conflict over what problems are worthy of governmental intervention as well as what alternatives are appropriate responses to those problems. Insurance reforms may be designed mostly by analysts and advocates steeped in the mechanics of finance and the health care system, but even these actions are a result of "how people fight over visions of the public interest or the nature of the community—the truly significant policy questions."[67] The policies that emerge reflect the intellectual, institutional, and political contexts in which debates arise and are resolved.

Ideas

What in these state insurance reforms can be attributed primarily to the influence of ideas? It is clear that the main idea underpinning insurance reforms is how to modify market structures and transactions to achieve a "fairer" distribution of medical care and medical care costs. People who happen to work for small businesses should not have to pay more for health insurance, nor should insurance be unavailable to the very people who need it most. In the typology of social groups proposed by Anne Schneider and Helen Ingram, this "dependent" population, unable to organize itself in the health care market, would be regarded as deserving of intervention by policymakers.[68] There seems to be genuine concern that health insurance maintain at least some degree of risk sharing and not degenerate further toward a pure market commodity. This accounts for why guaranteed issue and renewal of policies, restrictions on exclusions for preexisting conditions, and at least weak limits on how much premiums can vary are nearly universal elements of state reforms.

The ideas driving reform include not only fundamental principles, but also more narrow and concrete elements of policy design. Among the concepts that permeate the recent insurance reforms in some states are pooling purchasing power, limiting or compensating for adverse risk selection, and empowering consumers to make prudent choices in the insurance market.

The concept of a purchasing cooperative to put small groups on equal footing with larger buyers of health care seems to be an appealing and rational idea. It has been discussed in its current form since at least the late 1980s,[69] yet relatively few states have made these entities a conscious element of public policy. It is difficult to tell whether the small number of cooperatives reflects a view that organizing buyers of private goods and services is an inappropriate role for government; or is an artifact of states having waited to see if the federal government was going to create the Clinton plan's version of health alliances, only to have the subsequent chilling effect of defeat push virtually all health care reform issues off the agenda; or whether other forces are actively opposing them. But the "managed competition" model does appear to have considerable power, because states with purchasing cooperatives have adopted or are developing most of the Jackson Hole Group prescription for standard benefits, employee choice, employee contributions toward premiums, risk adjustment, and information on quality for purchasers. The main departure from the Jackson Hole model, ironically, is that cooperatives have insisted on selective contracting and negotiating premiums with insurers instead of trusting that the new structure of purchasing alone will produce cost containment.

Institutions

Institutions can be said to influence reform when ideas are substantially adapted to existing organizations and practices. The most direct influence can be observed if certain reforms are adopted only where existing organizations are available to give policymakers confidence that the reforms will be quickly and effectively implemented.

The evidence on this sort of direct influence is mixed, but some of the state purchasing cooperatives that are up and running are built around existing agencies. The Minnesota Employees Insurance Program and the Washington Health Care Authority represent good examples of successive institutional development, where the agency operating the state employee benefit program added purchasing pools for other governmental entities and for private businesses and individuals. A somewhat different example is the California Managed Risk Medical Insurance Board (MRMIB), which was assigned to create a small-group purchasing cooperative after successfully implementing two other small state programs to extend subsidized insurance to high-risk individuals and to infants and mothers. In the Minnesota and Washington programs, the new populations are minor additions to existing responsibilities, while in MRMIB the small-group cooperative (currently over one hundred thousand enrollees) dwarfs the original subsidized programs.

Patterns in the state reforms can also indirectly reflect institutional forces where provisions must be adapted to current practices. This is clearly the case when even publicly sponsored purchasing cooperatives use insurance agents and brokers rather than push for direct enrollment of subscribers. There is, theoretically, little need for the kind of services provided by agents and brokers in a system of purchasing cooperatives, but California officials—who have tried hard to eliminate the middlemen—admit that it is extremely difficult to change a system "where 99.9 percent of insurance is bought through agents and brokers."[70] Small-business owners are used to going through their local agents for all insurance needs; the slow pace of change suggests that they are unaware that they may purchase insurance directly through the state cooperative, they are reluctant to take away income from their personal insurance agent, or they feel that the additional information and advice that agents can provide on health plans is of sufficient value to maintain that relationship.

Institutional influences also help explain the current divergence in the boundaries of purchasing cooperatives—why the great majority of public cooperatives are statewide entities and almost all the private cooperatives are regional or community based. Quite simply, governments usually organize things from the top down and the private sector organizes things from the bottom up. The considerable size of enrollment in the California and Florida cooperatives may also show that governmental sponsorship speeds up the implementation process, either because it provides greater material resources to the process or, more likely, because public endorsement signals insurers that the cooperative will provide them a substantial pool of potential customers, making it more immediately rewarding to do business there.

Finally, the underdevelopment of risk adjustment and consumer information on health plan performance reflect the fact that this kind of technology and institutional infrastructure for quality-based market competition is not yet available in either the public or private sector.[71] A project in the California purchasing cooperative suggests that moving from conventional reinsurance to an agreeable method of risk adjustment is a tedious, complex process because there are no widely accepted guidelines or experience on which to ground these policies.[72]

Interests

Health insurance reforms, like other matters of public policy, are also determined by the various interests at stake. The observation that governmental sponsorship is related to a significantly higher number of participating insurers and subscribers in purchasing cooperatives raises the question of why, in the early stages of HPPC development, the public-sector approach is more successful than strictly voluntary organization. It is clear that establishing purchasing pools for small groups and individuals is a collective-action problem that often requires governmental support, because the stakes for a given participant are not great enough to justify the costs of organizing a cooperative in the private sector. Thus, until a "learning curve" in HPPC development has been established, private sector cooperatives will appear only in the presence of skillful entrepreneurs[73] or in places like the Twin Cities, where a small-group cooperative can form as a "little brother" to an established purchasing group like the Buyers Health Care Action Group for the region's large employers.[74]

Aside from purchasing cooperatives, the interests served by insurance reforms in the areas of access, rating of premiums, and marketing can be interpreted in different ways. These reforms may fit the category that James Q. Wilson defines as "client politics"—where providing purchasing parity for small groups and lower premiums to high-risk individuals costs little to the rest of the population. Alternatively, they may be interpreted as "entrepreneurial politics"—where generating a fairer and more competitive marketplace requires imposing substantial regulation and costs on the insurance industry (and indirectly, health care professionals and institutional providers).[75]

The political calculus of who will receive benefits and who will bear burdens is not determined strictly by which interests are organized and mobilized. Choices of policy design can be determined either by visible, mobilized interests or by implicit interests that might mobilize in reaction to unfavorable policy decisions.[76] In addition, Charles Lindblom has noted that business interests in the political system are privileged because of their importance to economic prosperity and its impact on electoral politics.[77] Finally, how interests are treated by policymakers depends in part on their "social construction," that is, whether they are widely considered deserving of legal, economic, or moral support by government.[78] But even clients who are perceived as especially needy or deserving do not necessarily gain if the costs will fall on politically powerful groups. A problem for policymakers on health insurance issues is that, in Schneider and Ingram's typology, "dependent" interests (deserving but not powerful) are matched against "contending" interests (undeserving but powerful).[79] This will likely result in primarily symbolic burdens on the contending interests of the insurance industry, according to Schneider and Ingram.

The adoption of many elements of small-group reform in forty-five states suggests that this brand of policy is politically popular, both on its own merits and as a nearly consensual alternative to more comprehensive reforms that pose deeper and broader threats to the existing allocation of resources in the health care system. In their current form, these provisions are not a severe threat to the insurance industry—indeed, the industry has worked closely with the National Association of Insurance Commissioners (NAIC), a group representing state officials that works closely with the insurance industry, to promulgate model legislation for the small-group market.

Few states have gone beyond the NAIC recommendations and mounted a direct challenge to current insurance practices. As the data in Table 3.6 (on pages 90–91) demonstrate, only nine states have adopted legislation with a relatively full scope of regulations on access to coverage, rating of premiums, and marketing and purchasing of plans. And within each area of regulation, there are few states opting for the strongest possible provisions. While the visible individual tragedies played up by the media and by groups like Families USA in recent years have had an impact in moderating the influence of self-interest, only a handful of states have adopted policies approaching community rating of insurance and only one state required pure community rating. Because the current voluntary system falls well short of universal coverage, no state is in a position to eliminate exclusions on the coverage of preexisting conditions without risking massive disenrollment in the small-group market. To date, even the effort to reduce industry incentives for selective marketing and avoiding subscribers with potentially high-cost conditions has been minimal. The recent effort to institute risk adjustment of premiums in the California purchasing cooperative serves as a reminder that this highly technical area of reform is also a highly political process: states must gain the cooperation of insurers to create a risk adjustment mechanism at all, and even then the adjustment and resulting transfer of revenues between plans is limited to boundaries of risk that the plans themselves are willing to negotiate.[80] Finally, no state has gone so far as to make purchasing cooperatives the main field of competition for the small-group market by preventing insurers from offering nonstandard benefit plans outside of the cooperative.[81]

Overall, the state reforms reflect the power of insurers and agents in that government has been able to somewhat bend, but certainly not yet reconstruct, the insurance system for individuals and small groups. How the pro-competitive insurance reforms will progress in the future is also unknown. Employee choice and purchasing cooperatives are tangible benefits that the California experience shows are political winners with the public. A vivid demonstration of this occurred when the governor and the legislator who sponsored the reforms, representing different political parties and philosophies, held dueling press conferences in the summer of 1994 when the purchasing cooperative announced a decrease in its average premiums for its second year of operation. It became an example of both limited government and intervention on behalf of the underdog—a desirable combination able to tap both conservative and liberal impulses.

National Reform: The Kassebaum-Kennedy
Proposal and Congressional Action

Since forty-five of the fifty states adopted small-group health insurance reforms during the first half of the 1990s (see Figure 3.1 on page 92), one might expect federal legislation to build upon those state initiatives and move the nation a modest distance farther along the road to health care reform.

In truth, the bipartisan bill cosponsored by Senator Nancy Kassebaum (R-Kans.) and Senator Edward Kennedy (D-Mass.) proposed creating federal requirements for provisions that already have relatively broad acceptance in the states. Their proposal did enhance some provisions and insulate against efforts to reverse the state initiatives, but the goal of advancing national health reform was well beyond the grasp of this legislation.[82]

The final legislation approved by Congress in August 1996 was even less ambitious than the original Kassebaum-Kennedy bill. What began as the Health Insurance Reform Act ended up merely as the Health Insurance Portability and Accountability Act, and true to its label, it enhances portability of health insurance coverage while doing little else. The main distinction is that the federal act, unlike the state reforms, reaches beyond the small-group market and applies its standards to all groups, large and small, who have conventional insurance plans or are self-insured.

The Health Insurance Portability and Accountability Act prohibits health plans from excluding, for more than twelve months, coverage of any medical condition for which medical advice, diagnosis, care, or treatment was recommended or received within six months of the effective date of coverage. The twelve month exclusion must be reduced or eliminated altogether for individuals who have been insured prior to obtaining the new coverage. This standard is consistent with many existing state small-group market reforms on the use of preexisting condition exclusionary clauses. Tougher state requirements are expressly permitted by the bill.

Complementing the restrictions on the use of preexisting condition

Table 3.6

Scope of Small-Group Market Reforms, 1990–95

No Small-Group Reform	Minimal Access Reform Only[a]	Only General Access Reforms[b]	Access and Rating Reforms Only[c]	Access and Marketing Reforms Only[d]	Access, Marketing, and Rating Reforms[e]
Alabama	Arkansas	Illinois	Maine[f]	Alaska	California[h]
Georgia		Indiana	New Jersey	Arizona	Colorado
Hawaii		Louisiana	New York	Delaware	Connecticut
Michigan		Massachusetts	Vermont	Idaho	Florida
Pennsylvania		Mississippi	New Hampshire	Iowa	Kentucky
		Nevada		Kansas	Maryland
		New Mexico		Minnesota	Oregon
		Ohio		Missouri	Virginia
		West Virginia		Montana	Washington
				Nebraska	
				North Carolina	
				North Dakota	
				Oklahoma	
				Rhode Island	
				South Carolina	
				South Dakota[g]	
				Tennessee	
				Texas	
				Utah	
				Wisconsin	
				Wyoming	
Total 5	Total 1	Total 9	Total 5	Total 21	Total 9

Table 3.6 *(continued)*

(continued)

Notes:

[a]"Minimal" access reforms are defined as adopting two or fewer of the following reforms: guaranteed issue, guaranteed renewal, enhanced portability, limits on the use of preexisting condition clauses.

[b]"General" access reforms are defined as adoption of three or more of the following reforms: guaranteed issue, guaranteed renewal, enhanced portability, limits on the use of preexisting condition clauses.

[c]Adoption of "access" and "rating" reforms includes states that have adopted minimal or general access reforms *and* adopted community rating or modified community rating.

[d]Adoption of "access" and "marketing" reforms includes states that have adopted minimal or general access reforms *and* mandate the offering of standardized health benefit plans or have created or legislatively enabled the creation of health plan purchasing cooperatives.

[e]Adoption of "access," "rating," and "marketing" reforms includes states that have adopted all three types of reforms as defined above.

[f]Maine passed legislation in 1996 that enables the creation of health plan purchasing cooperatives.

[g]With respect to access reforms, South Dakota has adopted only guaranteed renewal.

[h]California has adopted modified community rating only with regard to its health plan purchasing cooperative.

Figure 3.1 **Small-Group Market Reforms**

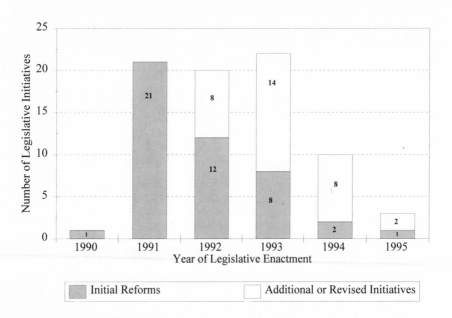

clauses are provisions that preclude health plans from charging individuals within a group different premiums than other individuals on the basis of health status, medical condition, claim experience, receipt of health care, medical history, genetic information, evidence of insurability, or disability. These rating restrictions enhance equity within insured groups and mean that the costs of insurance must be borne by the group as a whole rather than the individual.

Congress, unlike the majority of the states, was unable to adopt insurance rating reforms designed to reduce risk selection and risk competition by health insurers, or to broaden the insurance pool. With little agreement among the states as to the specific formula for such reforms, it is perhaps not surprising that insurance rating reform, traditionally an area exclusively regulated by the states, was left alone. Given that a majority of states found such reforms to be appropriate and necessary, however, the promotion of medical savings accounts (even on a trial basis for 750,000 people) makes federal action incongruous with state actions, since these accounts create incentives for healthy individuals to remove themselves from the general health insurance pool and presumably drive up premiums for the remainder of the insured population.

Ultimately, Congress also hesitated to advance regulation of insurance purchasing and marketing. The earlier Kassebaum-Kennedy bill included several provisions for the formation of private health plan purchasing cooperatives and marketing information provided by insurers to HPPC enrollees. Its most notable contribution would have been to encourage purchasing cooperatives in all states and provide a stronger set of operating principles than exists in most states today. It conceived of the HPPC as an institution that empowers consumers by providing enrollees a choice of health plans and giving them partial control over the operation. This is a contrast to the vision in which purchasing cooperatives are creatures of American business, with a primary if not sole objective of reducing employer costs for health benefits.

As in a majority of the reform states, the Senate version of the Kassebaum-Kennedy proposal mandated the disclosure of specified information to prospective groups and enrollees. It departed significantly from the state reforms, however, by specifying broader rules for the formation and operation of HPPCs. The Kassebaum-Kennedy proposal would have required each state to adopt a certification program for HPPCs and, if it failed to do so, possibly be subject to a federal certification program. The HPPCs were to be controlled by a board composed of both employers and enrollees, and provide an ombudsman for enrollees. This was a notable shift from private purchasing cooperatives or other group purchasing arrangements that primarily serve the interests of the employers that sponsor them. In addition, the Kassebaum-Kennedy proposal mandated individual choice of insurers and that HPPCs must provide comparative cost and quality information, the latter now generally ignored by private cooperatives. Finally, HPPCs would have been prohibited in most circumstances from being for-profit, if the profits did not inure to the benefit of the HPPC participants, including the enrollees.

The final legislation, however, eliminated provisions for insurance purchasing reforms. With this downsizing and the already timid approach to rating reforms, the congressional initiative amounts to this: It ratifies a single, widely accepted, and relatively uncontroversial component of state health care reform initiatives—portability of coverage—from the possibility of state repeal. In all other respects, it fails to encompass even the modest achievements of the majority of recent state reforms. Clearly, the goal of advancing national health reform awaits a new round of legislative activity beyond the tenure of the 104th Congress.

Conclusion

What general conclusions are possible about the potential impact of the recent wave of state insurance reforms? They eliminate or impose substantial restrictions on the "bad practices" in the insurance industry, which will allow millions of individuals fairer economic treatment in the health care system. But an important question to be asked about insurance reforms is, if states or the federal government build them in a voluntary system, will anybody come? The reforms help only if the intended beneficiaries have some purchasing power in the first place. A recent survey of small employers showed that 60 percent were simply not willing to contribute anything toward employee health benefits, regardless of accessibility and cost.[83] So the impact of these reforms will likely be modest, if only because they fail to address the heart of the insurance access problem.

It is too soon to tell what the ultimate numbers will look like, but in a market of tens of millions of individuals there are tiny enrollments in most of the state purchasing cooperatives. Except in California and Florida, there are no more than thirty thousand subscribers participating in any cooperative. These numbers may change if purchasing cooperatives demonstrate they are capable of delivering substantial savings to employers. The California program opened with prices substantially below the market average and actually reduced its average premiums in each of the first two years. Other purchasing cooperatives have shown they can be a catalyst for cost containment as well. Some advocates argue that the presence of the cooperatives serves cost containment well beyond the savings they deliver to their own enrollees. As a parallel but visible system operating alongside the conventional insurance market, the prices they negotiate are signals to the rest of the market. Therefore, a cooperative may be generating spillover benefits by saving money for outside groups and individuals who use the cooperative's premiums as a reference point in their own purchasing.

The bottom line is that government is willing to modify the market on behalf of deserving interests or its own budgets (and taxpayers' dollars) but that there are severe constraints on how far it can go. These constraints are due in part to limited knowledge, in part to entrenched institutions, and in part to interests that can mobilize vast resources to defeat or reduce initiatives in scope, scale, and duration. This may be the most valuable lesson from the recent pattern of success and failure in health care reform: rational analysis and political agreement on fundamental problems and goals are not sufficient to guarantee strong governmental action toward a more equitable system. Only the threat of large-scale reform ensures that these incremental achievements do not turn into hollow victories, and in the absence of this threat it will require ongoing skill and leadership to turn these new institutions into building blocks for a system that can meet much broader aspirations.

Notes

This is a revised version of a paper presented at the Annual Meeting of the American Political Science Association, Chicago, September 2, 1995.

1. Paul Starr, *The Social Transformation of American Medicine* (New York: Basic Books, 1982); David Rothman, "A Century of Failure: Health Care Reform in America," *Journal of Health Politics, Policy and Law* 18 (summer 1993): 271–86.

2. On the causes and consequences of the failure of the Clinton plan and other proposals for national reform, see Hugh Heclo, "Clinton Health Plan: Historical Perspective," *Health Affairs* 14 (spring 1995): 86–98.

3. Deborah Rogal and W. David Helms, "Tracking States' Efforts to Reform Their Health Systems," *Health Affairs* 12 (summer 1993): 27–30; Daniel M. Fox and John K. Iglehart, ed., *Five States That Could Not Wait: Lessons for Health Reform from Florida, Hawaii, Minnesota, Oregon, and Vermont* (New York: Milbank Memorial Fund, 1994); Pamela A. Paul-Shaheen, "The States and Health Care Reform: The Road Traveled and the Lessons Learned from Seven That Took the Lead" (Ann Arbor: typescript, 1995).

4. Daniel M. Fox and Howard M. Leichter, "The Ups and Downs of Oregon's Rationing Plan," *Health Affairs* 12 (summer 1993): 66–70; Howard M. Leichter, "Health Care Reform in Vermont: The Next Chapter," *Health Affairs* 13 (winter 1994): 78–103; Robert A. Crittenden, "State Report: Recent Action in Washington and Oregon," *Health Affairs* 14 (summer 1995): 302–5; Edwin Chen, "Health Care on Agenda Again," *Minneapolis Star Tribune,* June 26, 1995, 4A.

5. Heclo, "Clinton Health Plan."

6. Theda Skocpol, "The Rise and Resounding Demise of the Clinton Plan," *Health Affair* 14 (Spring 1995): 66–85; Sven Steinmo and Jon Watts, "Its the Institutions, Stupid! Why Comprehensive National Insurance Reform Always Fails in America," *Journal of Health Politics, Policy and Law* 20 (Summer 1995): 329–72.

7. Advisory Council on Social Security, *Commitment to Change: Foundations for Reform* (Washington, D.C.: Government Printing Office, 1991); Judith Feder and Larry Levitt, "Steps toward Universal Coverage," *Health Affairs* 14 (spring 1995): 140–49.

8. Intergovernmental Health Policy Project, *Fifty State Profiles: Health Care Reform* (Washington, D.C.: George Washington University and the Henry J. Kaiser Family Foundation, October, 1995), 29–34.

9. Catherine G. McLaughlin and Wendy K. Zellers, "The Shortcomings of Voluntarism in the Small-Group Insurance Market," *Health Affairs* 11 (summer 1992): 28–40; Joel C. Cantor, Stephen H. Long, and M. Susan Marquis, "Private Employment-Based Health Insurance in Ten States," *Health Affairs* 14 (summer 1995): 199–211.

10. California Legislature, Assembly, *Analysis of the Conference Committee Report on A.B. 1672,* August 26, 1992.

11. Diane Rowland, Barbara Lyons, Alina Salganicoff, and Peter Long, "A Profile of the Uninsured in America," *Health Affairs* 13 (spring II 1994): 283–87.

12. Deborah A. Stone, "The Struggle for the Soul of Health Insurance," *Journal of Health Politics, Policy and Law* 18 (summer 1993): 287–317.

13. Alain C. Enthoven and Sara J. Singer, "Market-Based Reform: What to Regulate and by Whom," *Health Affairs* 14 (spring 1995): 105–19; Paul M. Ellwood and Alain C. Enthoven, "Responsible Choices: The Jackson Hole Group Plan for Health Reform," *Health Affairs* 14 (summer 1995): 24–39.

14. Chen, "Health Care on Agenda."

15. The rhetoric put forth by Governor Pete Wilson of California in his brief presidential campaign—that his state's insurance reforms are the solution to the nation's

health care problems—concerned officials who cooperated with Wilson to enact those reforms in 1992 based on an explicit understanding that they represented only modest progress. In a related example, Michigan health experts reported that policymakers did not move to adopt proposals for health insurance reforms, believing they would undermine more comprehensive proposals that eventually died—leaving the state with no reforms whatsoever.

16. Deborah A. Stone, *Policy Paradox and Political Reason* (New York: HarperCollins, 1988); D. J. Palumbo and D. J. Calista, "Opening Up the Black Box: Implementation and the Policy Process," in *Implementation and the Policy Process: Opening Up the Black Box* (Westport, Conn.: Greenwood Press, 1990); Christopher J. Bosso, "The Practice and Study of Policy Formation," in *Encyclopedia of Policy Studies,* 2d ed., ed. Stuart S. Nagel (New York: Marcel Dekker, 1994).

17. Feder and Levitt, "Steps toward Universal Coverage," 143.

18. Kenneth E. Thorpe, "A Call for Health Services Researchers," *Health Affairs* 14 (spring 1995): 63–65.

19. Charles E. Lindblom, "The Science of 'Muddling Through,' " *Public Administration Review* 19 (spring 1959): 79–88.

20. Thomas R. Oliver and Emery B. Dowell, "Interest Groups and the Political Struggle over Expanding Health Insurance in California," *Health Affairs* 13 (spring II 1994): 123–41; Emery B. Dowell and Thomas R. Oliver, "Small-Employer Health Alliance in California," *Health Affairs* 13 (summer 1994): 350–51. A study of the California reforms, and in particular the creation and early operation of the state-sponsored health insurance purchasing cooperative for small employers, is part of a larger study of "Public Entrepreneurship and Health Policy Innovation" supported by an Investigator Award in Health Policy Research from the Robert Wood Johnson Foundation.

21. Kenneth E. Thorpe, "Expanding Employment-Based Health Insurance: Is Small Group Reform the Answer?" *Inquiry* 29 (summer 1992): 128–36; W. David Helms, Anne K. Gauthier, and Daniel M. Campion, "Mending the Flaws in the Small-Group Market," *Health Affairs* 11 (summer 1992): 7–27; Rowland, et al., "Profile of the Uninsured in America."

22. U.S. Congress, General Accounting Office, *Private Health Insurance: Problems Caused by a Segmented Market,* GAO/HRD–91–114, 1991; General Accounting Office, *Access to Health Care: States Respond to Growing Crisis,* GAO/HRD–92–70, 1992; Helms, et al., "Mending the Flaws in the Small-Group Market"; Thorpe, "Expanding Employment-Based Health Insurance."

23. Judith Glazner, William R. Braithwaite, Steven Hull, and Dennis C. Lezotte, "The Questionable Value of Medical Screening in the Small-Group Health Insurance Market," *Health Affairs* 14 (summer 1995): 224–34.

24. Mark A. Hall, "The Political Economics of Health Insurance Market Reform," *Health Affairs* 11 (summer 1992): 108–24, 120. The rise in premiums due to adverse selection—where people who need more services are the ones most likely to purchase insurance—is exacerbated by the "moral hazard" introduced by insurance coverage: once people have insurance coverage, they are more likely to use covered services than if they pay for each service out of pocket.

25. Enthoven and Singer, "Market-Based Reform," 117.

26. Free riding refers to the fact that many uninsured persons still receive medical treatment if they are injured or become ill. The costs of treating the uninsured are covered by providers, by public or philanthropic funds, or by raising premiums for insured individuals.

27. Stone, "The Struggle for the Soul of Health Insurance," 293.

28. Glazner, et al., "Questionable Value of Medical Screening." This study reviewed

the claims experience of employees in firms that were subject to medical screening compared with those that were not screened and found no significant difference in the average claims per employee over a six-year period. If agents and brokers in the small-group market carry out informal screening of firms in anticipation that some applications will be rejected, however, then medical screening may have value to insurers in discouraging firms with the worst risks from applying for coverage in the first place.

29. Henry J. Aaron and Barry P. Bosworth, "Economic Issues in Reform of Health Care Financing," in *Brookings Papers on Economic Activity: Microeconomics 1994,* ed. Martin Neil Baily, Peter C. Reiss, and Clifford Winston (Washington, D.C.: Brookings Institution, 1994), 271.

30. Stone, "Struggle for the Soul of Health Insurance," 297–308.

31. The chairman of the California Managed Risk Medical Insurance Board says that the experience with the state's high-risk insurance pool (which provides subsidized coverage for individuals who have been rejected by private insurers) demonstrates that traditional medical underwriting is likely to overestimate medical care use by individuals with preexisting conditions. The state program has been able to cover nearly twice as many individuals as anticipated in the original actuarial projections. Clifford Allenby, chairman of the California Managed Risk Medical Insurance Board, interview by author, Sacramento, California, September 6, 1994.

32. Horizontal equity is a criterion for social policy that requires "equal treatment for equals"—that persons in similar circumstances be treated alike by governmental regulations. One obvious application is the effort to eliminate tax shelters so that people with similar wealth will pay similar amounts of taxes. See Duncan MacRae, Jr., and James A. Wilde, *Policy Analysis for Public Decisions* (North Scituate, Mass.: Duxbury Press, 1979), 65–67.

33. Stone, "Struggle for the Soul of Health Insurance," 291.

34. The current private insurance system explicitly subsidizes coverage for spouses and large families, for example. Single individuals pay substantially higher insurance premiums per person than individuals with dependents, and beyond a certain number of children there are no increases in premiums at all.

35. Hall, "Political Economics of Health Insurance Market Reform," 120; Stone, "Struggle for the Soul of Health Insurance," 292; Enthoven and Singer, "Market-Based Reform," 106.

36. Alpha Center, "Federal/State Collaboration Needed to Make Health Care Reform Work," *State Initiatives in Health Care Reform* 7 (July/August 1994): 1.

37. Aaron and Bosworth, "Economic Issues in Reform of Health Care Financing," 270; Enthoven and Singer, "Market-Based Reform," 108.

38. Aaron and Bosworth, "Economic Issues in Reform of Health Care Financing," 271.

39. Price elasticity is the economic term for the sensitivity of consumer demand to changes in the price of a product. If the volume purchased changes little in relation to changes in price, then the product is said to be price inelastic. A product is considered price elastic if a specified difference in price creates an even larger difference in the volume purchased. For an application, see Thomas C. Buchmueller and Paul J. Feldstein, "Consumers' Sensitivity to Health Plan Premiums: Evidence from a Natural Experiment in California," *Health Affairs* 15 (spring 1996): 143–51.

40. Enthoven and Singer, "Market-Based Reform," 111.

41. Deborah J. Chollet and Rebecca R. Paul, *Community Rating: Issues and Experience* (Washington, D.C.: Alpha Center, 1994); Enthoven and Singer, "Market-Based Reform."

42. Thorpe, "Expanding Employment-Based Health Insurance."

43. Enthoven and Singer, "Market-Based Reform," 111.

44. Paul M. Ellwood, Alain C. Enthoven, and Lynn Etheredge, "The Jackson Hole Initiatives for a Twenty-First Century American Health Care System," *Health Economics* 1 (1992): 149–68.

45. Alpha Center, *State Initiatives in Health Care Reform,* 12.

46. These are the figures cited by officials in the Maryland Department of Health and Mental Hygiene; similar figures are cited in Enthoven and Singer, "Market-Based Reform."

47. Ibid., 108, 112.

48. Joseph P. Newhouse, "Patients at Risk: Health Reform and Risk Adjustment," *Health Affairs* 14 (spring I 1994): 132–46.

49. For an example of a new system of risk adjustment developed for the small-group market, see Sandra Shewry, Sandra Hunt, John Ramey, and John Bertko, "Risk Adjustment: The Missing Piece of Market Competition," *Health Affairs* 15 (spring 1996): 171–81.

50. The purchasing cooperative can be viewed as a variation on the Federal Employees Health Benefits Plan, which began operation in the early 1960s (Scott Fleming, former vice president of the Kaiser Foundation Health Plans, interview by author, Berkeley, Calif.: July 14, 1995). It served as the original model for a series of proposals to extend market competition throughout the insurance market. Alain C. Enthoven, *Health Plan* (Reading, Mass.: Addison-Wesley, 1980); Alain C. Enthoven, *Theory and Practice of Managed Competition in Health Care Finance* (New York: Elsevier Science Publishers, 1988); Ellwood, Enthoven, and Etheredge, "Jackson Hole Initiatives"; Ellwood and Enthoven, "Responsible Choices."

51. Kenneth E. Thorpe, "Inside the Black Box of Administrative Costs," *Health Affairs* 11 (summer 1992): 41–55; Elliot L. Wicks, Richard E. Curtis, and Kevin Haugh, "The ABCs of HIPCs," *Journal of American Health Policy* (March/April 1993): 29–34; Enthoven and Singer, "Market-Based Reform," 105–19; Cantor, Long, and Marquis "Private Employer-Based Health Insurance." The cost of acquiring a new subscriber is somewhere between $1,000 and $3,000 in the conventional small-group market, well above the costs of acquiring new business through a purchasing cooperative. John Ramey, executive director of the California Managed Risk Medical Insurance Board, interview by author, Sacramento, California, July 11, 1995.

52. Enthoven and Singer, "Market-Based Reform," 106.

53. We assume that, in the near future, no state will require all employers and individuals to purchase health insurance through a cooperative.

54. Ralph Schaffarzick, former member of the California Managed Risk Medical Insurance Board, interview by author, July 12, 1995.

55. Albert O. Hirschman, *Exit, Voice, and Loyalty* (Cambridge: Harvard University Press, 1970).

56. Martin Landau, "Redundancy, Rationality, and the Problem of Duplication and Overlap," in *Public Administration: Politics and the People,* ed. Dean L. Yarwood (New York: Longman, 1987); Jonathan B. Bendor, *Parallel Systems: Redundancy in Government* (Berkeley: University of California Press, 1985), 24–65.

57. Harvey Sapolsky, James Aisenberg, and James A. Morone, "The Call to Rome and Other Obstacles to State-Level Innovation," *Public Administration Review* 47 (March-April 1987): 135–42.

58. U.S. Congress, General Accounting Office, *Health Reform: Purchasing Cooperatives Have an Increasing Role in Providing Access to Insurance,* GAO/T-HEHS–94–196, 1994; Judith Yates Borger, "Employers Take Aim at Health Plans," *St. Paul Pioneer Press,* July 30, 1995, 1A; Ramey interview.

59. Kenneth E. Thorpe, "The American States and Canada: A Comparative Analysis

of Health Care Spending," *Journal of Health Politics, Policy and Law* 18 (summer 1993): 477–89; Robert Hackey, "Regulatory Regimes and State Cost Containment Programs," *Journal of Health Politics, Policy and Law* 18 (summer 1993): 491–502; Michael Sparer, "States and the Health Care Crisis," *Journal of Health Politics, Policy and Law* 18 (summer 1993): 503–13.

60. Ramey interview.

61. Institute for Health Policy Solutions, *State Experience with Community Rating and Related Reforms: A Report for the Kaiser Family Foundation* (Washington, D.C., 1995).

62. American Academy of Actuaries, *An Analysis of Mandated Community Rating* (Washington, D.C., 1994).

63. The data on privately operated HPPCs are based on a review of operational design of the following: Health Connections (Connecticut) as of April 1995; Illinois Employer Benefits Alliance as of July 1, 1996; Northwest Indiana Health Alliance as of July 1996; Independent Health Alliance of Iowa as of July 1996; MN Business Coalition (Minnesota) as of May 10, 1996; Long Island Association Health Alliance as of February 1995; Council of Smaller Enterprises (Ohio) as of summer 1995; Health Care Alliance of Texas as of July 1996; Care of Utah as of July 1996; and Employer Health Purchasing Coop (Washington State) as of July 1996. Information on specific design elements for the individual HPPCs is available from the authors.

64. Sandra Shewry, deputy director of the California Managed Risk Medical Insurance Board, interview by author, Sacramento, California, July 11, 1995.

65. Maryland, which has no HPPC legislation, has mandated that insurers can offer only standardized health benefit plans in the small-group market.

66. Telephone interview with program staff of the Independent Health Alliance of Iowa, July 1996.

67. Stone, *Policy Paradox and Political Reason,* 7.

68. Anne Schneider and Helen Ingram, "Social Construction of Target Populations: Implications for Politics and Policy," *American Political Science Review* 87 (June 1993): 334–47.

69. Enthoven, *Theory and Practice of Managed Competition.*

70. Shewry interview.

71. Newhouse, "Patients at Risk."

72. Shewry interview.

73. Robert H. Salisbury, "An Exchange Theory of Interest Groups," *Midwest Journal of Political Science* 13 (February 1969): 1–32.

74. The Twin Cities Business Health Care Action Group reorganized in 1995 as the Buyers Health Care Action Group when the state of Minnesota joined the existing health insurance purchasing program for large private employers.

75. James Q. Wilson, *Political Organizations* (New York: Basic Books, 1973); James Q. Wilson, The Politics of Regulation," in *The Politics of Regulation* (New York: Basic Books, 1980), 357–94.

76. R. Douglas Arnold, *The Logic of Congressional Action* (New Haven: Yale University Press, 1990), 70–71.

77. Charles E. Lindblom, "The Market as Prison," *Journal of Politics* 44 (May 1982): 324–36.

78. Schneider and Ingram, "Social Construction of Target Populations," 334–47.

79. It can be argued that the social construction of small-business interests would be "advantaged" (deserving and powerful), but until the debate over the Clinton health plan, small business was not very engaged on health insurance issues and was a fringe interest as a result. Oliver and Dowell, "Interest Groups and Political Struggle Over Expanding Health Insurance," 132.

80. Shewry, et al., "Risk Adjustment," 172–73.

81. The state of Maryland, in its small-group insurance reforms in 1992, adopted a mandatory standard benefit package; it has not established a purchasing cooperative to further restructure competition among insurers, however.

82. Senator Kassebaum introduced her original bill, S. 1028, on July 13, 1995. It came to the full Senate on April 18, 1996, and a substitute version of the bill, H.R. 3103, was unanimously approved by the Senate on April 23, 1996. Reconciliation with the insurance reform legislation passed in the House of Representatives was completed in conference committee and was approved by both houses of Congress on August 2, 1996. H.R. 3103, the Health Insurance Portability and Accountability Act of 1996 was signed into law by President Clinton on August 21, 1996.

83. Cantor, Long, and Marquis, "Private Employment-Based Health Insurance."

4

Medicaid Managed Care: Lessons from New York and California

Michael S. Sparer

Since the Republican landslide in the 1994 midterm elections, health care reformers are looking increasingly to the states for health policy innovation. This optimism is encouraged by the few states (including Hawaii, Minnesota, and Tennessee) that are now implementing major reform initiatives.[1] An alliance is even forming between many who have long argued that health reform should be led by the states and those who prefer a national solution but believe it unlikely.

There is little chance, however, that any state will soon enact universal insurance. Indeed, state legislators in 1997 are less likely to overcome the barriers to reform than were their federal counterparts in 1994. Even states that are health reform leaders are retreating. Washington state, for example, recently repealed a law that required all employers to provide employees with health insurance by 1999.

The most obvious obstacle is money: states are unlikely to find new dollars for reform given the current antitaxation ideology. On the contrary, most states will be unable even to maintain the status quo, given the cuts in federal Medicaid dollars that will soon be enacted.[2] Other obstacles include the antigovernment Republican revolution in many statehouses, entrenched interest group opposition (including the threat of a business exodus), and ongoing institutional barriers to legislation (such as the separation of powers). Finally, were any state miraculously to elude these barriers, there are also intergovernmental obstacles such as the Employee Retirement Income Security Act (ERISA), which prohibits states from regulating or taxing those companies that self-insure (and nearly 70 percent of all employees now work for companies that do).[3]

Given these political issues, states will probably concentrate on incremental initiatives. Most will enact small-group insurance reforms. Some will encourage individuals to open tax-deferred medical savings accounts. Others will develop purchasing pools for state employees. A few will establish insurance subsidy programs for small numbers of the uninsured (generally women and children). And nearly all will cut Medicaid eligibility and encourage (or require) remaining clients to enroll in managed care.[4]

The enthusiasm for Medicaid managed care began in the late 1980s. Medicaid costs at that time were increasing nearly 30 percent annually. Although pressure to reduce costs was enormous, there were few options for doing so. States could cut program eligibility, but there was a nationwide recession and the program covered less than 50 percent of the poor anyway.[5] States could decrease benefits, but even "easy" cuts, for example in podiatry and chiropractic services, tend to save little but generate intense political heat. States could reduce provider reimbursement, but not only do hospitals and nursing homes contest in court any proposed cuts, payment often is already so low as to jeopardize client access. The only plausible alternative, according to many state officials, was to promote more cost-effective health care, and the preferred strategy was managed care.

Adding to its appeal, managed care advocates promised improved quality and reduced costs. After all, Medicaid beneficiaries receive health care, most often, in the emergency rooms of large safety-net hospitals. Clients enrolled in managed care, however, cannot only avoid expensive and often inappropriate emergency rooms, but should instead receive inexpensive and more appropriate primary care.

To be sure, not all states embrace managed care with equal fervor. At one extreme are a few states, such as Tennessee, that claim that savings generated by mandatory Medicaid managed care programs will finance insurance coverage for large segments of the uninsured. Florida, Missouri, and Oregon are also trying to finance insurance expansions through managed care savings. Other states, such as California, hope to require Medicaid clients to enroll in managed care but have not proposed substantial insurance expansions. And most states take an even more incremental approach, encouraging but not requiring clients to enroll in managed care. Nonetheless, the number of Medicaid clients enrolled nationwide in managed care has increased dramatically, from 750,000 (3 percent of all enroll-ees) in 1983 to 7.8 million (23 percent of all enrollees) in June 1994.[6]

The variation in initiatives is due, in part, to the complicated and contro-versial state-based politics that accompanies any effort to radically restruc-ture a health care delivery system. Consider the impact on the influential medical provider community. Safety-net providers[7] are concerned not only that they will lose needed revenue as clients enroll in health maintenance organizations (HMOs), but that they will still need to care for the uninsured and the high-cost Medicaid clients that HMOs avoid. HMOs (and private physicians), which have traditionally treated a commercially insured mid-dle-class population, must decide whether to expand their operations to accommodate an influx of poor persons. Labor unions worry that nonpro-fessional health care workers either will lose jobs or be forced to work for nonunionized commercial HMOs.

Medicaid clients also are affected by new managed care initiatives. Cli-ents who are accustomed to a particular service pattern (such as reliance on the local emergency room) must now join large managed care plans, with restricted lists of providers. Clients, many of whom do not speak English and who have little formal education, must sift through and evaluate the terms and conditions of the various managed care plans. Not surprisingly, consumer advocates worry that the various plans are ill equipped to treat the Medicaid population, and that clients eventually will fall back into the (now weakened) medical safety net.

In this context, policy analysts need to evaluate and analyze the early returns from state Medicaid managed care initiatives. Which states are moving most quickly and why? How does variation in state policy-making environments influence managed care policy? How does the medical safety net fare in a managed care world? What are the characteristics of managed care plans, and how does variation in such characteristics influence outcomes? Does managed care save money, encourage improved access to care, and ensure better-quality care? Can managed care work for so-called special populations, such as the mentally ill, substance abusers, and the chronically ill?

Surprisingly, few studies have examined any of these issues.[8] Moreover, the political dimensions of Medicaid managed care are studied least of all. In this chapter, however, my focus is on politics: first, the variation in state policy-making environments; and second, the influence of such variation on state efforts to protect the medical safety net. I explore these issues using a comparative case study of the managed care initiatives in two states, California and New York. Why these states? First, they have the nation's two largest Medicaid programs and two of the largest managed care initiatives. Second, the Medicaid programs in the two states are extraordinarily different: in California, state Medicaid officials enjoy considerable bureaucratic autonomy and have long kept Medicaid expenditures relatively low; in New York, in contrast, Medicaid bureaucrats operate within a fragmented, decentralized, and interest-group-dominated political system, and Medicaid expenditures have soared as a result.[9] Finally, although California has adopted a strategy designed in part to protect safety-net public hospitals, New York has not.

California, 1966–91: Managed Care Scandals and a Crumbling Safety Net

Beginning in the late 1960s, the Medicaid program in California (known as Medi-Cal) initiated a large-scale effort to enroll beneficiaries in managed care organizations. The effort, the first of its sort in the nation,[10] was intended to reduce rising Medi-Cal costs: Each participating HMO received, for every client it enrolled, a fee set at 80 percent of the cost of an average Medi-Cal client. Indeed, although then governor Ronald Reagan suggested that Medi-Cal cost savings would result from the competition between private-sector health plans, the real savings, if any, would stem from tightly regulated reimbursement formulas.

There was, however, a problem: managed care capitation rates were extraordinarily low, arguably too low to attract health plan participation. The low rates were due, in large part, to the state's successful effort to keep Medi-Cal fee-for-service reimbursement levels quite low: the low reimbursement meant low expenditures per beneficiary, which meant low managed care rates.[11] To address this issue, state officials offered the managed care community an informal deal: although the rates would be low, there also would be minimal state oversight of health plan activity.

It soon became clear, however, that the mainstream managed care organizations, with their commercially insured middle-class clientele, had little interest in enrolling large numbers of Medi-Cal clients. One reason for this reluctance was the low Medi-Cal fees: even with minimal state oversight, the plans were pessimistic about their ability to operate a profitable Medi-Cal operation. The mainstream organizations were also concerned that enrolling Medi-Cal clients could encourage commercially insured clients to disenroll, particularly if the organization included more than a token number of Medi-Cal clients.

With the mainstream managed care organizations reluctant to participate, the business community created, virtually overnight, dozens of new managed care plans that competed among themselves for the Medi-Cal clientele. The operators of many of these new organizations had little or no experience as health plan administrators, but they were attracted by the promise of guaranteed income and by the lack of state regulatory oversight. They began to market their wares door-to-door in low-income communities. Soon tens of thousands of Medi-Cal clients were signing up.

The emphasis on managed care posed a serious threat to the county health system, drawing Medi-Cal clients away from county facilities and leaving the facilities to care for the increasing uninsured population. The vulnerability of the county system increased even more in 1971, when the state (in yet another cost-containment effort) dramatically increased the county share of Medi-Cal costs and simultaneously eliminated a program that helped counties pay for the cost of caring for the uninsured.[12] Soon thereafter, several counties either closed or sold their hospitals. State officials at that time had little interest in stabilizing the crumbling county system. The goal instead was to create a low-cost Medi-Cal managed care delivery system.

By the early 1970s, however, many of the newly formed managed care plans were embroiled in controversy and scandal. There were at least four problems. First, many of the plans relied on unlawful marketing techniques. Some door-to-door marketers, for example, told clients that enrollment was mandatory (it wasn't). Others promised benefits and perks well beyond the Medicaid package. Second, client access to care was often inadequate, particularly after normal working hours. Moreover, even when clients did get an appointment, they often waited hours for poor-quality care. Third, client efforts to disenroll were often ignored, or at least were excessively delayed. Fourth, many of these new organizations were inadequately capitalized (some went bankrupt rather quickly), whereas others were rife with fraud and profiteering.[13]

California's legislature responded to the crisis with a series of incremental efforts to regulate the managed care market.[14] At about the same time, federal investigators reported the problems with California's managed care initiative and suggested that Congress should regulate Medicaid managed care programs.[15]

Shortly thereafter, Congress enacted the HMO amendments of 1976, which imposed substantial federal restrictions on state managed care initiatives. The law required, for example, that only federally qualified HMOs receive full-risk Medicaid contracts. The law also required that no more than 50 percent of any HMO's clientele be Medicaid or Medicare recipients (thus nearly eliminating the "Medicaid-only" HMO).[16] Because most of the Medi-Cal plans were not federally qualified, and most had more than 50 percent Medicaid enrollees, the new federal legislation (together with the tightened state regulation) deflated the Medi-Cal managed care initiative. By the late 1970s, for example, the number of managed care organizations with Medi-Cal contracts had declined from sixty-five to twenty-one.

As the managed care initiative ended, Medi-Cal clients again sought care from the county hospital safety net. But counties were ill equipped to respond to the increased utilization. Rising health care costs had caused the counties to raise property taxes, which prompted the tax revolt of 1978 (otherwise known as Proposition 13) that rolled back property tax levels and sharply limited future increases.

The state legislature, which at that time had the luxury of a $3.7 billion budget surplus, responded to the counties' fiscal crises by assuming the counties' share of Medi-Cal expenditures and by enacting the County Health Services Fund, which provided state funds for county health costs. The pendulum had shifted: The managed care initiative was over, and the emphasis was instead on restoring the fiscal health of the county health system.

The environment changed again in 1981, however, when then president Ronald Reagan decided that the Medicaid program should delegate more authority to the states and that states should be encouraged to experiment with managed care initiatives. As a result, federal legislation in 1981 substantially increased state discretion over Medicaid policy and greatly loosened federal restrictions on Medicaid managed care programs. For example, non-federally-qualified HMOs could now receive full-risk Medicaid contracts, the limit that required HMOs to have no more than 50 percent Medicaid and Medicare clients was increased to 75 percent, and states were authorized to offer six months of guaranteed eligibility to those Medicaid clients who enrolled in managed care.

The changed federal environment was particularly appreciated in California, which was then suffering from a severe recession, the cost of the county bailout, and a decline in federal aid. The state's budget surplus was replaced by a budget deficit, and in 1982 the state enacted a major Medi-Cal reform package. The 1982 reforms are best known for requiring hospitals to bid for Medi-Cal contracts (the so-called selective contracting system).[17] But the legislation also followed the federal lead and authorized some incremental expansions in Medi-Cal's now small managed care program. The new efforts fell into two categories. First, there were efforts to encourage clients to enroll voluntarily in a new Primary Care Case Management program (PCCM). This program provided physicians with a fixed fee for both providing primary care services to enrollees and for supervising client efforts to receive specialty care. The expectation was that, over time, participating providers would become full-risk prepaid plans.

Second, the 1982 legislation authorized three counties to require local Medi-Cal clients to enroll in managed care. Two of these counties, Santa Barbara and Monterey, received permission to operate county-organized health systems (COHSs). The COHS in these counties would receive from the state a fixed fee for every local Medi-Cal resident. The COHS would then contract with local providers to care for the Medi-Cal population. These clients were required to belong to the COHS, and the COHS served only the Medi-Cal population.[18] The third county aided by the 1982 legislation, San Diego, received permission to require its Medi-Cal clients to pick from a menu of private managed care plans.

Despite the renewed interest in Medicaid managed care, the new initiatives proceeded slowly. The Monterey COHS was abandoned shortly after it started, a victim of poor planning and inadequate funding (California Department of Health Services 1985). San Diego's effort to require Medi-Cal clients to choose from a menu of managed care plans was undermined by the California Medical Association, which objected that the plan would disrupt thousands of senior citizens' medical care. And only one PCCM provider ever became a full-risk provider, despite the state's hope that all of the nearly two dozen such providers would do so.[19]

Perhaps the only success stories of the 1980s initiatives were the COHSs in Santa Barbara and San Mateo (the San Mateo COHS was authorized in 1983 and began operation in 1987). By all accounts, the two programs have reduced costs by cutting client inpatient utilization and by persuading primary care providers to reduce specialist referrals. Moreover, clients and providers alike generally consider the programs to be unusually consumer-friendly.[20]

Despite the success of the COHS model, however, the number of Medi-Cal clients enrolled in managed care increased only incrementally during the 1980s, reaching approximately 355,000 by 1990.[21] Ironically, one problem was the state's success in keeping regular Medicaid rates (based on a fee-for-service methodology) quite low. Because managed care rates are required by law to be less than fee-for-service rates, finding reputable providers willing to accept the necessarily low capitation rate was particularly difficult.

At the same time, the state's governor during much of the 1980s, George Deukmejian, had little interest in health care policy. His priorities were cutting taxes, building prisons, and shrinking social welfare programs. Under Deukmejian's leadership, state health officials avoided major new initiatives, and the Medi-Cal delivery system remained predominantly fee-for-service.

New York, 1966–91: Managed Care as Afterthought

During the 1970s and early 1980s, only twenty thousand of New York's 2 million Medicaid recipients were enrolled in managed care, and nearly all of them were in a single plan, the Health Insurance Plan of New York (HIP). The low Medicaid managed care penetration rate was consistent with the low managed care penetration rate in the state's commercial market as well.[22] State policy before 1985 even prohibited investor-owned HMOs from operating in New York.[23]

Influential interest groups also opposed Medicaid managed care. New York City's public hospitals and academic medical centers relied heavily on Medicaid funds received for emergency-room care; an emphasis on managed care would substantially reduce those funds. Organized labor worried that if managed care hurt the hospital sector, nonprofessional hospital workers would be the first to lose their jobs. Consumer advocates argued that managed care would reduce access to care, citing the California scandals as evidence.

Finally, New York's Medicaid program, more than any other state's, has long favored institution-based specialty care and disfavored the community-based primary care needed for a managed care network. This bias is most noticeable in reimbursement policy. New York ranks fiftieth among the states in the ratios of Medicaid physician fees to both Medicare-allowed charges and private fees,[24] reimbursing the absurdly low sum of $11 for a routine office visit.[25] At the same time, however, New York provides skilled nursing facilities with an average of $112.93 per day per Medicaid client, compared with the national mean of $56.50,[26] pays more than $6,000 per Medicaid client for inpatient hospital care, the third highest among the states,[27] and spends nearly 16 percent of the nation's entire Medicaid budget.[28] Managed care cannot thrive, however, if revenues are directed away from primary care gatekeepers to specialists and institutions.

The rocky politics of Medicaid managed care during this era is illustrated by the disappointing effort to initiate a mandatory managed care program in northern Manhattan. The story begins in 1980, when then mayor Ed Koch proposed closing two large public hospitals, Sydenham and Metropolitan. Leaders in the African-American community, labor unions, physicians, and the Catholic Church fiercely opposed the proposal. As a compromise, Koch suggested that Sydenham be replaced by a collection of ambulatory clinics and that Metropolitan be replaced by a city-run HMO, called CitiCaid, which would be mandatory for local Medicaid recipients and available to the local uninsured. Koch's opponents, however, were equally opposed to a mandatory managed care program, arguing that it discriminated against poor (and mainly minority) recipients. Koch backpedaled again, proposing that CitiCaid be a purely voluntary program. Only then did the opposition lessen, and in September 1985 the program accepted its first enrollees.

Given the strong anti-managed-care coalition, state policymakers recognized that a successful managed care initiative needed to be incremental, voluntary, and nonthreatening to safety-net providers. With this in mind, in 1984 the state legislature provided start-up funds for safety-net providers to form prepaid health service plans (PHSPs), a new type of HMO that could enroll Medicaid and other publicly funded beneficiaries but could not compete in the commercial market. The state's policy assumptions were that safety-net hospitals would form PHSPs, which would compete for Medicaid clients, and that revenue lost by emergency rooms would be recovered by the health plans.[29]

The PHSP program has had some success. Montefiore Hospital, for example, converted three clinics into a freestanding PHSP, called the Bronx Health Plan, which by late 1993 served approximately twenty-five thousand members. Other PHSPs formed as well and have done well financially, despite receiving, for every beneficiary enrolled, less than 90 percent of the cost of an average Medicaid client. One reason for the success is that New York's fee-for-service costs are high, so a capitation rate based on those rates is also high. For example, New York HMOs receive from Medicaid $140 to $160 per month for an average child,[30] a rate that is close to that paid by most commercial payers.[31] A California HMO, in contrast, receives from Medi-Cal $80 to $100 per month for a similarly situated child, a rate much less than regular commercial rates.[32] Perhaps surprisingly, however, the PHSP program never generated the hoped-for hospital participation. Indeed, most of the PHSPs emerged from small community health centers, and not from large acute care hospitals, and most did not develop until the early 1990s.[33]

But although the hospital industry hoped to maintain the status quo, the HMO industry anticipated major marketplace changes. Several of the nation's large for-profit HMOs accelerated their efforts to enter the New York state market. The legal basis for their exclusion was tenuous: state officials interpreted a law that excluded investor-owned hospitals to also exclude investor-owned HMOs, even though HMOs were governed by an entirely different set of state laws. With the HMOs threatening litigation, and state officials questioning the exclusion, the health department in 1985 changed its policy and permitted investor-owned HMOs to enter the state. Given the growing interest in Medicaid managed care, however, the department added a requirement that the newly licensed HMOs must "demonstrate a willingness" to enroll Medicaid clients.[34] But not surprisingly, few commercial HMOs were interested in the Medicaid population (their goal instead was to tap into the state's lucrative private market), and the state did little to enforce its new (and vague) regulation.

With the 1984 Medicaid managed care initiative lagging, and with the newly licensed commercial HMOs generally avoiding Medicaid clients, New York's policy environment was drifting away from its flirtation with Medicaid managed care.[35] The drift ended, however, when a New York City task force on Medicaid recommended that the city adopt a mandatory managed care demonstration project. The proposal, like the earlier CitiCaid initiative, was sharply attacked by the hospitals, the unions, and advocates. Once again, city officials proposed a compromise: a pilot project in a small section of southwest Brooklyn. This time, however, the state legislature, unhappy with the progress of the 1984 initiative, was willing to authorize the demonstration. The 1984 legislation also provided start-up funds for county-based physician care case management programs, and it established a program, called utilization thresholds, in which clients who "overused" the medical system would be assigned a case manager. Despite these changes, however, the managed care evolution remained incremental: The southwest Brooklyn project was limited to twenty-five thousand enrollees, the physician care case management programs were even smaller, and there was no real effort to encourage commercial HMOs to accept Medicaid clients. By the end of the 1980s, fewer than fifty thousand Medicaid clients were enrolled in managed care.

California in the 1990s: A Renewed Emphasis on Managed Care

By the early 1990s, increasing Medi-Cal costs convinced California officials of the desirability of a renewed emphasis on managed care. The newly elected governor, Pete Wilson, supported the effort, and in 1991 the state legislature, in the waning moments of the legislative session, enacted a new Medi-Cal managed care initiative. That the legislation was pushed through by the administration with little debate or discussion caused concern among traditional opponents of managed care (the counties, physicians, and consumer advocates), but the initiative was sufficiently incremental that opposition was relatively muted. For example, the legislation authorized three new COHSs, which was hardly a surprise because in the previous year Congress had approved the limited COHS expansion. The legislation also allowed a revised version of the San Diego managed care experiment (now called "geographic managed care") in two counties. Finally, and most controversially, it required that Medi-Cal clients who do not affirmatively choose a fee-for-service physician be enrolled in managed care by default.

The task of implementing the new legislation was assigned primarily to the California Department of Health Services (DHS), the state agency generally in charge of the Medi-Cal program. The California Medical Assistance Commission, created in 1982 to administer the hospital selective contracting program, was to work with DHS to implement the new COHS efforts and the new geographic managed care program.

In early 1992, DHS established a goal of expanding the number of Medi-Cal clients in managed care from 530,000 (or about 11 percent of the total Medi-Cal enrollment) to 1.25 million (27 percent of the total) by early 1997. DHS then decided that to meet this goal it would (1) ensure that the presentation to clients at the time of enrollment emphasized managed care, (2) implement the default enrollment by early 1994, (3) authorize managed care plans to provide nonmonetary incentives to prospective enrollees, (4) expand the PCCM program, (5) pressure HMOs to accept Medi-Cal clients, (6) provide case management for high-cost clients, and (7) work with the California Medical Assistance Commission in developing the new COHS and geographic managed care programs.

Almost immediately, the implementation effort faced problems. First, legal services lawyers challenged the legality of the new default program.[36] Second, most HMOs were still reluctant to accept Medi-Cal clients. And third, and most important, counties (particularly the larger ones) not only were reluctant to participate in either the COHS or geographic managed care experiments but they opposed the entire initiative.

County-state relations soured again in 1991, when the legislature enacted a state-local realignment, under which state aid for county health programs was discontinued, county responsibility for indigent health care was expanded, and counties were given additional tax revenue (primarily from the state sales tax) to compensate for lost revenues. Even in the best of economic times the counties would have lost money under realignment, but with the recession bringing reduced sales tax revenue and increased demands on the county safety net, many counties soon faced a severe fiscal crisis.

The counties were helped, however, by a 1987 federal law, implemented fully in 1990, that provided additional Medicaid funds to those hospitals that treat a disproportionate number of low-income persons.[37] Suddenly, most county hospitals were receiving millions of dollars in supplemental Medi-Cal payments. Indeed, by 1993 California's safety-net hospitals (both public and private) were receiving more than $1 billion annually in disproportionate-share funds. These hospitals then used the increased reimbursement to recoup lost state funds and to care for the uninsured.

The increased reliance on disproportionate-share funds only increased county opposition to managed care. If the Medi-Cal population moved primarily into commercial HMOs, the county hospitals would not only lose much of their insured clientele but they would sacrifice their disproportionate-share funding. The counties would be left with a predominantly uninsured patient base and inadequate funding to subsidize their care.

Given the county opposition, the state persuaded (or coerced) only one county, Sacramento, to participate in geographic managed care and three small counties to develop COHSs—Orange, Solano, and Santa Cruz. Not surprisingly, none of these four counties has a county hospital.[38] In July 1992, however, the politics of managed care changed dramatically, when a large for-profit HMO, the Foundation Health Plan, claimed that it could cover the entire Medi-Cal population and save the state hundreds of millions of dollars while doing so.

Foundation Health Plan's bid for an exclusive Medi-Cal contract was supported by influential legislators (most prominently Willie Brown) and state budget officials. But nearly every interest group opposed the bid, as did the state's Medi-Cal agency (DHS). Public and private hospitals worried about losing patients and disproportionate share funding. HMOs worried that a competitor would accumulate several million new clients (even though they had little interest in such clients themselves). Physicians worried about a large-scale shift to managed care. Community clinics, and other small safety-net providers, worried about losing their primary source of income. Consumer advocates worried that Foundation Health Plan would provide Medi-Cal clients with poor-quality health care. The California Medical Assistance Commission worried that if Foundation Health Plan succeeded, the COHS model, which it supported and administered, would soon decline. And state Medi-Cal officials (in the DHS) worried about losing control of the program itself.

As part of its effort to defeat the Foundation Health Plan bid, DHS officials began a campaign to demonstrate that they, too, could rapidly increase the state's managed care capacity. During the summer of 1992, for example, DHS proposed legislation that would require that 5 percent of every HMO's client population be Medi-Cal beneficiaries. Although the California Association of HMOs strongly opposed the 5 percent mandate, its members agreed to accept an additional one hundred thousand Medi-Cal clients.[39] DHS also persuaded the California Association of Public Hospitals to agree that its members would enroll more than 1 million beneficiaries into newly created hospital-based HMOs. And the DHS increased its effort to persuade small groups of physicians to join the PCCM program, or to provide other forms of Medi-Cal case management.

In the end, the coalition opposed to the Foundation Health Plan bid was strong enough to defeat it. But in September 1992 the legislature enacted a bill that both required DHS to speed up the transition to managed care and provided DHS with considerable discretion in meeting that goal. For example, the legislation authorized DHS to enact "emergency" managed care regulations without going through normal notice and comment procedures.

Perhaps ironically, the same forces that coalesced to defeat the Foundation Health Plan bid also led, albeit unintentionally, to a dramatic increase in DHS authority.

To be sure, DHS at first exercised its expanded authority gingerly. Medi-Cal director Molly Coye promised that DHS would work closely with all interested parties in managing the movement toward managed care. Even as Dr. Coye spoke, however, her staff was developing an aggressive and ambitious expansion program, one that focused on expanding the PCCM program and on encouraging more private-sector HMOs to accept Medi-Cal clients. DHS staff at that time placed little emphasis on expanding public-sector managed care programs (the public hospital initiative, for example, was suddenly a low priority).

The emphasis on private-sector expansion created a political uproar in October 1992, when Santa Clara officials learned, after the fact, that DHS staff had signed a contract with PruCare, a large PCCM program, to provide care to Medi-Cal clients in Santa Clara County. The PruCare negotiation mobilized the opposition: not only would the contract undercut the county hospital, and other safety-net providers, but PruCare itself was an organization accused of both providing poor-quality care and engaging in marketing abuses. Indeed, and rather ironically, DHS released a report critical of PruCare's activities in southern California just as the agency was signing the contract with PruCare in Santa Clara.

Given the controversy over PruCare, Coye declared a moratorium on new managed care contracts in November 1992. She also asked several members of her staff to develop and defend a more formal managed care policy, and to do so within a few months.

Several DHS officials favored an expanded COHS program, as did the California Medical Assistance Commission (which hoped to supervise any new COHSs), much of the provider community (although not the HMOs), several influential counties (which hoped to make the best of a bad situation), and several consumer advocates. The HMOs favored an expansion of the geographic managed care program, under which several plans could compete for Medi-Cal business.

Ignoring the interest-group proposals, DHS released a draft strategic plan on January 13, 1994, that proposed an entirely new managed care structure: "interested parties" in eleven of the state's largest counties would develop "health care consortia," which would then offer Medi-Cal clients a choice of managed care plans.[40] By July 1994, 2.4 million Medi-Cal clients would be enrolled in managed care, an increase from 606,000.

The response to the DHS draft plan was negative. The counties argued that the consortia model was a COHS without the counties in charge (indeed, it was impossible to tell who would be in charge of forming and administering the consortia), and that the proposal inadequately protected disproportionate-share funds received by county hospitals. HMOs and other providers objected to a requirement that organizations in the consortia drop any rate-related lawsuit brought against the state. The HMOs also believed the proposal delegated too much authority to the counties. Consumer advocates argued that the proposal relied too heavily on private-sector HMOs and PCCMs. The California Medical Assistance Commission complained that it had been given too small an administrative role. And nearly every group suggested that the plan contained unrealistic time frames (for example, interested parties had fewer than four months to form a consortium).

At the same time, however, DHS itself was questioning the wisdom of delegating substantial authority to a sole source (whether called a consortium, a COHS, or something else). The DHS's concern was prompted by an ongoing rate dispute with the San Mateo COHS. The dispute began in early 1992, when a state audit claimed that San Mateo's reserves and reimbursement rate were too high.[41] State officials[42] then demanded a substantial rate reduction. In response, the COHS threatened to shut down its operations. This threat enabled the COHS to negotiate a more favorable deal. However, it also convinced many DHS officials that an expanded managed care initiative should avoid sole-source contracts.

To rethink its strategy, DHS assigned six staffers to spend six weeks in a "hideaway location" and not to emerge until a final plan was in place.[43] The goal was to limit interest-group influence. Once again, the staffers devised a completely new idea, the so-called two-plan model. The plan has five key features. First, twelve of the state's largest counties would develop a local initiative, or a government-run HMO.[44] But to ensure competition (and to avoid another San Mateo), there would also be a mainstream or private-sector plan in each county. Second, the private-sector plan could be a single HMO (like the Foundation Health Plan) or a joint venture with several HMOs. Third, the government-run plan would be guaranteed a minimum number of Medi-Cal clients so as to protect county hospital disproportionate-share funding. Fourth, when the new system is in place (in mid-1996), PCCMs would no longer be licensed, and HMO enrollees would have to join one of the two plans. Fifth, and finally, DHS (and not the California Medical Assistance Commission) would administer the new system.

DHS officials argue that the new approach would reduce the state's administrative burden, eliminate excessive competition, and protect safety-net providers, primarily by preserving disproportionate-share funding. The state is now seeking federal permission to implement the plan. The opposition remains fierce. The HMO industry objects to the decision to permit only one private-sector plan in each county and to the requirement that the local initiative be guaranteed a minimum number of clients. At the same time, the counties, although they support the two-plan concept, argue that private-sector HMOs are using the transition period to enroll scores of low-risk Medi-Cal clients, leaving the high-risk (and more expensive) clients for the evolving public plans. And consumer advocates worry about the speed with which the state is proceeding. By July 1994, for example, more than 850,000 Medi-Cal clients were enrolled in managed care, and the state plans to increase that figure to 2.8 million by late 1996. A recent federal audit suggested that the state is moving too fast and that it lacks the resources (from staff to data systems) to adequately supervise the transition.[45]

There is controversy, too, over the state's efforts to keep HMO capitation rates very low. Unlike New York, where there is near parity in the public and private rates, Medi-Cal capitation rates are about 33 percent less than the average commercial rate;[46] and there is a three-year freeze on such rates and a strong likelihood that rates will be decreased even further.[47] Even federal officials are worried that the rates may be too low.[48] Not surprisingly, the HMOs claim they lose money on the low rate, but sign clients up anyway, in an effort to develop market share. State officials reply that the rates are adequate. But the low rates do raise again memories of the 1970s, when bargain-basement managed care rates encouraged bargain-basement plans.

Finally, there is also controversy over the DHS's effort to freeze out the California Medical Assistance Commission, especially as the commission is well versed in administering managed care programs. Indeed, maintaining its bureaucratic autonomy is a high priority for the DHS, as demonstrated also in its opposition to the Foundation Health Plan bid and to the San Mateo model. Given this mission, the DHS's decision to support the two-plan model, despite both interest-group and bureaucratic opposition, is hardly surprising. Nor are its efforts to keep capitation rates low. Moreover, the state-dominated managed care initiative emerging today contrasts sharply with the decentralized and fragmented initiative now under way in New York.

New York in the 1990s: Managed Care Takes Center Stage

In June 1991, New York's legislature enacted a sweeping managed care initiative, declaring that 50 percent of the state's 2.5 million Medicaid clients would be enrolled in managed care before the end of the decade. With only seventy-five thousand clients then in managed care, the initiative promised to revolutionize the state's Medicaid program. Surprisingly, however, the bill generated relatively little opposition: neither consumer advocates nor public hospital officials nor labor leaders lobbied hard against the proposal. Their acquiescence, although unexpected, was attributed to four factors.

First, the movement toward managed care was sweeping Medicaid programs around the nation. With program costs increasing nearly 30 percent a year, and with clients still receiving most of their care in hospital emergency rooms, the idea of managed care seemed irresistible. Clients would receive better and less expensive care. The alternatives—cutting eligibility, benefits, or provider reimbursement—were particularly unattractive.

Second, the legislation delegated to the counties the task of developing a plan to enroll local Medicaid clients into managed care programs. The delegation of authority persuaded county leaders (and public hospital officials) that local interests would not be ignored. A county could, for example, encourage (or require) a local public hospital to participate. It could encourage HMOs to be active participants. Or it could build on local provider networks of all sorts to develop the most promising delivery system.

The decision to delegate also enabled state legislators to sidestep some particularly difficult policy issues. The safety-net hospitals, for example, urged that HMOs be required to reimburse hospitals even when an HMO client receives nonurgent care in an emergency room. After all, not only are emergency rooms required by law to treat all who seek care but the Medicaid reimbursement rate for an emergency-room visit ($95) is much less than the cost of treating a true emergency. But the HMO lobby insisted that managed care works only if clients stop using emergency rooms inappropriately, and that paying for nonurgent care reinforces all the wrong incentives. The legislature, however, instead of resolving the emergency-room reimbursement debate, delegated it to the counties.

Third, the legislation phased in managed care over several years. The transition had two parts. Counties would have three years to develop their own managed care plans; nineteen of the state's fifty-seven counties would develop a plan in year one, nineteen in year two, and the final nineteen in year three. This timing enabled those counties most ready for managed care to move quickly but gave more time to others. Moreover, each plan had to meet transition targets: 10 percent of enrollees should be in managed care after one year, 25 percent after three years, and 50 percent after five. This timing allowed counties to plan over the long term for how best to accomplish the transition.

Fourth, and most important, the transition to managed care would be voluntary, at least until a particular county decided otherwise (and received federal permission to do so). The southwest Brooklyn demonstration project would remain the state's only mandatory managed care initiative. Medicaid clients elsewhere would be encouraged, but not required, to enroll in managed care. To be sure, most analysts (including those in the state's department of social services) doubted that a purely voluntary program would meet the 50 percent target. But the claim that a managed care initiative would inevitably restrict client freedom of choice was, for the time being, removed from the debate.

The more immediate problem was to develop a managed care infrastructure to accommodate the newly enrolled clients. The counties could require public hospitals to develop a managed care capacity, but they lacked similar leverage over the HMO community. Although HMOs were required by law to show "a willingness" to accept Medicaid clients, the provision was too vague to be effective.

Perhaps surprisingly, however, HMOs were soon competing fiercely for the Medicaid business. Some observers attributed the change to a state law, enacted in early 1992, that imposed a 9 percent surcharge on the hospital bills of those HMOs that had too few Medicaid clients.[49] Without a doubt, the surcharge was a factor. Several HMOs accepted their first Medicaid clients only because they had to. But the HMOs continued to enroll many Medicaid clients, even after a federal court held that the surcharge violated ERISA.[50]

The better explanation is that HMOs now understand the economic rationale for enrolling Medicaid clients. Medicaid in New York is a generous payer, and enrolling Medicaid clients generates profits. The high rates have two explanations. First, managed care rates are based on Medicaid fee-for-service costs, and New York's fee-for-service costs are more than twice the national average.[51] Second, managed care rates are developed through direct negotiations between Medicaid and plan officials. Such plan-specific rates are unusual: most states set a single rate for all plans (with adjustments for age, sex, and beneficiary's residence) or determine rates according to a competitive bidding process. New York officials, however, negotiate a rate with plan representatives once a year.[52]

In this changing Medicaid marketplace, the safety-net hospitals (particularly New York City's public hospitals) are forced to compete as well. One option is to persuade HMOs to refer patients to their facilities. But most HMOs prefer to contract with low-cost voluntary hospitals. The public hospitals must become managed care entities and compete directly for Medicaid enrollees. New York City's Health and Hospitals Corporation, for example, which administers the city's eleven acute care hospitals, determined that its economic viability depended on how successfully it expanded its managed care capacity. Other safety-net hospitals reached a similar conclusion.

Given the sudden competition for Medicaid business, the number of clients enrolled in managed care expanded remarkably, from sixty-two thousand in early 1991 to more than six hundred thousand today (or 24 percent of the eligible population). All fifty-seven of the state's counties have exceeded their enrollment targets. The managed care initiative seems to be working well.

However, several issues remain troublesome. First, 75 percent of managed care enrollees have joined traditional HMOs. HIP, Oxford, and Managed Healthcare Systems have done particularly well. The hospital-based HMOs, however, such as MetroPlus (formerly CitiCaid), have had slow beginnings. This only increases concerns about the long-range viability of the public hospital system, particularly because neither the state nor (more surprisingly) the city has developed a long-term plan to protect the medical safety net. Indeed, and in contrast, city officials (such as Mayor Rudy Giuliani) seem more interested in privatizing the city's hospitals than in helping them survive in a managed care setting. The health policy environment has clearly changed: hospital influence has declined while the influence of commercial HMOs has increased.

Second, questions arise about the quality of care provided by many of the managed care plans, few of which are experienced in serving a low-income population. A recent state investigation concluded, for example, that many Medicaid beneficiaries have difficulty scheduling initial medical appointments.[53] Similarly, many beneficiaries are unable (or unwilling) to travel long distances to authorized providers. Others, without telephones, cannot follow treatment regimens that require telephone authorization. And still others cannot find authorized providers who speak their native languages. For all these reasons, many enrollees still seek care in public hospital emergency rooms.

This is not to suggest, of course, that all managed care plans are ill equipped to treat the Medicaid population. But many have entered the market surprisingly quickly, in the hope of capturing a large share of low-risk, low-cost Medicaid clients, and therefore have focused as much on marketing as on service. With many plans competing for clients (in some communities there are more than a dozen competitors), and with health plan marketing surprisingly deregulated (one observer referred to the competition as the "Wild West"), the potential for fraud is high. Indeed, state officials recently suspended direct enrollment by health plans in New York City because of these concerns.[54]

Even with these problems, New York's Medicaid program is in the midst of a remarkable transition, moving quickly and surely in the direction of managed care. Moreover, the state's new Republican governor, George

Pataki, is anxious to increase the movement toward managed care and has proposed that all Medicaid recipients be required to enroll in managed care within the next two years. Although the fate of the governor's proposal is at this time uncertain, the state's transition to managed care is sure to continue.

Moving Medicaid Recipients into Managed Care: Lessons from California and New York

In both California and New York, competition for Medicaid business is fierce. This competition reverses (virtually overnight) the long-standing reluctance of commercial HMOs to court Medicaid clients. It also challenges the assumption that the managed care industry is too small to accommodate the Medicaid population. Moreover, competition today is not (primarily) between newly formed fly-by-night organizations, as was the case in California during the early 1970s. Rather, several of the nation's largest HMOs, such as U.S. Healthcare and Oxford in New York and CIGNA and Foundation Health Plan in California, are vigorously pursuing Medicaid clients.[55]

Some observers attribute the newly competitive environment to the states' legislative activity, both the managed care initiatives and the measures targeted directly at the HMO industry, such as the surcharge in New York and the threatened mandate in California. Although these actions surely had an impact, competition in New York continued (even increased) after the courts voided the surcharge, and California's HMOs now seek to enroll far more than the one hundred thousand Medi-Cal clients stipulated in the 1992 agreement.

The better explanation is that HMOs, initially pressured by government to enroll Medicaid beneficiaries, now recognize the wisdom of doing so. Medicaid clients (at least the low-risk, low-cost variety) generate profits. They also increase patient volume, which in turn increases negotiating leverage with hospitals and other providers.

The rapid expansion of Medicaid managed care can, if done well, improve the quality of care received by beneficiaries, encouraging more primary care and less emergency-room use. There are, however, serious risks. Most HMOs have little experience caring for the poor.[56] Capitated payment systems contain incentives to underserve. Safety-net providers, which still need to care for the uninsured (and perhaps high-risk Medicaid clients), probably will lose needed revenue. In other words, Medicaid managed care is not necessarily good or bad health policy. Rather, policy success depends on a host of variables, several of which are illustrated by the comparison of California and New York.

First, the previous policy-making environment shapes the current managed care initiative. New York, for example, has a decentralized and pluralistic Medicaid program. New York's managed care initiative follows suit. Policy is set largely by the fifty-seven counties. Rates are set on a case-by-case basis, after bargaining and negotiation. The marketing and enrollment process has been largely unregulated. Many plans compete, including several that serve only Medicaid clients. California, in contrast, has a more centralized and autonomous Medicaid bureaucracy and a more centralized managed care initiative. State officials control managed care policy. There is little bargaining over rates. Only two plans will be permitted to compete in much of the state.[57]

Second, previous fee-for-service expenditure patterns will influence future managed care spending. Fee-for-service Medicaid in New York is costly, and the managed care rates now in place reflect those patterns. Conversely, fee-for-service Medicaid in California is inexpensive; in fact, the state ranks forty-eighth in expenditures per beneficiary,[58] and its managed care payment rates are also low. This also suggests that New York could save even more money from managed care than California can.

Third, provider capacity is an important problem. In both states, for example, it remains unclear whether the participating HMOs have contracts with enough community-based providers (both physicians and others) to adequately serve their newly enrolled populations. This is especially true if Medicaid regulators can minimize adverse selection[59] and compel the HMOs to take some of the sickest and most difficult-to-treat Medicaid clients (such as infants born addicted to cocaine, persons with the acquired immunodeficiency syndrome, and the mentally ill homeless). Fourth, even low-risk, low-cost Medicaid clients, such as healthy women with young children, often need special attention: many neither speak English nor have a telephone, most have long used the local emergency room as their only provider, and nearly all live in medically underserved communities. There are ongoing questions, however, about the ability of many health plans to meet these needs.

Fifth, the profitability of Medicaid clients may well diminish. For example, Medicaid officials try to reduce reimbursement rates whenever they conclude that a managed care organization is making excessive profits. The San Mateo experience is illustrative: when the county-administered health insurance organization kept costs down and profits up, both federal and state officials insisted on a rate reduction. Officials at New York's Bronx Health Plan report a similar pattern. Moreover, if the federal contribution to Medicaid declines (as seems likely), there will be additional pressure to decrease HMO reimbursement rates. This is especially true in New York, where HMOs receive relatively generous reimbursement. In addition, if

Medicaid officials ever reduce adverse selection, the profitability of Medicaid clients will diminish even further. But as the profitability of Medicaid clients declines, so will their attractiveness to HMOs, particularly as the reform environment is now less threatening.

Sixth, and last, the potential lack of a long-term HMO commitment increases the need to preserve a strong medical safety net. California and New York have adopted different approaches, however, to this issue. In California, state Medi-Cal officials have used their considerable bureaucratic discretion to develop a managed care model (the "two-plan model"), designed in large part to protect safety-net institutions. In New York, in contrast, state officials have neither designed nor implemented a safety-net protection plan. Instead, the state delegated to the fifty-seven counties the task of designing and implementing the managed care initiative, and the safety net (particularly in New York City) fends for itself.

In short, the comparison of New York and California suggests again that New York's Medicaid program is less regulatory than its reputation suggests, whereas California's program is hardly a model of free-market competition. The comparison shows also that states, despite complaints of federal micromanagement, retain wide discretion to shape their Medicaid programs. Indeed, the comparison documents the need for a strong federal role, a policy prescription surely at odds with the current trend toward increased state authority. Federal officials, for example, need to ensure that states implementing Medicaid managed care develop a safety-net protection plan (such as California's). Without federal supervision of this sort, the ability of safety-net providers to survive may depend largely on the state in which they operate.

Notes

Research for this chapter was supported by a Caldone Award for Junior Faculty Development and the Columbia University School of Public Health. The text originally appeared in the *Journal of Health Politics, Policy and Law* 21 (fall, 1996): 433–60. It is reprinted here by permission of Duke University Press.

1. Hawaii is the only state in the country that requires employers to provide health insurance to their employees. Hawaii is also implementing the State of Hawaii Insurance Plan, which subsidizes insurance coverage for large segments of the state's previously uninsured. For a good summary of the state's reform activities, see Deane Neubauer, "Hawaii: A Pioneer in Health Systems Reform," *Health Affairs* 12, no. 2 (1993): 31–39.

Minnesota is now implementing the MinnesotaCare program, under which families with incomes less than 275 percent of poverty and individuals with incomes less than 100 percent of poverty are eligible for a state-subsidized health insurance policy. For a good summary of the state's reform activities, see Howard M. Leichter, "Minnesota: The Trip from Acrimony to Accommodation," *Health Affairs* 12, no. 2 (1993): 48–58.

Tennessee is now implementing the TennCare Program, which provides a choice of managed care plans to nearly 1.5 million low-income persons, one-third of whom were previously uninsured. For a good summary of the program so far, see Marsha Gold, Hilary Frazier, and Cathy Schoen, *Managed Care and Low Income Populations: A Case Study of Managed Care in Tennessee* (Washington, D.C.: Henry J. Kaiser Family Foundation and the Commonwealth Fund, July 1995).

2. At the time of this writing, for example, Congress had passed a budget that would (if signed by the president) reduce federal Medicaid expenditures by $182 billion over the next seven years.

3. For a description of ERISA and its impact on state health reform efforts see Patricia A. Butler, *Roadblock to Reform: ERISA Implications for State Health Care Initiatives* (Washington, D.C.: National Governors' Association Center for Policy Research, 1994).

4. For a good description of the various state reform strategies, see Intergovernmental Health Policy Project, "Health Care Reform: Fifty State Profiles" (Washington, D.C.: George Washington University, July 1994).

5. Moreover, during this period Congress actually required states to expand their coverage of certain groups, particularly children and pregnant women.

6. Kaiser Commission on the Future of Medicaid, *Medicaid and Managed Care: Lessons from the Literature* (Washington, D.C.: Henry J. Kaiser Family Foundation, 1995).

7. The medical safety net includes those hospitals (both public and nonprofit) and community health centers that have traditionally cared for both Medicaid clients and the uninsured, along with a few individual practitioners who serve a primarily indigent population.

8. The best review of the literature is from the Kaiser Commission, *Medicaid and Managed Care.*

9. In New York, for example, a typical nursing home receives more than $120 per day per Medicaid recipient; a similarly situated facility in California receives only $65 per day per recipient. Michael S. Sparer, "States in a Reformed Health System: Lessons from Nursing Home Policy," *Health Affairs* 12, no. 1 (1993): 8.

10. California was a good state in which to test the viability of Medicaid managed care. Californians have long enrolled in managed care organizations, such as the Kaiser Permanente health clinics, in numbers far greater than their counterparts in other states. Given the state's large managed care industry, Medi-Cal officials argued both that mainstream care in California is managed care, and that the state had the managed care infrastructure to accommodate the expansionary effort.

11. Medi-Cal officials enjoy considerable bureaucratic autonomy and have used that discretion to implement an effective cost-containment program. Michael S. Sparer, *Medicaid and the Limits of State Health Reform* (Philadelphia: Temple University Press, 1996).

12. The 1971 legislation also provided Medi-Cal eligibility for those adults previously unable to meet the categorical requirements for eligibility (so-called medically indigent adults or MIAs). State officials predicted that 800,000 new adults would thereby become Medi-Cal eligible, providing cost savings for the counties and counteracting the increased county Medi-Cal share. In the next several years, however, only 250,000 persons joined the MIA program, leaving the counties still responsible for nearly 600,000 indigent adults. Only now the counties are going without state aid in paying for these programs.

13. David F. Chavkin and Anne Treseder, "California's Prepaid Health Plan Program: Can the Patient Be Saved?" *Hastings Law Journal* 28 (1977): 685–760.

14. In 1972, for example, the legislature enacted the Waxman-Duffy Prepaid Health Plan Act, which regulated for the first time the marketing activities of the new managed care organizations. Then, in 1975, the legislature enacted the Knox-Keene Health Care Service Plan Act, which required the state's Department of Corporations to license all prepaid health plans, including those with Medi-Cal contracts.

15. U.S. General Accounting Office, *Better Controls Needed for Health Maintenance Organizations under Medicaid in California,* Report #B–164031(3) (Washington, D.C.: Government Printing Office, September 1974); General Accounting Office, *Deficiencies in Determining Payments to Prepaid Plans under California's Medicaid Program,* Report #MWD–76–15 (Washington, D.C.: Government Printing Office, August 1975); General Accounting Office, *Relationships between Nonprofit Prepaid Health Plans with California Medicaid Contracts and For-Profit Entities Affiliated With Them,* Report #HRD–77–4 (Washington, D.C.: Government Printing Office, November 1976).

16. The law exempted federally funded community health centers from the 50 percent requirement.

17. Under selective contracting, state officials estimate the number of hospital beds needed for Medi-Cal patients, hospitals bid for Medi-Cal contracts, and hospitals without contracts provide only emergency-room care to Medi-Cal patients.

18. Before 1985, COHSs were exempt from the requirement that no more than 75 percent of an HMO's clients could be receiving Medicaid or Medicare. Today, the remaining COHSs (in Santa Barbara, San Mateo, and Solano) have congressional exemptions from the 75-25 percent rule.

19. Both consumer advocates and some state officials have complained about the quality of care provided by the PCCMs. First, there were many anecdotal reports of PCCMs providing poor access to care (long waits for appointments, no evening appointments, and so on). Second, there were suggestions that some PCCMs discouraged necessary inpatient care (because they received a fiscal bonus for reducing such care). And third, the state had very little regulatory control over PCCM behavior, because the Knox-Keene legislation (which governed HMOs) did not cover PCCMs.

20. Jack Meyer, *Case Study of Health Plan of San Mateo* (Washington, D.C.: New Directions for Policy, August 1991).

21. Congressional Research Service, *Medicaid Source Book: Background Data and Analysis* (Washington D.C.: Government Printing Office, 1993 Update), 1028.

22. In 1984, for example, there were fewer than 1 million New Yorkers enrolled in managed care.

23. Article 21 of New York's Public Health Law prohibits investor-owned hospitals from operating in New York. Before 1985, this law was interpreted to also prohibit investor-owned HMOs.

24. John Holahan, Martcia Wade, and Michael Gates, "The Impact of Medicaid Adoption of the Medicare Fee Schedule," *Health Care Financing Review* 14 (1993): 15.

25. Eli Ginzberg, "Improving Health Care for the Poor: Lessons from the 1980s," *Journal of the American Medical Association,* February 9, 1994: 465.

26. James Swan, Charlene Harrington, Leslie Grant, John Luehrs, and Steve Preston, "Trends in Medicaid Nursing Home Reimbursement," *Health Care Financing Review* 14 (1993): 126.

27. Prospective Payment Assessment Commission, *Medicaid Hospital Payment Congressional Report,* C–91–02 (Washington, D.C.: Prospective Payment Assessment Commission, October 1, 1991).

28. Kaiser Commission, *Medicaid and Managed Care,* 8.

29. The legislation also authorized counties to establish Physician Case Management Programs, under which individual physicians would receive enhanced fees in exchange

for serving as managed care gatekeepers. This program resembled California's PCCM program. But the legislation neither provided start-up funds for this initiative nor otherwise encouraged counties to participate. Not surprisingly, only one county (Erie) signed up.

30. Paul Tenan, New York State Department of Health, interview by author, July 13, 1993.

31. Katherine Allen, New York State HMO Conference, interview by author, July 19, 1993.

32. Bill Caswell of MaxiCare, and Michael Owens of CIGNA, interview by author, February 14, 1994.

33. New York State Department of Health and New York State Department of Social Services, *Report to the Legislature on the Implementation of the Medicaid Reform Act of 1984* (New York: New York State Department of Health, 1984).

34. 10 New York Code of Rules and Regulations, Part 98.

35. The disillusionment with managed care was prompted, in part, by a short and unsuccessful effort to require Medicaid beneficiaries in Rochester to enroll in managed care. This initiative began in 1985 and ended in 1987, a victim of inadequate capitation rates, poor program design, and inefficient program administration. Research Triangle Institute, Center for Health Research, *Nationwide Evaluation of Medicaid Competition Demonstrations, Volume 7: Analysis of Administrative Costs in the Medicaid Competition Demonstrations* (Research Triangle Park, N.C.: Research Triangle Institute, May 31, 1988).

36. Legal services lawyers representing Medi-Cal clients argued that DHS needed federal permission to implement a default program. Although the state disagreed, it ultimately sought federal approval. In November 1993, the federal government approved the default but urged the state to work with federal officials and consumer advocates to develop the health care options materials that would be presented to clients at enrollment. As of November 1995, the default had yet to be implemented, and the health care options materials developed by the state were being challenged in federal court.

37. Federal legislation enacted in 1981 required states "to take into account" the situation of those hospitals that serve a disproportionate number of low-income persons. Despite this command, however, many states refused to provide the subsidies. In 1987, Congress required states to provide subsidies to hospitals that met federally defined criteria. The 1987 law went into effect in 1990.

38. During the summer of 1994, approximately 150,000 clients in the Aid to Families with Dependent Children and Medi-Cal programs were enrolled in managed care plans as part of the Sacramento Geographic Managed Care Initiative. The COHS in Solano was also implemented in 1994 and now has enrolled more than 43,000 clients. The COHS in Orange County began operation in October 1995 and has enrolled more than 170,000 clients. The COHS in Santa Cruz has yet to enroll clients.

39. The basis for the one hundred thousand figure was a series of telephone calls, made by the executive director of the California Association of HMOs, in which several health plans agreed to enroll small numbers of additional Medi-Cal clients. At that time, the industry was reluctant to accept Medi-Cal clients, and the one hundred thousand figure was considered high. Soon thereafter, however, as health care reformers emphasized managed competition and managed care, the HMOs' willingness to accept Medi-Cal clients increased, and HMO officials declared the one hundred thousand figure to be a floor, not a cap.

40. If the consortia failed to develop, the state would implement a geographic managed care model.

41. Federal officials have since used this audit to demand the return of $5 million. This federal claim remains unresolved.

42. The California Medical Assistance Commission conducted these negotiations.

43. The six, one of whom worked for the DHS's parent agency, the California Health and Welfare Agency, were of course in regular contact with their bureaucratic supervisors.

44. The plan initially called for thirteen county participants, but San Diego later received legislative permission to enact a separate program modeled after geographic managed care.

45. Health Care Financing Administration, *Report on Medi-Cal Managed Care* (San Francisco: Health Care Financing Administration, 1994).

46. Jonathan Lewis, director of the Los Angeles Health Advantage and former director of the California Association of HMOs, interview by author, February 9, 1994; Caswell and Owens interview.

47. By law, Medi-Cal HMOs cannot receive more than the average client costs the fee-for-service program. In the last few years, however, as Medi-Cal has added many low-cost clients, such as women and children, the average cost per client has declined, so much so that many HMOs now receive more than 100 percent of the fee-for-service amount.

48. Richard Chambers, of the federal Department of Health and Human Services, letter dated September 26, 1995 to John Rodriguez, of the California Department of Health Services (on file with the author).

49. State officials had enacted the law as a way to raise an estimated $35 million in revenue; the impact on HMO behavior was (by most accounts) an unintended benefit.

50. *Travelers Insurance Company v. Cuomo,* 813 F. Supp. 996 (S.D.N.Y. 1993), aff'd 14F.3d 708 (2d Cir. 1994), remanded for reconsideration 115 S. Ct. 1671 (1995).

51. Kaiser Commission, *Medicaid and Managed Care,* Table 16.

52. There are actually several rates for each plan, with each rate covering a different age and sex band. The rates also cannot exceed a maximum of 95 percent of the average cost per beneficiary in the preceding year.

53. Elisabeth Rosenthal, "Albany to Require Improvements in Service by Medicaid H.M.O.'s," *New York Times,* November 17, 1995, A1.

54. Ian Fisher and Esther B. Fine, "Forced Marriage of Medicaid and Managed Care Hits Snags," *New York Times,* August 28, 1995, B1.

55. To be sure, not all of the key players are well established in New York; for example, Managed Healthcare Systems evolved primarily to participate in this competition.

56. Before 1990, for example, fewer than fifty thousand New York Medicaid beneficiaries were enrolled in managed care.

57. To be sure, the policy environments are not fixed. New York state regulators are increasing their oversight of marketing. State officials are even talking about moving to a competitive-bid rate setting model.

58. Kaiser Commission, *Medicaid and Managed Care.*

59. Adverse selection occurs when HMOs enroll low-risk, low-cost clients, leaving the high-cost clients for others. HMOs (and other insurers) often market their product only to their preferred customers. The best way to eliminate adverse selection would be to implement an effective system of risk adjustment (paying HMOs with high-risk clients more than those with low-risk clients). But because the technology of risk adjustment is still in its infancy, states need to regulate closely HMO marketing and enrollment patterns.

5

The Federal-State Relationship in Health Care Reform: A View from the Trenches

Jean I. Thorne

As academics have been busy dissecting various health care reform proposals over the past several years, many of us who have been charged with actually developing and implementing workable programs have often wondered at the disconnect between the worlds of policy analysis and of "making it happen." Listening to scholarly presentations about the ideal world of health system reform, I have often thought how those providing their ideas and critiques might benefit from having to fight the battles to change programs. Having directed Oregon's Medicaid program through eight years of extraordinary change, I can provide some insights into both what it took us (and to a lesser extent, other states) to move the federal-state relationship to allow for reform at the state level and how that relationship may affect future plans.

The past several years have seen increased activity at the state level in beginning to grapple with health care reform. For many of us, this work was initiated by efforts to better control state expenditures for the Medicaid program, a program that is jointly funded by the federal and state governments. In attempting to deal with Medicaid, lawmakers have been confronted with the hydraulic effects that actions in the Medicaid program have on other parts of our health care system. As we began to understand the dynamics of this complex system, many states identified the need to address a number of issues if we were to be successful in both increasing health care access and controlling health care costs. We developed our plans and forged political consensus to carry out those plans. Unfortunately, we have also found that the ability of states to undertake reforms of this system are often hindered by the involvement of the federal government in financing or regulating activities over which states have little or no control.

Our current system of health care financing is not the result of comprehensive planning, but of a number of separate actions taken over many years. It has only been in the last two decades that states have begun to play a significant role in the financing and regulation of health care activities. For most of our history government played little role in the financing of health care services, except for special populations such as merchant seamen, Native Americans, and members of the armed services. The payment for health care services was a matter between the provider and the patient. As concerns about the potential costs of health care grew, medical insurance became a popular mode for protecting one's assets. Over the years, medical insurance became part of many employers' compensation packages. Although government played a role in protecting individuals through the regulation of insurance, it had little direct role in financing the costs of those medical services.

The Growth of Medicaid as an Issue for States

The advent of Medicare and Medicaid in the mid-1960s dramatically changed the dynamics of health care policy. The center of the debate at that time was the creation of the Medicare program, which was established as a means to protect the elderly and disabled from the potentially devastating costs of a serious illness. The program was financed and directed by the federal government. Although the Medicaid program was established at the same time, there was less congressional debate because it was seen as a less significant policy or financing issue. The program was designed to provide assistance to states in paying for the health care costs of those families on the federal-state welfare program (Aid to Families with Dependent Children), as well as to low-income elderly, blind, and disabled persons. Medicaid is a federal-state partnership in which the national government matches state expenditures for services provided to Medicaid-eligible clients. To participate in Medicaid, states are required to meet certain federal mandates involving eligibility, benefits, delivery, and payment for services. In effect, if states wanted the federal government as a partner, they had to accept certain federal requirements.

Over the years, states were given the opportunity to receive federal matching funds on an increasing number of "optional" services for special groups. Some of the more significant options were given to states by Congress in the mid-1980s, as states were allowed to expand coverage to low-income pregnant women and infants whose income was above a state's welfare standards but below the federal poverty level. Many states, in efforts to address concerns about infant mortality, began to expand their programs to cover some of these women and children.

By the late 1980s, however, Congress began to turn many of these additional options into mandates. No longer was it the choice of states to cover these groups, it was now a requirement imposed by the federal government. Initially, states were required to cover pregnant women and infants under age one to the poverty level. This was later expanded to cover pregnant women and children to age six up to 133 percent of the poverty level. Congress then added a requirement to cover children to the poverty level born after September 30, 1983, phasing in coverage to children to age nineteen. Under changes to the Early, Periodic, Screening, Diagnosis, and Treatment (EPSDT) statutes of 1989, states were required to provide any "medically necessary" service to a Medicaid client under age twenty-one, even if the state otherwise did not include the service because it was "optional" or if it imposed certain limitations on the service (such as hospital day limits or physician visit limits).

One of the more interesting mandates arose out of the 1988 Medicare Catastrophic Act. The act was initially designed to expand Medicare coverage to cover prescription drugs, as well as to make other changes to inpatient hospital coverage. This expansion was financed by an increase in the premiums paid by Medicare beneficiaries. One requirement in the bill was that state Medicaid programs had to pay the cost of Medicare premiums for the elderly who were under the federal poverty level, even if they were otherwise not eligible for Medicare. Once Medicare recipients realized that the law would increase their premiums, the outcry that ensued forced Congress to repeal the law—except for portions that placed additional requirements on Medicaid.

As the burden of the federal mandates accumulated, states began to rebel. Whereas the federal government could impose additional requirements and finance their increased costs by deficit spending, states did not have that luxury. All states but Vermont are required to have balanced budgets. When the federal government expanded requirements in the Medicaid program, it also expanded the obligation of states to pick up their share of that tab (up to 50 percent of the costs for some states). States were then faced with the need to make decisions about how to balance these additional costs, either through cuts elsewhere in the Medicaid program, reductions in other state-financed programs (such as education), or by raising revenues. Although the decisions by Congress to provide additional coverage to certain groups can easily be justified as worthy public policy, the states were then left with the tough decisions as to how to finance these additional requirements. In sum, states were forced to make trade-offs because of unilateral actions by the federal government.

At various times, the nation's governors called on Congress to not impose any additional unfunded mandates. They were finding that the costs of the Medicaid program were consuming an ever increasing share of their state expenditures, at a time when they had decreasing amounts of flexibility to control those costs. Against this backdrop, some states, such as Oregon, began to identify the need to not only reform their Medicaid program, but to do so within a larger context of reforming the entire health care system.

How Oregon Came to Health Care Reform

In Oregon, our road to health care reform was initiated by a decision made by the 1987 legislature to discontinue funding of organ transplants for Medicaid clients, while at the same time expanding coverage to some of those for whom there were new Medicaid options, namely poor pregnant women and children. This decision was made in the closing days of the legislative session, with little public discussion. It was not until a young boy who might have benefited from a bone marrow transplant died months later that the legislature and the public became fully engaged in a debate about our health care priorities. (For a more complete account of the Oregon reform story, see Howard Leichter's chapter (6) in this volume.)

The focus of the debate was initially on the Medicaid program. Coverage for transplants had been singled out because of a loophole in federal law that allowed states not to cover them. Beyond that, there was little ability for states to decide not to cover a service, even if it was of marginal value, if an argument could be made that it was "medically necessary." As special legislative committees met during 1988 to discuss the transplant controversy, they became increasingly aware of the requirements and limitations of Medicaid. The discussions were led by the Senate president, John Kitzhaber (D), an emergency-room physician. Kitzhaber recalled the decisions made by the previous legislatures to redefine Medicaid eligibility, cutting off coverage for thousands of poor Oregonians as a way to balance the state's Medicaid budget. He noted that soon after, he began to see poor persons coming into his emergency room who had previously been covered by Medicaid, yet now were forced to wait until their medical condition was so severe that they could not be turned away by the hospital. Not only were the conditions more severe than they might have needed to be, they were more costly. The costs of this care were then shifted to other payers, since these people were often unable to pay their hospital bills. This, in turn, partially fueled increases in the premiums paid by private payers (primarily employer-sponsored insurance). Employers then complained about the rising cost of health insurance. In some cases, they then decreased or even dropped coverage for their employees or dependents, adding to the number of uninsured.

It became increasingly clear that our lack of a comprehensive health care policy resulted in a vicious cycle that could not be attacked from merely one angle. To address the cost problems of the Medicaid program in isolation might merely mean that the cost and access problems would become worse elsewhere. Since there appeared to be little interest in dealing with the need for health care reform at the national level, our state decided that it was critical to begin addressing it at the state level. To do this in a comprehensive manner, however, would necessarily require that we also deal with the Medicaid program, which was not completely under our control.

During the 1989 legislative session, a political consensus formed among a broad array of interest groups to develop and pass comprehensive health reform. Business, labor, medical providers, insurers, and consumers came together to agree on a set of principles that would guide the reform of our health care system. A set of strategies was agreed upon that included an expansion and reform of the Medicaid program, the establishment of a high-risk pool for the medically uninsurable, tax credits for small employers who began offering coverage to their employees, and an eventual employer mandate designed as a "play-or-pay" system (i.e., provide coverage for employees and dependents or be required to pay into a state pool). At the next legislative session, small-market insurance reform and expanded technology assessment programs were included as part of this comprehensive strategy, which by then had become known as the Oregon Health Plan. Through this set of efforts, we believed that we could achieve near universal coverage as well as control costs. It was a strategy that was designed to include expanded roles for both the public and private sectors.

Oregon's Road to Medicaid Waivers

Both the tax credit program and high-risk pool were initiatives we could undertake without federal approval. The initial major undertaking, however, involved the reform of the Medicaid program. The principles guiding our

Medicaid reform were relatively simple: (1) cover those under the poverty level, without regard to family status, disability, or age; (2) provide a benefit package based on a process involving the prioritization of health care services, allowing us to concentrate our public dollars on those services doing the greatest good; (3) deliver those services through prepaid managed care organizations; and (4) pay for the services at rates designed to cover costs in a managed environment. Not one of those policies could be carried out under federal Medicaid law. If we wished to reform our Medicaid program in this way, it would require federal waivers. In consulting with the federal Health Care Financing Administration (HCFA), we found that the secretary of health and human services had the authority to grant us the necessary waivers under Section 1115 of the Social Security Act. Section 1115 gives the secretary broad waiver authority in support of "research and demonstration" programs. Up to that point, only one state (Arizona) had been granted a waiver to undertake such sweeping changes, but that state had also not previously participated in the Medicaid program. We recognized that we would be covering new ground, but we did not anticipate the controversy that would surround our request, both at the White House and in Congress. Looking back, it is clear that many of the issues we confronted in our quest for waivers were precursors to the current debate about the future of the Medicaid program.

The center of the controversy over Oregon's plan was with our proposal to determine benefits based on a priority list of health services. An independent commission was charged with developing a list of health services ranging from "most important to least important." The statute required that the commission include significant public input on the values that should guide its decision making. Once that list was developed, it was to be priced by an actuary and given to the state legislature. The legislature could not alter the placement of items on the list but could only decide where to "draw the line," thus defining both the benefit package and the program's budget. Those services higher on the list would be covered, those falling below the line would not. The strategy behind this approach was one that recognized that it was more important to provide the most effective services to a broader group of individuals than to provide every available service to a smaller group of individuals.

Oregonians had acknowledged the flaws in our health care system during the debates of 1988. By and large, they understood that not all health services were equally effective, that we had a significant portion of our population that had no health care access, and that trade-offs were necessary. The passage of this bill during the 1989 legislative session was not controversial within Oregon. The reaction outside Oregon, however, was much different. National client advocacy organizations decried Oregon's plans to "ration" health care. A congressional hearing was held on the "Oregon Medicaid rationing experiment." The national press portrayed Senate president Kitzhaber as "Dr. Death."

Few of these opponents acknowledged Oregon's plans to increase the number of poor Oregonians to be covered by Medicaid by almost 50 percent (120,000 people). The focus was not on those faceless people who currently had nothing; it was only on those who already had coverage but would lose their entitlement to some less effective or less important services.

The commission charged with developing the priority list had a daunting task. No one had ever tried to prioritize the vast array of available services before. They were told by many opponents that it just could not be done. The commission had its share of stumbles along the way, but eventually came to the 1991 legislature with a comprehensive list that was understandable and supportable. The legislature made its funding decision, drawing the line on the list of services. The waiver request was submitted in August 1991. HCFA officials had indicated that they believed a decision could be made within four to six months; we planned to begin operation of the program in July 1992.

Over the year following submittal of our waiver request, state staff and various stakeholders spent endless hours responding to seemingly interminable questions, not only from HCFA but from other parts of the national government. Members of Congress requested the Office of Technology Assessment (OTA) to review the process Oregon used to create its priority list to determine what flaws might lie behind it. Others in Congress requested the General Accounting Office (GAO) to conduct a study to gauge whether Oregon had sufficient provider capacity to absorb the additional people who would be eligible for Medicaid under the proposed plan. Symposiums were held and numerous articles were written on Oregon's "rationing plan." Detailed inquiries were made to determine whether the managed care system being developed could provide quality care to Medicaid enrollees, and permanent office space was set aside for the various groups of investigators who had been commissioned to examine the Oregon plan.

During all this time, not only did the workloads of those of us in the state required to respond to these inquiries grow, so did our frustrations. What was most remarkable to us was the level of scrutiny that our plans were undergoing, compared to the level of scrutiny afforded the system already in place. For instance, while investigators from OTA reviewed in detail the processes and results of the prioritized list, we wondered how much review had been given to the federally prescribed benefit structure. Federal law allows states the "option" of covering such services as prescription drugs and physical therapy, while "mandating" that medically necessary physician services be provided, although the latter could be subject to arbitrary limits. Had OTA ever been asked to determine the impact of those requirements and allowances on Medicaid clients? While the GAO spent months trying to determine whether there was adequate capacity to serve additional Medicaid enrollees, we wondered whether having a physician shortage would mean that additional poor persons should be told that they would be given no coverage at all? While others examined whether our managed care standards and oversight were adequate to assure quality, we wondered why no one seemed to ask that question of a fee-for-service system where providers were paid less than cost and merely refused to serve Medicaid clients. The questions to which we were responding did not seem to be comparing our plans with what was already in place, but rather to a "perfect" system. Why were we being reviewed and dissected in such excruciating detail, while the current system with its obvious flaws was not?

We began to ask these questions and to show our critics the real picture behind what we were trying to accomplish in Oregon. We had them actually review the list of services that would no longer be covered. We explained how our Medicaid reforms fit within a broader picture of health care reform. As we did that, we found that some of our critics were finally willing to say that what Oregon was doing "wasn't so bad." But lurking behind these comments was another question: "What if Alabama (or Mississippi or Louisiana) wants to do it?" Critics acknowledged the trade-offs involving "rationing" within the context of an overall plan to expand access, and that the services that would no longer be covered were not so critical. Their concerns, however, appeared to be with less "progressive" states that might wish to use "rationing" in isolation from other reforms.

As we attempted to force our critics to define their objections to what we were doing, it became increasingly clear to us that the arguments were not about the details of Oregon's plan, but about moving power to the states. Congress had been able to respond to appeals by various interest groups by forcing mandates upon states. Congress could be the "good guy" in these appeals, while states were forced to make the hard fiscal choices in response to these mandates. Interest groups believed they could achieve their goals more effectively and efficiently dealing with Congress than with fifty separate state legislatures. Supporters of mandates appeared to see their role as protector of the poor from the villainous states. By looking at the Medicaid program within a vacuum, however, they were unable to see the harm that could be done to the poor by states being forced to make fiscal choices that might affect other state-financed programs.

Opposition to our plans was not confined to Capitol Hill. Our request in fact was not to Congress, but to the Bush administration. The initial time-line of four to six months dragged on as discussions about the Oregon waiver request moved to the White House. Those familiar with the discussions told us that there were two camps—those who supported states' rights and those who believed that "rationing" of health care could not be supported in any way, even if it meant the continued lack of coverage for 120,000 poor people. The presidential election campaign moved into full swing as we continued to wait for a decision.

Eleven months after we submitted our waiver request, we were told that there might be "problems" with the Americans with Disabilities Act (ADA), specifically that the process used by the Health Services Commission (HSC) might have inherently discriminated against persons with disabilities. We asked federal officials to tell us what services that were not covered would be considered a violation of the ADA. We were told that it was not the results that were of concern, but the process that developed those results. Although we argued that current law allows states to not cover optional services, many of which are used disproportionately by disabled persons, federal officials responded that such a comparison was inappropriate. Since the HSC's process included looking at the ability of a treatment to improve functioning (as one means of determining effectiveness), such an assessment was supposedly inherently discriminatory.

One year after we submitted our waiver request, it was denied on the basis of the ADA. Even though the Bush administration sent a team of lawyers to explain to the commission how the process violated the ADA, I believe that few people involved in the process ever believed those to be legitimate or credible arguments. Even national disability advocates, who later visited Oregon and reviewed our list and plans in more detail, were willing to admit that Oregon's plan was "not so bad, but what if another state were to do it" in a different way?

Seven months later, after changes to the process and the arrival of the Clinton administration, we were granted our waivers. It had been almost four years from the time the law had passed. What had happened during those four years? We changed governors, although both were Democrats, our House of Representatives, which had been solidly Democratic in 1989, was now under Republican control, and the author and staunchest legislative advocate of the plan had retired from the Senate. Senate Democrats held a 20-to-10 margin in 1989; in 1993 they held a 16-to-14 margin. Lastly, a national debate on health care reform had begun, a debate that was becoming increasingly bitter and partisan.

As we brought our approved waiver to the legislature in 1993, Oregon lawmakers began to back off from their commitment to universal coverage.

Although they were eventually willing to fund the Medicaid expansion and insurance reform, the Medicaid changes became tied up with debate on the employer mandate. It was this issue that was one of the major reasons the 1993 session was the longest one in Oregon history. By the time the 1993 session adjourned, the Medicaid plan was funded, but the employer mandate was delayed, with a statutory provision included that would automatically repeal the mandate if a congressional exemption from the Employee Retirement Income Security Act (ERISA) was not received by January 2, 1996.

Impact of the National Health Care Debate on States

Most states that were struggling on their own to reform health care most likely welcomed the national attention that was given to the issue soon after President Clinton took office. Although citizens in our state had become educated to the need for health care reform in the late 1980s, the issue had not captured a national audience until the early 1990s. As individual states, we were attempting to deal with issues that did not confine themselves to state borders. Concerns about in-migration to take advantage of our programs and business out-migration to flee employer mandates were very real to lawmakers. Most of those involved in state health care reform at that time would have acknowledged that there were some issues best dealt with on a national level. In 1993, many state legislatures hesitated to take action on a state level, waiting to see what national solutions would emerge.

The national debate, however, was a far cry from the types of debates that had occurred in our own state legislatures. In Oregon, we had brought together the various interest groups to agree on principles. Each of those groups was willing to accept the need for trade-offs and compromise. We had a solid coalition supporting the plan, although some groups may have had reservations about certain components of it. They were all involved throughout the process of working through the broad outlines and the eventual details of the proposals.

At the national level, however, there was no such coalition building and little rational discussion. Well-financed interest groups were willing to sponsor national advertising campaigns designed to scare the public about proposed solutions. Health care reform is inherently an emotional and personal issue—a matter affecting life and death. Within Oregon, we acknowledged those emotions and then worked to move the debate beyond that. At the national level, those who would suffer financially knew just how emotional an issue it could be and used that to fight against proposed reforms. The American public appeared to become more afraid of the solution than of the problem. Not only did non-positive action come of the national debate, health care reform is now barely mentioned at the national level. And back home in our states, the scared public and the scared lawmakers decided health care reform was not so important after all. The past two years have seen most states that had attempted comprehensive health care reform either retreating or treading water.

Current Federal-State Issues

Although there are still efforts at the national level to take some smaller steps, especially in the area of insurance reform, most of the attention is no longer focused on expanding health care coverage, but rather on cutting federal Medicaid expenditures. As Republicans took control of Congress in 1995, they announced their plans to balance the federal budget by the year 2002. As a major part of that effort, they proposed turning the Medicaid program into a block grant to states, allowing the states very broad flexibility to manage the program. Rather than Congress having to decide how to control expenditures, states could figure it out. They could decide who to cover, what to cover, how to deliver it, and what to pay for it. The pendulum would swing completely from the heavy hand of federal control to little federal involvement beyond passing out more limited funding. What is especially ironic is that just as federal mandates of the late 1980s caused state costs to increase, Congress was now expecting the states to determine how to save federal dollars in the program.

The debate that has ensued around the federal role in Medicaid is not surprising to those of us who have struggled with the federal government to reform our programs. Although those who favor allowing states total flexibility may portray this as restoring balance to our federal system in which the states will play a more active role, one could question whether that is an easy way out of a difficult and complex problem. On the other end of the spectrum are those who strongly defend the current program, expressing grave concerns about whether states can be trusted, but who might allow slightly more flexibility (although primarily in areas where states have already taken action through waivers, such as in managed care programs and home- and community-based services to the elderly and disabled). I know of no states, regardless of their governor's party affiliation, who would support the existing program. On the other hand, given the resistance to change we have seen on the part of many policymakers in Washington, it is tempting to advocate that they just give us the money and get out of our way. But if the Medicaid program truly is a federal-state partnership, should not the federal government play some role in assuring some level of accountability, if not consistency? The current debate in Medicaid involves the issue of determining how much the states can be trusted to run responsible programs, but it also involves determining the appropriate federal role in assuring accountability. At what point do federal requirements step over the line of appropriate safeguards into micromanagement of programs? There is no easy or clear answer, as those of us in Oregon have discovered.

Outlook for the Future

The prospects for significant national health care reform are bleak. States now understand that and know that if major changes are to occur, it will be up to them. In the short run, however, states will most likely be primarily focused on how to deal with eventual reductions in federal Medicaid funding. Our challenges now will be to hold on to the gains we may already have made in health care reform and to begin taking additional incremental steps to move closer toward universal coverage. That goal, however, appears more elusive today than it did only two years ago.

Comprehensive health care reform may have to wait until the public again becomes convinced that it is necessary. Health care reform takes political will. It is a difficult and emotional issue, as well as one in which substantial amounts of money are at stake. Unless the public understands the critical nature of the need for reform, it will be difficult to garner the political support that will be necessary to make it happen. But even then, the difficulty we will face as states in attempting to reform the system is the realization that we cannot control the allocation and use of all health care dollars within our state, even if we are able to achieve political consensus. It is unlikely that we can ever achieve comprehensive reform on a state-by-state basis, but it is certainly within our abilities to make significant inroads into the issue.

6

Rationing of Health Care in Oregon: Making the Implicit Explicit

Howard M. Leichter

In 1989 Oregon became the first state in the nation to adopt legislation that explicitly rations or prioritizes health care for the poor. The Oregon Health Plan (OHP), originally called the Oregon Basic Health Services Act, guarantees health care to all those whose incomes fall below the federal poverty level, but limits that care to what expert opinion, community sentiment, legislative judgment, and fiscal reality deem a "basic level of services." In the words of the law's chief architect, John Kitzhaber, "Everyone will be in the health care lifeboat. Not everyone will eat steak, but at least everyone will eat." The fact that it is primarily the poor who are deprived "steak" in the Oregon health care lifeboat is just one of many facets of the plan that trouble its opponents.

The Oregon plan has left few observers neutral. It has been characterized as "bold," "pioneering," "rational," a "brave medical experiment," "fundamentally flawed," "unfair," and "unethical." What proponents and opponents of the Oregon law agree on is that the current "system" is seriously, and probably irreparably, flawed. Something must be done to control spiraling health care costs and to expand access to an estimated 40 million uninsured Americans. Where observers and participants disagree is over the question whether the Oregon plan offers a fair, workable, and responsible solution.

This chapter focuses on the most publicized and controversial aspect of the Oregon plan, namely, the prioritizing of health services for the Medicaid population. This facet of the reform has been in effect now for three years and, at least by the standards set by the state, has been a success. Yet, as I describe below, back in 1989 Oregon policymakers envisioned the prioritization plan as one part of an overall scheme that would result in near universal access to health care in the state. On this and other points they have had to retreat. In this regard the Oregon story is like the others detailed in this book, a case of expectations far exceeding accomplishments.

The Oregon Health Plan

At the heart of the Oregon reform is Senate Bill (S.B.) 27, which explicitly confronts the most critical challenges facing the nation's health care system. Its purpose is to: (1) "provide access to health services for those in need," (2) "contain rising health services costs through appropriate incentives to providers, payers, and consumers," (3) "reduce or eliminate cost shifting," and (4) "promote the stability of the health services delivery system and the health and well-being of all Oregonians." To accomplish these ambitious and seemingly contradictory goals, the state defined a minimum entitlement to basic health services, which it initially applied to those people with incomes below the federal poverty level, and later (in 1991) extended to persons covered under programs for the aged, blind, disabled, medically needy, and children in foster care, as well as to those in drug and alcohol dependency programs.

By extending medical assistance to all those below the poverty level Oregon has departed from prevailing national practices. Medicaid eligibility typically has been a function not merely of income but of gender, age, family status, and type of illness. For example, prior to the OHP, poor women without children and low-income men were ineligible for Medicaid in Oregon and most other states. Moreover, each state sets an income eligibility requirement that is expressed in terms of a percentage of the federal poverty level. In the case of Oregon this meant that only those who had incomes of 58 percent of the federal poverty level or less were eligible for Medicaid. For example, in 1996 poverty level for a family of four was $15,156. Under the prereform system the state would only extend Medicaid benefits to those families with incomes under $8,790.

To bring all the poor into the Medicaid lifeboat, contain costs, and fairly compensate health providers for their services, the state limits the amount of money and, therefore, the range of services available to its Medicaid recipients. To insure the "social and political consensus" that the law's supporters felt was vital to the clinical and political success of the program, an elaborate mechanism was designed to allocate health resources. The law created an eleven-member Health Services Commission (HSC) to conduct public hearings and encourage public involvement in preparation for the prioritization of health services. The HSC is required to seek testimony from health care providers and consumers, as well as advocates for disadvantaged groups. The commission then submits its recommended priorities to the governor and a Joint Legislative Committee on Health Care by July 1 of the year preceding each regular legislative session. Accompanying the list of priorities is a report by an independent actuary on the rates for each of the services/treatments. The Joint Legislative Committee on Health Care recommends to the full legislature whether to accept or reject the commission report; it cannot change the priorities. Should the legislature accept the report it must decide how much it is willing to spend on health care for the next biennium. This money is then used to buy a package of health services for each recipient from as far down the priority list as the legislative allocation will allow. Oregon has gone through this exercise now on three occasions: in 1991, 1993, and 1995. The most recent list contained 744 condition/treatment pairs ranging from "severe/moderate head injury" (no. 1) to "disorders of refraction and accommodation" (no. 744). The 1995 legislature funded the program at a level that would allow for 581 of these conditions to be covered in the basic health services package for the 1996–97 fiscal year. To help contain costs, health services are purchased primarily from managed care providers—over 80 percent of Oregon's Medicaid recipients are in managed care, such as health maintenance organizations (HMOs) and physician care organizations (PCOs).

Should a revenue shortfall occur, as it did in 1995, or should the number of persons below the poverty level increase, the state may not drop people from the program, as it had in the past, or reduce payments to providers below the cost of providing services. Instead, the legislature must retreat back up the list of priorities until it reaches the point where there is enough money to provide services for all those eligible under Medicaid. This happened in 1995, when the legislature approved a list with twenty-five fewer services than it covered in 1993 (a total of 581, down from 606).

In addition to the Medicaid law, the 1989 Oregon legislature enacted two companion bills that were intended to facilitate access to health insurance for two other groups of Oregonians. The first consists of about ten thousand to twenty thousand people who are considered "medically uninsurable" due to preexisting medical conditions. Senate Bill 534 created an insurance pool subsidized by the state and private insurers from which these people can purchase health insurance. Thus far, however, average annual enrollment in the program has been only just over four thousand people.

The more important, but ultimately unsuccessful, of the two bills was S.B. 935. This applied to working Oregonians, and their dependents, who had incomes above the federal poverty level but had no health benefits and did not qualify for medical assistance. Had it been implemented, the law would have affected about two-thirds of uninsured Oregonians (approximately 260,000 people) and gone a long way toward achieving universal access to health care in the state. Under S.B. 935 the state would require or mandate all employers currently not offering insurance to either provide health insurance to their employees (i.e., "play") or contribute to a state insurance fund that would purchase insurance for uninsured workers (i.e., "pay"). Significantly, the law provided that the benefits offered to these employees "must include substantially similar medical services as those recommended by the Health Services Commission" under S.B. 27. In effect, then, had the law been implemented, the prioritization list developed by the HSC would have had relevance for a much broader population than merely those on Medicaid. Implementation of the "play-or-pay" provision, however, required that Congress exempt Oregon from the Employee Retirement Income Security Act, or ERISA. Initially intended to protect the pensions of retired workers from fraud and mismanagement, ERISA has been interpreted by the courts to prohibit states from regulating the health benefits of self-insured companies or taxing self-insured plans to raise money, for example, to cover the uninsured. Because about 65 percent of all companies, and about one-half of all companies with more than fifty employees, choose to self-insure, ERISA has had the effect of severely crimping the capacity of states to adopt comprehensive reforms. The original law provided that the "play-or-pay" option would be dropped if the state did not receive an ERISA exemption by January 1, 1996. With the Republicans gaining control of Congress in 1994, the prospects of an ERISA exemption virtually disappeared.

Yet it was not merely congressional opposition that thwarted the mandate. Pressure from Oregon business groups led to a postponement of the employer-based insurance program from January 1994 until March 31, 1997, for companies with over twenty-five employees, and January 1, 1998, for those with twenty-five or fewer employees. Then, the 1995 Republican-controlled state legislature rescinded the employer mandate. Although the bill was vetoed by Democratic governor John Kitzhaber, who as senate president had been the architect of the original legislation, the veto was largely a symbolic gesture; there was no chance that Congress was going to grant Oregon an ERISA waiver by the January 1, 1996, deadline. The play-or-pay option passed quietly into the night on December 31, 1995.

Despite the failure of play-or-pay, the Oregon rationing plan remains a bold experiment in health care policy and delivery, and one that continues to draw national and international attention. The remainder of this chapter is devoted to exploring this innovative program.

The Politics of Rationing

The Transplant Controversy

Oregon's road to prioritizing and rationing health services began in the 1987 legislative session, when the state decided to eliminate funding of organ transplants for Medicaid recipients. This decision went all but unnoticed when it was adopted by the legislature. Oregon had first authorized funding of transplantation operations for the poor in the 1983–85 legislative session. Between 1985 and 1987 the state paid for nineteen transplants at a cost of about $1.2 million. The transplant program was covered by Medicaid with the state absorbing 38 percent of the costs and the federal government the remaining 62 percent.

In the first two years of the program requests for transplant operations were approved on a case-by-case basis. The state could reject any transplant request, and could stop the program when it had exhausted the allocated funds. In 1985, however, Congress required that states file a plan indicating which procedures they would fund and were then obligated to fund *all* transplant requests that fell under the plan.

In 1987 the Oregon Department of Human Resources requested $2.2 million from the legislature to fund thirty-four transplant operations in the 1988–89 biennium, nearly double the cost of the previous two-year period. In a memorandum to the joint House and Senate Ways and Means Committee, the Adult and Family Services Division (AFS) suggested, "At some point AFS must face the question of continuing transplant coverage, or investing in more basic health care which could potentially benefit a much larger number of people. Such a decision would require the full support of the Legislature."[1]

A House and Senate Ways and Means subcommittee decided to take transplant funding out of the regular budget and place it on an optional priority list along with other requests for special social programs. The subcommittee had about $20 million at its disposal and requests that totaled about $48 million. Transplants had to compete with programs dealing with the mentally ill and disturbed, the deaf, head-injury victims, juvenile delinquents, and senior citizens. The subcommittee ran out of money before it got to transplants. The decision to eliminate transplant funding was hardly noticed by the legislators; State Representative Mike Kopetski, who introduced the human resources budget in the House, called attention to the deletion of the transplant program twice in his speech. Not a single legislator questioned the decision.

If the initial transplant decision went largely unnoticed, the next one did not—it brought the attention of the nation upon the state. On December 2, 1987, a seven-year-old boy from Portland, Coby Howard, died of leukemia. The boy had become a familiar personality across much of the state over the preceding two months as his family, school friends, and teachers tried to raise $100,000 for a bone marrow transplant. The highly publicized effort became necessary when Oregon officials informed Coby's unemployed and uninsured mother that the state no longer covered transplant operations under its Medicaid program and that they would not grant Coby an exemption from this new policy. The private fund-raising campaign was $30,000 short of its goal when Coby Howard died.

In a January meeting of the Legislative Emergency Board, which acts on behalf of the full legislature during the interim period, Representative Tom Mason introduced a motion to appropriate $220,000 to the state's Medicaid program to fund five transplant operations for people whose requests for such procedures had already been denied. The proposal was opposed by the Oregon Senate president, John Kitzhaber, who presided over a subcommittee meeting on the proposal on January 28, 1988. He, and House Speaker Vera Katz, took the unusual step of attending the subcommittee meeting to vote on the funding request.

Senator Kitzhaber said that the issue before the Emergency Board was not whether the state could find $220,000 to fund these five requests. Clearly it could. He argued, however, that the "basic issue is one of equity." There were thousands of working Oregonians who had no private insurance, and still other nonworking Oregonians ineligible for Medicaid. Neither of these groups were eligible for these transplants. "I think what this [transplant] policy does, is it gives to Medicaid recipients certain services that are not, in fact, available to a large number of other Oregonians and I think that there's a basic inequity involved there. What you're really doing is you're asking many taxpayers to buy services for people on public assistance that they can [not] even get for their own children."[2]

Another critical issue was one of priority. Since it is impossible to satisfy all demands, it becomes necessary to make choices on how best to spend state dollars. "What we can do," argued Kitzhaber, "with our limited money, is to reduce the number of deaths to the maximum. Save as many people as we can, because we can't save them all."[3] Despite an emotional plea by Representative Mason that Oregon not become "known as the state that lets children die," his motion failed on a tie vote. President Kitzhaber and Speaker Katz voted against the motion. The next day, however, the full Emergency Board was scheduled to meet and Mason vowed to bring the issue before it.

That evening Ted Koppel featured the Oregon transplant decision, and Senator Kitzhaber, on his *Nightline* show. He began the program with footage of Coby Howard and said, "When the State of Oregon decided to stop funding organ transplants, it allowed this boy to die." Koppel later asked: "Is the cost of modern medical technology forcing public officials to play God?"[4] It was in the rather heady atmosphere of national media attention, then, that the full Emergency Board met the next day. The arguments about equity, priorities, costs, and compassion were the same; and so were the results. The motion was defeated. In the course of the debate Senator Kitzhaber set the stage for the next act in this drama. "Now I guess I just want to close by saying that we are going to have to ration health care," he said.

Accordingly, rationing health care is precisely what Senate president Kitzhaber proposed in the following legislative session. Kitzhaber submitted a plan to reform health care in Oregon to a specially created Senate Committee on Health Insurance and Bioethics in January 1989. Kitzhaber, a liberal Democrat who was first elected to the Oregon House in 1978 and had been in the Senate since 1981, had served three terms as Senate president. His experience as an emergency-room physician added a good deal of credibility to his role as the premier legislative authority on the state's health policy system, and aided him in gaining support within the medical community. The Oregon health reform plan was in every sense of the term "Kitzhaber's Plan."

The bill was, by his own admission, a "mere skeleton," really just a "concept." As a result, even before the health committee met, Kitzhaber submitted several amendments to his own bill. These amendments were the first of many as the legislation evolved. The changes were not so much the result of controversy or fierce opposition, but rather of the innovative and uncertain nature of the reform. Indeed, throughout the hearings conducted on the bill between February and June 1989, legislators heard little disagreement over the need for reform from health care providers and insurers, social advocacy groups, union leaders, and members of the public health and welfare bureaucracy. This is not to suggest that there were no differing views on how to accomplish the goals of increasing access and slowing cost increases, but merely to emphasize that virtually everyone agreed with the most fundamental assumption underlying the legislation, namely that the current system was unsustainable.

Although there was agreement on principle, there was certainly disagreement on specifics. The most important concern, and the one that would become the rallying point for opponents both in the state and in Congress, was over the trade-off between access and benefit levels. Central to Kitzhaber's plan was the notion that not everyone would be able to get all the possible medical care they might need, but that everyone should have some basic level of care. Under the current system those covered by Medicaid effectively enjoyed the same full range of health services as those who had private insurance. Indeed social advocates wanted very much to protect the benefit level currently provided under Medicaid. The problem was that about 450,000 Oregonians neither qualified for Medicaid nor were covered by private insurance. Officials estimated that S.B. 27 would pick up about 120,000 to 130,000 of these people—the actual number in 1996 was 114,000—when it was fully implemented by extending coverage to all those with incomes below the federal poverty level. The high-risk pool and the employer mandate would cover most of the remaining uninsured.

However, to achieve the goal of universal access would require limiting or rationing benefits to those brought into the Medicaid program under the new plan. The purpose of the prioritization process was to identify, through professional, social, and political consensus, those health services that constitute an adequate or basic level of care—and that the state could afford.

But here was the rub: Would the benefit package be adequate? What would be covered, what omitted? Unless a great deal of money was added to the Medicaid budget, something that did not appear likely, adding 120,000 people to the Medicaid pool would require reducing current benefit levels. Some who testified indicated that although they supported universal access, if presented with a choice between universal access with a "thin" package of benefits, and something short of universal access with a more substantial package, they would prefer the latter.

Moreover, some charged that the plan would create a two-tier health care system, with guaranteed access to finite services for the poor, and virtually unlimited services for those who could afford to purchase insurance on their own. As a result of these concerns, opponents in both the social advocacy and health provider communities wanted some assurance that the basic benefits package would be comprehensive enough to provide an adequate and acceptable level of health care. As a result a House committee amended the Senate version of the bill to include a broad definition of basic health services. This included "so much of each of the following as are approved and funded by the Legislative Assembly: (1) provider services and supplies; (2) outpatient services; (3) inpatient hospital services; (4) and health promotion and disease prevention services." This rather general list apparently assuaged the concerns that some had about the bill.

Universal access to health care for the poor and a basic level of services were at the heart of both the philosophy of the legislation and the concerns of the groups affected. But the politics of health care reform in Oregon produced other, more parochial, concerns. Who, for example, would be eligible to provide services, and which groups would be represented on the Health Services Commission and thus have a direct say in the prioritization process? In the first instance, there was predictable interest on the part of dentists, drug and alcohol counselors, mental health specialists, social workers, pharmacists, chiropractors, and osteopaths, among others, that their services be included in the package authorized under the law.

Second, both provider and consumer groups wanted assurances that they would have an opportunity to influence the prioritization process through representation on the Health Services Commission. Advocates for children, the elderly, the disabled, the mentally ill, Medicaid recipients, persons with chemical dependencies, as well as all varieties of health care providers wanted to have a representative on the commission. Following intense lobbying the bill that emerged provided for a commission of eleven members, five of whom would be physicians with clinical expertise in the areas of obstetrics, perinatal care, pediatrics, adult medicine, geriatrics, or public health. In addition, one of the physicians would be a doctor of osteopathy, there would be a public health nurse, a social services worker, and four "consumers of health care."

Since not every interest could be accommodated by representation on the commission, the HSC was given the charge to "solicit testimony and information from advocates for seniors, handicapped persons, mental health services consumers, low-income Oregonians, and providers of health care, including but not limited to physicians licensed to practice medicine, dentists, oral surgeons, chiropractors, naturopaths, hospitals, clinics, pharmacists, nurses, and allied health professionals."

Following its largely uncontested odyssey through the three legislative committees, Senate Bill 27 was approved with overwhelming bipartisan support in both the Senate (19 to 3) and the House (58 to 2).

Coming Up with "The List"

Two very difficult tasks lay ahead before the state could implement the Oregon Health Plan. The first was to obtain a Medicaid waiver from the federal government. I will return to this part of the story shortly.[5] The second task was for the Health Services Commission to construct a list of health care priorities for the legislature. To accomplish this the HSC used three formats. The first was a series of eleven public hearings held around the state allowing interested parties to express their views. The second was to authorize Oregon Health Decisions (OHD), a highly respected citizens advocacy group, to conduct community meetings in every county of the state "to build a consensus on the values to be used to guide health resource allocation decisions." Ultimately forty-seven community forums were held during which participants filled out a questionnaire soliciting their opinions on the relative importance of certain health situations and categories and engaged in group discussions. Like much else about the process, health care interest groups dominated this stage too. Although it was the hope and intention of OHD to have a cross section of Oregonians, this did not turn out to be the case. Of the slightly more than one thousand people who attended the meetings almost 70 percent were "mental health and health care workers."[6] Although the term "workers" is not defined, over one-third of the participants had incomes of $50,000 or more, and two-thirds were college graduates. The HSC has acknowledged and responded to the criticism that those who participated in the process were unrepresentative of the recipient population. Thus in 1993 when, under legislative mandate, it set about to devise clinical practice guidelines as part of the priority list, the HSC contracted Oregon Health Decisions to convene focus groups to gauge consumer reaction to such guidelines, and requested that participants be chosen at random "so that the group would represent the demographics of Oregon."[7]

The third mechanism provided the most systematic solicitation and application of citizen values in the prioritization process—and proved the most controversial. The commission authorized a statewide, randomly dialed telephone survey of one thousand Oregonians. To conform to the principle of incorporating community values in the ranking process, and not simply rely on treatment-outcome data, the commission decided to use a Quality of Well-Being Scale (QWB). Respondents were asked to rate thirty-one health situations from zero (a situation that "is as bad as death") to one hundred (a situation that describes "good health"). Among the situations respondents were asked to rate were: "You cannot drive a car or use public transportation, you have to use a walker or wheelchair under your own control, and are limited in the recreational activities you may perform, but have no other health problems," and "You can go anywhere and have no limitations on physical or other activity, but wear glasses or contact lenses."[8]

The results of the survey were then formally incorporated into a mathematical cost/utility or "net benefit value" formula that included data on expected outcomes of given treatments for hundreds of health conditions. The "net benefit value" equation was in the form of a word formula where:

$$\text{Net BenefitValue} = \frac{\text{Net Benefits}}{\text{Net Costs}}$$

Benefits included the length of time the patient benefits from a treatment, the public values regarding certain health states (e.g., death, return to asymptomatic state of health, etc.), and the probability that a health state will result from a particular treatment. Costs include "diagnosis, hospitalization, professional services, non-medical but prescribed services and ancillary services."

In February 1991, the HSC made public its first "Prioritized Health Services List." The list contained medical conditions and treatments, grouped into seventeen major categories ranging from "acute fatal, prevents death, full recovery," (e.g., various forms of pneumonia) to "fatal or nonfatal, minimal or no improvement in QWB" (e.g., "terminal HIV disease with less than 10 percent survival rate at five years"). Reflecting both the current wisdom among the medical community and the values expressed in the community forums, preventive medicine was given high priority on the list.

In April the Health Services Commission received the actuary's report on the priority list. The commission recommended to the legislature that it fund a benefit package that would include, at least, all "essential" services (i.e., categories one through nine in the seventeen-category list) and most "very important services." On June 30, 1991, the Legislative Assembly approved a budget that included an additional $33 million for the Medicaid program. This allowed the state to add seventy-eight thousand new Medicaid recipients and extend health services to them through line 587 out of 709 condition/treatment pairs on the priority list. Having secured funding, the state now needed federal approval to implement the plan.

The Elusive Waiver

From the outset state officials knew they would need a federal waiver to implement the program. Under Medicaid rules a state cannot drop any mandated services, or in any other way deviate from Medicaid rules, without federal approval, and the Oregon plan would not cover all services currently under mandate.

What followed next was, for state officials, the most frustrating part of this long process. This part of the story reveals the extraordinary frustrations experienced by state officials as they have tried to reconcile the competing demands of the uninsured, various stakeholders, the federal government, and partisan politics. (See Jean Thorne's chapter in this volume.) The odyssey of the Oregon experiment became a metaphor for the federal bureaucratic morass that has dogged and undermined state health policy innovations, and the precariousness of the states' ability to finance these innovations.

On August 19, 1991, Oregon requested that the Health Care Financing Administration (HCFA) waive certain Medicaid rules so that it could implement a demonstration project built around the principle of universal access to a basic package of health care services for all Oregonians under the poverty level. State officials were buoyed in this effort by what they thought were sympathetic and supportive comments from Gail Wilensky, then director of HCFA. When, in March 1992, Wilensky moved from HCFA to the White House as a policy adviser on health and welfare issues, "a quiet cheer went up among Oregon state officials," who expected Wilensky "to be a key backer of Oregon's Medicaid-waiver request."[9]

It was not the first, nor was it be the last, time state officials were disappointed. To begin, as the time of decision moved closer, opponents became more vocal. For example, Congressman Henry Waxman (D-Calif.), an early and consistent critic of the plan, wrote to Secretary of Health and Human Services Louis Sullivan that he found the Oregon plan "offensive" and wondered about "a government rationing proposal that affects only low income families."[10] In addition, groups within the state that had initially opposed the plan, including the Oregon Catholic Conference, Oregon Fair Share, and the Oregon Human Rights Coalition, renewed their criticism.

But most disconcerting of all to state officials was the new tone of the comments coming out of the White House and especially from Gail Wilensky, who was now talking about "troubling aspects" of the plan. In June 1992 the Office of Management and Budget announced that the promised spring decision would be delayed. Most political observers in the state attributed the delay, and Wilensky's backpedaling, to presidential election politics. The Bush administration simply did not want to endorse a "rationing" plan during a presidential campaign.

In the latter part of July Oregon officials learned of a new problem. Twenty national organizations representing people with disabilities had written to President Bush urging him to reject the waiver request on the grounds that the Oregon plan violated the 1991 Americans with Disabilities Act (ADA). White House staff had questioned state officials several months earlier about possible conflicts with ADA, but Oregon officials had heard of no further administration concerns along these lines.

Then on August 3, 1992, the secretary of health and human services, Dr. Louis Sullivan, informed Governor Barbara Roberts (D) that the state's plan was in conflict with ADA, and that he would not grant the waiver. In particular, Sullivan challenged the methodology of the Health Services Commission in drawing up the priority list. The specific problem was the statewide telephone survey in which Oregonians were asked to evaluate various health situations, and to rate them with regard to their impact on a person's "quality of life." The secretary objected to the procedure and the resulting list of priorities because it "contains considerable evidence that it was based in substantial part on the premise that the value of life of a person with a disability is less than the value of life of a person without a disability."[11] Reaction to the waiver rejection among the plan's supporters was predictable. Senator Kitzhaber described the secretary's action as "a disgusting performance," and Senator Bob Packwood declared, "We have been betrayed."[12] In addition, defenders of the plan reminded critics that the surveyed Oregonians were asked to judge the impact of various health conditions on their own quality of life, not that of others.

In his letter to Governor Roberts, Dr. Sullivan raised the prospect of eventual approval from the Bush administration: "I urge Oregon to submit a revised application which addresses these concerns, and I look forward to approving such a demonstration [project]."[13] This same message was communicated to HSC members when they met with officials from the Department of Health and Human Services in Portland at the end of August. Commission members were told that if they eliminated the survey and all references to "quality of life" from the prioritization process, "you have a very high likelihood of approval."[14]

State officials decided to prepare a revised list immediately, rather than await the outcome of the 1992 presidential election, and resubmitted the Medicaid waiver request on November 13, 1992—ten days after Bill Clinton was elected president. The HSC made three major changes to the prioritization process and subsequent list. First, it accepted the Bush administration's criticisms and eliminated the survey results and judgments about quality of life from the new prioritization. Second, it shortened the list from 709 to 688 condition/treatment pairs. This was accomplished largely by combining some categories and eliminating others. Finally, the HSC placed greater weight in the prioritization process on cost and on the judgment of the commissioners in assigning ranks.

The HSC proposed, and in early December the Legislative Emergency Board approved, drawing the line at number 568 on the list of 688 condition/treatment pairs.

Clinton Takes Over: "A Real Big Change"

With the newly revised list, state officials believed that they had put behind them any remaining ADA-related problems. And, with Clinton's victory they believed they were finally free of the political and bureaucratic frustrations they had endured during the last year of the Bush administration. They were wrong on both points.

First, on January 19, the day before Bill Clinton was inaugurated, a political appointee in the Justice Department sent a memorandum to the Department of Health and Human Services concluding that the revised plan continued to have "features that violate ADA."[15] This parting shot, by a Bush appointee, became a place marker from which opponents would renew their attacks on the Oregon plan when the new administration took over.

Once again the difficulty was with the methodology used to rank conditions/treatments, and alleged biases that resulted from that methodology. Under the new procedure, the Health Services Commission placed the highest priority on those health services that prevented death. However, to further discriminate among treatments that were equally efficacious on this criterion, the commission put a higher priority on those treatments that would "return the patient to an asymptomatic state of health after saving the life." It was these so-called "tiebreakers" that were the source of trouble. Specifically, the memorandum charged that the designation "asymptomatic" denigrated the quality of life of the disabled. The basis of this accusation was that the commission provided guidance in the original waiver request on "asymptomatic" status in a "Major Symptom(s) List." This list included references to decreased mobility or agility (e.g., missing, deformed, or paralyzed limbs), or some functional limitations on speech, sight, or hearing.[16] Since the disabled could not, by definition, be returned to an asymptomatic state (i.e., complete mobility, perfect vision, hearing, or speech), the tiebreakers were inherently discriminatory. As the Justice Department memo put it, " 'symptom' as defined by Oregon is, in many cases, another term for 'disability.' "

There was a second ADA-related concern raised by the memorandum and, ironically, it involved that part of the process about which reformers were most proud—the incorporation of citizen values as expressed in public hearings and community meetings in the priority setting process. This objection echoed a theme raised in the initial HHS rejection of the priority list, namely, that able-bodied citizens tend to devalue the lives of the disabled. This point was illustrated by specific reference to the low ranking assigned to infertility. Part of the justification for the low ranking was that, as the HSC report observed, "infertility services are not highly valued by Oregonians." Yet, according to the memorandum, infertility "is a disability within the meaning of the ADA." Hence, this was another example of "an intentional devaluation of treatment on account of a disability." The memorandum concluded that "the revised proposal is inconsistent with the ADA."

Oregon officials were not immediately informed of these objections—they would receive a copy of the memorandum weeks later when it was leaked by advocacy groups. As far as state officials were concerned, the revised and resubmitted November 1992 list eliminated any remaining ADA-related problems.

Furthermore, state officials had reason to believe that Clinton would be more sympathetic to their request than his predecessor. Candidate Clinton had endorsed the Oregon plan on a campaign stop in Portland in May 1992 and again during the second presidential debate in October. It was with cautious optimism, then, that members of the Oregon congressional delegation, including Congressman Ron Wyden (D) and Republican Senators Bob Packwood and Mark Hatfield, met with Donna Shalala, the new secretary of health and human services. Shalala was well informed about the content and status of the waiver request, and generally sympathetic but noncommittal in these early meetings in late January and early February 1993. It is not clear if she had seen the January 19 memorandum, which had been sent to counsel in HHS.

It was Senator Hatfield who forced the administration's hand. State legislative leaders and Medicaid officials explained to Hatfield that a waiver decision was needed quickly so the legislature could provide funding in the 1993–95 state budget. State political leaders wrote to Hatfield outlining their concerns and the need for a mid-March decision. Hatfield responded by announcing in mid-February that unless the administration made a decision on the waivers, he would attach an amendment to a National Institutes of Health authorization bill stipulating that if the waiver decision was not made by March 19, it would automatically be deemed approved. Hatfield and Shalala had a telephone conversation on February 17 in which the secretary agreed to the deadline. She reiterated this in a letter to Hatfield, which he read on the Senate floor.

It was around this time that Hatfield, and subsequently state officials, learned of the January 19 parting shot by the Bush administration in the form of the Justice Department memorandum. It was unclear at the time, however, what, if anything, the Clinton administration would do about these objections. There were as yet no Clinton appointees in the Justice Department, as Janet Reno was not confirmed as attorney general until March 12. Even if Clinton administration officials wanted to ignore the objections raised by the Bush appointee, the advocacy community would not let them because national and state disability groups obtained and leaked a copy of the memorandum. State and federal officials would have to revisit the list and the methodology used to construct it.

What followed was a period of intense consultations, largely through conference calls, between political appointees and bureaucrats from HHS and state officials. Then, on March 12, one week before Hatfield's deadline, key federal officials made an unpublicized trip to Salem. There, in a day-long marathon session with members of the governor's office (and, briefly, Governor Roberts herself), the Oregon Department of Human Services, and the Health Services Commission, state and federal officials tried to reach agreement on perfecting the waiver request.

State officials believed that the Clinton people were, in fact, "looking for a way to make this thing work."[17] Nevertheless, the federal officials were concerned about the potential of politically embarrassing legal challenges to the list unless it, and the methodology upon which it was based, were revised. Both state and federal officials wanted to avoid a situation in which the plan would face legal challenges before it could even be implemented.

Although state negotiators shared this concern, they were troubled by the prospect of further compromising the integrity of their reform. In particular, the Oregon group was reluctant to move too far toward pragmatic health commissioner judgments in setting the priorities. According to Jean Thorne of the Oregon Health Plan, "The more you move toward the subjective judgment of the commission the more difficult it is to replicate the list in the future, and the more prone it is to really substantial change based on who the commissioners are."[18]

The federal negotiators pressed the Oregonians on the objections raised by the January 19 memorandum and by advocates of disability groups. In particular, they urged the removal of "asymptomatic" status as a tiebreaker, and replacing it with the clinical judgment of the commissioners—it was suggested that the criterion "medical effectiveness" could be used as a discriminator in place of "asymptomatic." In addition, the federal officials wanted the state to address the problem of the low ranking of infertility on the basis of low citizen value. State negotiators, recognizing that failure to make the suggested changes would jeopardize waiver approval, agreed to poll the HSC members over the weekend—although they would not make a recommendation to the commissioners on whether or not to accept the proposed changes. On Monday, however, they were able to report back to their federal counterparts that the HSC agreed to change the methodology and revise the list as a condition for obtaining the waiver.

While all this was happening, a group of seventy social advocacy groups signed a letter urging President Clinton to reject the Oregon plan. Nevertheless, the president appeared committed to allowing the states flexibility in seeking innovative solutions to their problems without undue federal interference. Thus, on Friday, March 19, 1993, Secretary Shalala, in a letter to Governor Roberts announcing approval of the waiver, said that "the President believes that the Federal Government must give states the flexibility to design new approaches to their local problems, provided these proposals meet Federal standards."

The Oregon Health Plan: A Demonstration Project

Officially, what the Clinton administration did on March 19 was to approve the "Oregon Reform Demonstration" for a period of five years beginning April 1, 1993—this was later postponed to February 1, 1994—and waiving various Medicaid requirements. The state received permission to, among other things

- Establish a basic package of health services for all people up to 100 percent of the federal poverty level. The benefit package will be based upon a prioritized list of condition/treatment pairs, and not necessarily cover all medical services currently offered under Medicaid.
- Simplify participation in the program by basing eligibility solely on gross family income, rather than such factors as age, gender, or marital status.
- Restrict freedom of choice of providers so that the state could take advantage of the cost savings associated with prepaid, managed care delivery.
- Allow reimbursements to managed care providers to exceed standard Medicaid rates—which are deemed too low—in order to encourage physician participation in the plan.

Actual implementation of the Oregon Health Plan was now contingent on two factors. First, the state had to satisfy a list of twenty-nine terms and conditions as outlined in a memorandum accompanying formal written notification of the waiver approval. The majority of these dealt with the reporting, monitoring, and verification of administrative procedures, deadlines, and evaluations. In a more substantive vein, as expected and agreed upon, HCFA gave the state sixty days to "rerank the condition-treatment pairs without relying on data which it collected with respect to whether treatment returned an individual to an asymptomatic state."[19] Second, the HSC had to revise the criteria it used to locate infertility on the prioritization list. Although the state was not required to include infertility services at all, the ranking of this condition had to be based upon "content neutral factors that do not take disability into account."

Finally, the state had to adopt guidelines for health providers that make it clear "that before denying treatment for an unfunded condition for any individual, especially an individual with a disability or a co-morbid condition, providers will be required to determine whether the individual has a funded condition that would entitle the individual to treatment under the program." Federal officials, in short, wanted to minimize the likelihood of someone, particularly a disabled person, being denied care through some technical ambiguity or oversight. To resolve any questions that might arise concerning covered conditions and treatments, the state was required to set up a toll-free telephone information line for physicians and Medicaid clients who need clarification.

Although state officials were loath to rework the priority list yet again, for the most part the terms and conditions posed few problems and a revised list of 688 conditions/treatments was prepared. Finally on February 1, 1994, four and one-half years after S.B. 27 and its companion legislation were approved, the Oregon Health Plan began operation. How has it fared in the three years in which it has operated?

The Plan's Current Status

It is necessary, I think, to emphasize the most obvious and important measure of the OHP's status. There are as of this writing about 114,000 Oregonians, one-half of whom are women, who have access to a predictable and assured basic level of health care and who, in the absence of the plan, almost certainly would have to rely on charity or go without health care. Whatever its other successes or failures, this fact must stand out in any assessment of the Oregon Health Plan. On this measure alone, the OHP must be judged successful.

But there are other successes as well. The plan is credited with an approximately 5 percent decline in emergency-room visits, since 114,000 people no longer have to wait until they become seriously ill before they can have access to medical care; a 30 percent decline in hospital charity care that translated, in the first year, into a 19 percent cost reduction in charity write-offs for the state's hospitals, and a reduction in cost shifting and a leveling off of private insurance premiums; and an 8 percent reduction in the state's welfare rolls, since fewer people are falling into poverty because of illnesses that they must pay for out-of-pocket. In addition, the percentage of uninsured Oregonians declined between 1994 and 1995 from 17 percent to 14 percent, which state officials attribute, in large part, to OHP's expansion of Medicaid. Lastly, and significantly, there have been no reported cases of people being denied necessary medical care.

For all of its undeniable successes, the OHP has not been without its critics, setbacks, and failures. To begin, it must be remembered that one of the key features of the plan, the employer mandate, has been abandoned, thus leaving the largest uninsured segment of the population outside the health care lifeboat. The state's failure to extend health insurance to approximately four hundred thousand working Oregonians through the employer mandate means that the goal of universal access to health care among Oregonians remains unrealized. Fourteen percent of Oregonians, the majority of whom are "not quite poor"—that is, they have incomes between 100 and 200 percent of the federal poverty level—remain uninsured.

However, even that facet of the plan about which Oregonians are most proud and can claim the most success, namely, expanding Medicaid to all whose incomes are below the poverty level, has not been without its serious problems. The difficulty here is not that the prioritization process has not worked or that the plan has lost its political support, but rather that it must compete for limited state resources in an environment that is quite different than it was in 1989.

In 1990 Oregonians passed a citizen-initiated property tax limitation measure that, among other things, shifted most of the responsibility for funding K–12 education from localities (and property taxes) to the state general fund and lottery income. In addition, the ballot measure required the state to equalize funding among districts, bringing spending per student in the poorer, typically rural, districts up to that of the more affluent Portland-area schools. The state would thus have to come up with considerable additional money in 1995 to satisfy these demands.

This was not, however, the only initiative-inspired demand on state funds. In 1994 Oregonians, following a national trend of getting tough on crime and criminals, overwhelmingly approved (66 percent to 34 percent) a ballot measure that set mandatory sentences for certain felons and required juveniles fifteen years of age and older to be tried as adults. In a separate ballot initiative, voters also prohibited the legislature from reducing voter-approved mandatory prison sentences except by a two-thirds majority—a virtual impossibility. Both supporters and opponents of the two measures agreed that the result would be a near doubling of the state's prison population within five years and the need to significantly increase the number of prison beds. The estimated cost was about $1 billion by the year 2001.

Thus, as the 1995 legislative session began, the Democratic governor and the Republican-controlled legislature (Republicans enjoyed solid majorities in both the House [34 to 26] and Senate [19 to 11]) faced political and statutory demands to increase spending on education and corrections, while at the same time continuing to finance the OHP with existing general fund dollars. Although the state economy was healthy,[20] the property tax limitation, the absence of a sales tax, and a balanced-budget requirement meant that the additional funds had to come from existing programs. As the 1995 legislative session evolved Governor Kitzhaber and the Republican legislative leadership split over how much additional money should go into education and how much of this should come at the expense of the Oregon Health Plan. Kitzhaber feared that deep cuts in OHP funding would threaten the very existence of the plan. At one point during the legislative session, the governor told a group of Oregon Medical Association leaders that the plan was "in very, very deep trouble."[21] In order to protect the plan, the governor proposed several changes that would reduce the cost of the OHP. The changes the governor proposed, and the legislature ultimately accepted, were to reduce the services offered under the plan, increase eligibility requirements, and introduce co-payments and monthly premiums. Specifically, beginning January 1, 1996, the following changes have been made to the OHP:

- The 114,000 people covered under the OHP since February 1, 1994, now must pay five dollars per office visit, plus a fee of $8 to $28 per month, depending on their income and family size. Previously there were no co-payments or monthly fees.
- Eligibility, which is based exclusively on falling below the federal poverty level, is now calculated on income for three consecutive months, rather than just one month as in the original law. This provision is to prevent people from qualifying based upon just one bad month.
- Persons with liquid assets (e.g., savings, stocks, and bonds) in excess of five thousand dollars are now ineligible for the plan even if their incomes fall below the poverty level. The assumption here is that these people can afford to purchase private health insurance.
- Full-time college students are no longer eligible for the plan.

With the exception of eliminating coverage for college students, each of these changes required, and ultimately received, HCFA approval. Nevertheless some observers worried that the changes, and especially the co-payments and monthly premiums, would increase the likelihood of doing what the plan was intended to eliminate, namely, rationing care on the basis of the ability of people to pay. Defenders of the changes, including Governor Kitzhaber, believe the integrity and underlying principle of the plan remain intact. They note that the co-payment and sliding-scale premium are modest and that the former does not apply to maternity, family planning, or preventive services.

As noted earlier, the number of conditions/treatments on the priority list was initially reduced by the 1995 legislature from 606 to 581. Then in July 1996 the Legislative Emergency Board, which acts on behalf of the full legislature during the interim, further reduced the number to 573 in response to an $18.4 million shortfall in the OHP budget. This further reduction required HCFA approval, which was delayed, purposely, until after the 1996 presidential election.

Lessons from Oregon

The Oregon health care story is now four years old. No effort at health care reform has been as extensively chronicled as the "Oregon rationing plan"; indeed it is hardly possible to write about health care reform in this country without reference to Oregon. Anyone who thinks that reforming the nation's health care system will be easy or quick need only read the history of the Oregon experiment to be disabused of such a notion. Aside from the need for patience, what lessons can scholars and policymakers learn from the Oregon experience? I think there are two sets: one deals with process and one with content.

Lessons about Process

In terms of process, one lesson takes the form of a cliché: good intentions do not necessarily make good public policy. It is certainly one of the most extraordinary ironies of this entire story that those facets of their health reform that Oregonians were most proud of, and for which they received most praise, were where they proved the most vulnerable. Thus, for example, the decision to actively solicit and incorporate citizen values in the prioritization process started as a benevolent exercise in participatory democracy and ended up being characterized as a malevolent mechanism for denigrating and discriminating against disabled persons. Oregon's experience throws into question not simply citizen participation as a political strategy to gain widespread acceptance of innovative reform, but the desirability of such an approach. Are citizens well enough informed about the complexity of health and health care to have as intimate an involvement in the decision-making process as the Oregon experiment allowed?

Another procedural lesson to grow out of this story deals with specificity. Oregon lawmakers take pride in the fact that, unlike the invidious practice of stealth rationing that routinely denies access to health care to millions of poor and unemployed Americans, their plan openly, explicitly, and specifically set the limits of care the state would provide for its poorest citizens. Every two years legislators go through the highly public exercise of drawing a line on the list of priorities, announcing, in effect, "this much and no more." They thus stand accountable for their decisions. Although no state has followed Oregon's lead thus far, the fact that the plan has won the grudging support of even some of its most vocal critics has renewed interest in the clinical and political viability of the Oregon plan. This is especially true now that there is no longer any immediate hope that the national government will step in to save state governments from the staggering burden of health care cost increases.

On the Backs of the Poor? Lessons about Content

However, the Oregon Health Plan remains controversial because it raises a fundamental ethical question: Is Oregon using its poor population as a guinea pig to deal with the societal problem of runaway health care costs? Some critics, especially outside of Oregon, think that this is exactly what the state is doing. According to Arthur Caplan, a national authority on biomedical ethics, "It is wrong to make the poor, and only the poor, bear the burden of rationing."[22] And, indeed, it is hard to deny the charge that the law creates a situation in which some Oregonians have virtually unlimited access to health care, as they do now, while others have only limited, albeit "adequate," access. This, however, may be preferable and more humane than the system it replaced in which most had unlimited access, while others had none at all. In the absence of a nonemployment-based, universal system of health insurance, the fundamental issue at stake here is what principle should guide U.S. health policy for the poor: equity or equality. Specifically, should limits be placed on the level of medical services available to those on public assistance? Should we as a society say that fairness—equity—requires only as much health care as expert and popular consensus judges to be adequate? In the absence of unlimited resources it may be that it is impossible to guarantee equal access for everyone to all available medical technology, service, and treatment that can be brought to bear on a particular condition.

The dilemma is hardly a new one. Several years ago Charles Fried addressed this question and argued, "To say there is a right to health care does not imply a right to equal access, a right that whatever is available to any shall be available to all."[23] In place of the notion of equality of care, Fried suggests a "dynamically defined" "decent standard of care." The question then becomes what constitutes the currently defined "decent standard." Clearly, as Fried's operational directive suggests, such a standard must be a dynamic one, accommodating changing technology, available resources, as well as popular consensus and democratic values. The value of an adaptable standard of what is a decent minimum level of health care is also endorsed by Allen Buchanan. "The first advantage of the idea of a decent minimum," Buchanan argues, "is that it allows us to adjust the level of services to be provided as a matter of right to relevant social conditions and also allows for the possibility that as a society becomes more affluent the floor provided by the decent minimum should be raised."[24] All this sounds remarkably like the Oregon Health Plan. The question is, of course, whether we as a society are willing to openly acknowledge that fairness, not equality, will and/or should govern health resource allocations? The state of Oregon has answered the question in the affirmative. Yet it has done so primarily for the most marginal elements of society.

Other states have and will draw upon the substance, if not the process, of the Oregon experiment. Oregon lawmakers have indeed done what needs to be done. They have recognized, earlier than anyone else, that there are limits to what the public sector can provide in health care without bankrupting state budgets. They have gone through a much needed and long overdue exercise of defining what constitutes a minimum, basic, or adequate package of health care services. Although others may avoid Oregon's explicitness, they cannot avoid Oregon's conclusion about defining limits. Oregon officials have simplified the costly, cumbersome, and at times cruel and irrational standards for Medicaid eligibility. They have spoken the words that others dare not with regard to freedom of choice of providers. Americans will not only have to learn that there are limits on what they can have, but that there may also be limits on who will provide their health care. Managed care is the future of American medical delivery.

Rationing is already a routine and integral part of the American health care system. It occurs when health care providers refuse to treat Medicaid patients, or when legislators redefine Medicaid eligibility and benefits so as to reduce coverage of persons or procedures, or when the poor but uninsured delay seeing a physician for a health problem. It is stealth rationing—virtually undetectable except by those who go without care. What Oregon has done is to allocate health resources in an explicit, public, consensual, and accountable fashion. It is an appealing process, but one that does not mask the ultimately troubling reality of rationing health care.

Finally, Oregonians have taught the rest of the nation that we must begin to better assess the care we receive, and judge it in terms of what is most important: does it work? Oregon has been a classroom to which much of the nation has gone to learn about the future of health care in this country.

Notes

Portions of this article originally appeared in Daniel M. Fox and Howard M. Leichter, "Rationing Care in Oregon: The New Accountability," *Health Affairs* 10 (summer 1991): 7–27, and Daniel M. Fox and Howard M. Leichter, "The Ups and Downs of Oregon's Rationing Plan," *Health Affairs* 12 (summer 1993): 66–70. The material is reprinted by permission of Project HOPE. The People-to-People Health Foundation. *Health Affairs,* 7500 Old Georgetown Road, Suite 600, Bethesda, Md. 20814.

1. Adult and Family Services Division, "Organ Transplant Services," n.d.
2. Oregon Legislative Emergency Board, Human Resources Subcommittee, Transcript of meeting January 28, 1988.
3. Ibid.
4. *Nightline,* January 28, 1988.
5. For a detailed account of Oregon's efforts to secure a federal Medicaid waiver, see Lawrence D. Brown, "The National Politics of Oregon's Rationing Plan," *Health Affairs* 10 (June 1991): 28–51.
6. Romana Hasnain and Michael Garland, *Health Care in Common: Report of the Oregon Health Decisions Community Meeting Process* (Portland, Ore.: Oregon Health Decisions, 1990), 29.
7. Oregon Health Services Commission, *Prioritization of Health Services* (Salem, Ore.: Department of Human Resources, 1995): 32.
8. For a copy of the complete questionnaire see Health Service Commission, "Preliminary Report," (Salem, Ore.: March 1, 1990), Exhibit 2. For a critical analysis of the technical aspects of the prioritization process, including the QWB, see David C. Hadorn, "The Oregon Priority-Setting Exercise: Quality of Life and Public Policy," *Hastings Center Report* 21 (May–June 1991): 11–16.
9. Alan K. Ota, "Oregon Health Plan May Get Grease," *Portland Oregonian,* April 9, 1992.
10. Quoted in Michael Abramowitz, "Oregon Blazes a Trail," *Washington Post,* June 9, 1992.
11. Robert Ulrich, "State Health Care Plan Rejected," *Portland Oregonian,* August 4, 1992, A8.
12. Ibid.
13. Robert Pear, "Plan to Ration Health Care Is Rejected by Government. *New York Times,* August 4, 1992, A8.
14. Patrick O'Neil, "Officials Now Say U.S. May Approve Oregon Health Plan," *Portland Oregonian,* August 27, 1992, C4.
15. Timothy Flanigan, assistant attorney general, Office of Legal Counsel, Department of Justice, letter to Susan Zagame, acting general counsel, Department of Health and Human Services, January 19, 1993.
16. Health Services Commission, *Prioritization of Health Services,* 1991, Appendix D, p. D–23.
17. Lynn Read, Oregon Health Plan, interview by author, April 21, 1993.
18. Jean Thorne, Oregon Health Plan, interview by author, April 6, 1993.
19. Health Care Financing Administration, "Special Terms and Conditions," March 19, 1993, 2.
20. In fact so healthy was the state economy that tax revenues exceeded projections. However, in 1979 Oregon passed a "2 percent kicker" law that required the state to give individuals and corporations a tax rebate whenever revenues were 2 percent over pro-

jected income. Thus, although the state was expecting $320 million in extra revenue, the legislature could only spend this money if the so-called kicker law was rescinded. Republican legislative leaders made it clear that they had no intention of doing so.

21. Patrick O'Neill, "Stop Health Plan Cuts, Doctors Urged," *Portland Oregonian,* April 29, 1995, B7.

22. Arthur Caplan quoted in William Raspberry, "A Question of Fairness: Oregon's Health-Care Rationing Plan Should Apply to Everyone," *Portland Oregonian,* October 24, 1989, B7.

23. Charles Fried, "Equality and Rights in Medical Care," *Hastings Center Report* 6 (February 1976): 29.

24. Allen Buchanan, "The Right to a Decent Minimum of Health Care," *Philosophy and Public Affairs* 13 (winter 1984): 58.

7

Hawaii:
The Health State Revisited

Deane Neubauer

Introduction

In the late 1980s public officials in Hawaii believed that their state had entered into a "new era of health care." This view was based on a series of innovations that were intended to reduce the proportion of the population without health insurance, create a health care environment conducive to and supportive of health promotion and disease prevention, and promote public- and private-sector cooperation in the delivery of cost-effective publicly funded health care. These outcomes appeared to be the product of two critical variables: the emergence of a "health culture" in the state and a political leadership that was committed to pursuing an innovative health policy agenda. Since the gubernatorial election of 1994 Hawaii politics has been dominated by its most severe budget crisis since statehood, an event that has threatened to undo much of the liberal health care agenda that prompted the notion of Hawaii as "the health state." The winner of that election, Ben Cayetano, a long-time Democratic Party legislator and two-term lieutenant governor during the tenure of his predecessor John Waihee, has also proved a strong advocate of reinventing government, by which he means downsizing state departments and agencies, and seeking market-oriented solutions for traditional governmental concerns. This chapter chronicles these events, which themselves have been strongly influenced by the politics of national health care reform.

The chapter is organized in three parts. In the first I briefly describe the setting of Hawaii, the health state. This idea emerges out of a political-economic context that is different from that of Hawaii's sister states and that owes much to the historical nexus in the state of plantation agriculture and tourism. Hawaii has also produced a distinctive political culture in which the dynamics of politics in a small island state are readily identifiable. Central to these dynamics has been the development of the Democratic Party as the dominant political force during the statehood era, having held the governorship and dominated the legislature in every election. Until the last state election Hawaii was identified with a strong political liberalism, which in the 1980s had worked to limit the effects of Reaganism on state policy. This liberal domination is now changing, irrespective of the continued political hegemony of the Democratic Party. Health issues have been a true reflection of these ideological shifts.

In the second part of the chapter I describe several recent health policy innovations, linking them to the political setting. Of these the most important have been the Prepaid Health Care Act of 1974, the State Health Insurance Program (SHIP) in 1989, and Health QUEST in 1994.

Finally, I seek to assess the impact of recent Hawaii politics on the dual goal of promoting universal access to care while controlling costs.

The Setting

The idea of Hawaii developing a special character as a health environment began to take form with the election of John Waihee as governor in November 1986. Many requisite ingredients were already in place, perhaps most important the fact that Hawaii is and seeks to remain a healthy place. The fortunes of geography and climate have spared it many of the indignities of industrial and postindustrial development. Its three major industries—tourism, government employment, and agriculture—are clean endeavors when compared with smokestack environments. And whereas complex environmental issues continue to be associated with all three economic endeavors, such as the continued high use of pesticides and herbicides in pineapple and sugar production, and infrastructure stress resulting from too-rapid tourism growth, their visibility is nowhere near as great as those associated with traditional industrial development.

Furthermore, the population of Hawaii is on the whole remarkably healthy when judged by conventional indicators. With the exception of individuals of Polynesian descent, the longevity of other major ethnic groups—Caucasians, Japanese, Chinese, Koreans, and Filipinos—exceeds that of their mainland counterparts.[1] Hawaiians, part-Hawaiians, and other Pacific Island people have poorer health status as measured by a variety of indicators, and significantly lower life expectancy.[2]

Hawaii has also become an extremely attractive place to practice medicine. The ratio of practicing physicians to the general population is seventh highest in the nation, but the physician distribution is highly concentrated. Medical care is highly concentrated. The one-mile radius surrounding Queen's Medical Center, Honolulu's largest and most sophisticated medical facility, is said to contain the highest concentration cf physicians per unit measure in the world. Fully 80 percent of these are specialists. Local economic predictions hold that by the year 2010 health care will be the primary industry in the state, exceeding even tourism.

"Hawaii, the health state," then, builds from a convergent set of economic and social factors already in place: a benign environment that in comparative terms is relatively free of "environmental insults," a highly trained and plentiful health care workforce, a population that, although aging, has substantial resources to invest in health care, and a tourist industry anxious to gain a competitive edge by packaging these health attributes as a new and relatively unique industry value.

This latter aspect formed one of the more significant and interesting ingredients of Governor Waihee's vision of the health state. Hawaii would serve as a major destination for the residents of less attractive physical and social environments. As people become more concerned with health issues, the argument goes, Hawaii gains in comparative advantage through its ability to provide an alternative environment. "Recreation" under this formula would focus on its literal meaning: re-creating the individual in settings designed to reverse the effects of those stresses. Simple and conventional tourism would be restructured to include a completely healthy physical environment emphasizing outdoor activities of all types, supplemented by the full range of medical services and convalescent needs. All of these would be effectively advertised by the obvious good health of the resident population.

Steps toward achieving these early-twenty-first century goals are already under way. For example, the Ihilani Hotel at Ko'OLina, a major Japanese-financed resort community on leeward Oahu, provides such a full spa-type regimen complete with personal trainers, custom menus, and multiple workout and exercise facilities for about $3,000 a week. The Department of Business, Economic Development, and Tourism has recently completed a study that touts health tourism as a market niche for upscale Asian visitors.

Health tourism induces rhapsodic claims by state economic development coordinators and officials. A former dean of the School of Travel Industry at the University of Hawaii, Chuck Gee, has claimed that health tourism could become a three-billion-dollar annual industry. State Senator Stan Koki speaks of building a "Mayo Clinic of the Pacific," an idea also favored by Governor Cayetano. The Hawaii Community Development Authority argues that a health-related development in Kakaako, a former light industrial area near downtown Honolulu currently under redevelopment, could be "a new economic generator for a tropical paradise."[3]

To promote the outdoor life in Hawaii the state has underwritten attempts to acquire major sporting events that would advertise Hawaii as a healthy environment, including blue-water events like the America's and Kennwood Cups. A "corporate games" festival, inaugurated in October 1990, featuring teams representing transnational corporations competing in a wide variety of events is meant to symbolize the commonplace unification of corporate goals with the norm of fitness and health. The annual Aloha State Games featuring competition in forty-five sports from arm wrestling to canoeing to the decathlon and horseshoe pitching have become an annual vehicle for eliciting mass participation from both residents and visitors at all skill levels. The volunteer labor force alone for these games numbers in the thousands, and corporate sponsorship is both visible and strong. The Big Island Triathlon has become an annual global media event, and the twenty-fifth anniversary of the Honolulu Marathon in 1996 drew over twenty-five thousand runners, the majority from Japan. Golf now contributes more to the Hawaiian economy than either sugar or pineapple crops. These activities join an already long list of more conventional sports such as running, biking, swimming, canoeing, and walking events featured almost weekly, all of which contribute to the norm of extensive physical activity in an attractive setting.

Steps such as these to produce a value-added "health" component to tourism are but one aspect of a broader commitment the state has made to its conception of health, which extends from an activist concern with the mechanics of health insurance coverage to the core dynamics of its political economy. Increasingly, state economic planners are looking to the health care industry as an alternative to both traditional tourism and a declining agricultural sector. That health care should be perceived as an industry and a social service, both capable of being developed under the aegis of state planning, was consistent with the liberal political culture that emerged in Hawaii after statehood.

For most of continental America, statehood is but a dim aspect of its received history. For those living in Hawaii, it is a recent and important experience. Historically, statehood has been associated with a commitment to a tradition of political liberalism as new political forces moved into government imbued with the spirit of reform. Since 1959 Hawaii has been sensitive to the ideological tides sweeping the United States while at the same time remaining loyally identified with the commitments formed within the political coalition responsible for achieving statehood. This coalition, located within the Democratic Party, was anchored by Japanese-Americans emerging for the first time as a political force and led by highly decorated and recognized war heroes, who in the immediate postwar period added advanced degrees, many in law, to their military accomplishments. As a group they represented a newly developed middle-class faction that had grown out of a prewar history of turbulent plantation labor struggles.

The period dating from the overthrow of the Hawaiian monarchy in 1893 until the onset of World War II was one of unrelieved Republican Party dominance. It was also a period characterized by self-conscious social, economic, and political aggrandizement by a narrow Caucasian elite. For those struggling to gain the right to full and effective political participation, the Democratic Party was the obvious vehicle. When these emerging ethnic groups achieved legislative power in 1954, the political program from which they took their cues was mainland reform liberalism. The central organizing principle for this reform-minded coalition was the application and extension of political rights to ensure the place of its constituent, newly emerging groups.

The first ten years of statehood witnessed a significant boom in real estate and tourist industry development, attenuated by infusions of federal spending for the war in Vietnam. A prosperous and growing economy provided ample means to extend strong public commitments across the range of social services. One important example was greatly increased spending on public education at all levels, including the building of a state-wide system of higher education that was perceived as a channel for upward mobility for local students unable to follow the career path of their more prosperous peers who traditionally attended mainland institutions. State spending for the University of Hawaii increased almost 600 percent in the decade of the 1960s. Another dimension included the provision of relatively generous state support for public welfare, workers' compensation, and unemployment compensation. The International Longshore Workers Union (ILWU) had been a major vehicle for the unionization of plantation agriculture in Hawaii. With statehood it was highly influential in the creation of a liberal political agenda, including public welfare and strong, centralized state planning. Thus, much to the dismay of many business groups who preferred market-oriented solutions to development and social issues, Hawaii state government followed an activist and interventionist development model in which state planning played a central role.

By the 1970s Hawaii had earned the label in some circles of having an "undesirable" business climate, by which was meant a continuing penchant for supporting labor values and structuring new economic ventures through state mechanisms. But, tellingly, these rhetorical assaults were most strident within the small-business community. In macro political and economic terms, a compromise appears to have been engineered during these decades that provides for the shift of big-business support from the Republican to the Democratic Party within a broad understanding that the latter would embrace a program of continued economic development, essentially through tourism. Like all such "policy stories" this one is far more complex than suggested by this telling. The "compromise" has been itself a developmental undertaking without conscious articulation so much as the working out of the structural dynamics that inform the political economy. For example, during the administrations of George Ariyoshi (1973–86) efforts were made through governmental planning mechanisms to slow growth. Although some of these actions did provoke complaints from big business that the state was overregulated and fostered an "antibusiness" climate, the large firms in the economy at the same time accepted the fact that electoral fortunes had shifted decisively to the Democratic Party, and their financial support followed accordingly. In turn the Democratic political leadership has provided a development agenda essentially congenial to those interests. The result has been to deny the Republican Party access to its traditional source of electoral funding.

Since 1959 Hawaii has been effectively a one-party state, displaying unbroken Democratic Party dominance in both houses of the state legislature and the executive branch. Correspondingly, the Republican Party has grown proportionately weaker: the 1994 legislative elections returned only seven Republican members to the fifty-one-seat House of Representatives and two to the twenty-five-member Senate. This one-party dominance within the context of the grand political-economic compromise has meant that all major political disputes take place within and between the various ill-defined and shifting factions of the Democratic Party. To a significant extent, Hawaii legislative politics is personality driven.

The events of the Waihee administrations (1987–94) involved a rather unique confluence of factors involving both the structure of the political economy and the role of new political actors. Structurally, as suggested above, the Democratic Party became the repository of traditional liberalism and through its dominance protected the local environment from those features of Reaganism that took hold in many other states. Moreover, the economic environment during the Ariyoshi administration had been one of generally sustained, if moderate, growth that provided a generally supportive climate for continued governmental action.

This was followed during the first term of Governor Waihee by extraordinary budgetary surpluses, brought about by a booming tourist industry and striking real estate inflation initiated by Japanese investment. For example, housing prices on the most populous island, Oahu, doubled during the five-year period from 1986 to 1991. Governor Waihee had the great good fortune of achieving office at a time when state coffers were awash with money, a situation that well suited his activist political propensities. By 1991 the financial tide had begun to turn, although not all would recognize it so soon. Historically the economy of Hawaii has lagged behind mainland recessions and recoveries by two to three years. The U.S. recession of the late 1980s was just beginning to affect Hawaii when the Persian Gulf War broke out, resulting in a drastic decline in the tourist industry. Further, Hawaii's economy has become highly dependent on Japan. Initially, the impact of the U.S. recession was buffered by Japanese spending, which despite the collapse of the "bubble economy" had not fully dried up. By 1993 Hawaii was in a recession. The Waihee government and the legislature did what they could to cushion the blow of declining state revenues, but it remained for Cayetano to announce in his first "State of the State" message in January 1995 that the state was not only broke, it was in severe deficit. I shall return to how this confluence of economic events affected health care innovations.

One last point remains to be made before turning directly to innovation within the health sector. The personality of major actors in the health sector has significantly affected efforts to promote health care reform in the state. Waihee's election in 1986 brought to office Hawaii's first native Hawaiian governor, a graduate of the University of Hawaii Law School, a major player in Hawaii's last constitutional convention in 1978, and a person determined to make his mark on Hawaii's history by bold governmental action. As his health director, Waihee appointed John Lewin, an equally young and dynamic physician who had practiced in Hawaii for ten years and whose background was marked by political activism, a strong commitment to public health, prior experience in the Indian Health Service, and a desire to expand the boundaries of health promotion activity. In contrast with his predecessors, and like Waihee, Lewin's dynamism was focused on an activist role for government in addressing social problems, of which health was but one interrelated component. And, as events would later reveal, both Waihee and Lewin had their eyes on national office, a goal for which health care reform was to be the vehicle.

A supporting cast existed in the legislature. During the early Waihee years, the health committees of both houses were chaired by individuals keenly interested in health questions and not themselves representatives of the provider industry. In the House, Representative James Shon, a full-time legislator with a background in curriculum development at the University of Hawaii, chaired the Health Committee for three terms before losing his position subsequent to the 1992 election in a leadership dispute in which he backed a losing candidate. The penalty was severe, in that he was forced to serve for one entire session without any committee assignments, an almost unheard of penalty. In the Senate, Andrew Levin, a young attorney from the island of Hawaii, was widely viewed as "enlightened" with respect to social welfare issues. During the eight Waihee years he shared the Health Committee chair with Bertram Kobayashi, a Ph.D. in political science, who after retiring from the legislature was appointed by Cayetano as deputy director of the Department of Health in 1995. Although in no way constituting a group, Waihee, Lewin, Shon, Levin, and Kobayashi were ideologically sympathetic toward the policy initiatives that were to occur.

Health Policy Innovations

In the eyes of its creators, by addressing universal health care insurance coverage in a manner unique among the American states, the State Health Insurance Program (SHIP) was the keystone to the claim of Hawaii as the health state. Health QUEST, implemented in August 1994, and other efforts to innovate in coverage and cost control derive from the public policy position taken in the creation of SHIP. To most health professionals, the ability to develop SHIP was in turn entirely dependent on the prior success of the Prepaid Health Care Act.

The Prepaid Health Care Act

Passed in 1974, the Prepaid Health Care Act (Prepaid) mandates an employer-based insurance coverage system for all employees not covered by collective bargaining. It operates through plans offered by the existing insurance system, which is dominated by two major providers, the Hawaii Medical Services Association (HMSA), and Kaiser Permanente, the state's dominant health maintenance organization. Together HMSA and Kaiser provide almost 80 percent of all private health insurance in Hawaii, with the former almost four times larger than the latter.[4] The creation of Health QUEST has not changed these market shares, which have been in place for over twenty years. The Prepaid law stipulates that "the plan must provide health care benefits equal to or medically substitutable for benefits provided by plans having the largest number of subscribers in the state," thereby guaranteeing this relationship to the primary providers and ensuring that employees covered under this plan will not receive a lesser form of coverage.[5] The legislation also provided the opportunity for periodic negotiation of mandated benefits, services that must be provided in the basic universal package. Very large employers were permitted under the act to self-insure, but must also provide the basic benefit package.

Financing is shared equally by employees and employers with the exception that the employee in no case contributes more than 1.5 percent of total wages. Employees are not permitted to refuse coverage, and coverage is universal within the category of nonunionized employees, with a few designated exceptions such as real estate sales agents who receive all of their income from commissions. Business-sector opposition to early drafts of the plan was resolved with the inclusion of two key provisions. One permits employees covered by two plans—through, for example, spousal membership or multiple employment—to choose the coverage they wish to have apply. The more important provision was designed to meet the opposition of small-business owners upon whom the additional costs of providing care would fall most heavily. The act created a special premium supplementation fund for such marginal small employers. Supplementation is available only to employers of fewer than eight employees if the employees' share of coverage exceeds 1.5 percent of total payroll and if the amount of excess is greater than 5 percent of pretax income. In the first year of the act, the legislature appropriated $166,000 for supplementation. In practice, small employers have found it difficult to apply for supplementation and few do so. Requiring all employers to provide coverage permitted health insurers to create a de facto community risk pool that provides rates for small employers roughly comparable to those of larger employers.[6] It is instructive to note that a major motivation for the development of the Prepaid Health Care Act was the belief that other states and the federal government were also moving in the direction of mandating compulsory health insurance. The 1974 act was the concluding piece to a 1967 legislative request (Act 198, Session Laws of Hawaii, 1967) that the state's Legislative Reference Bureau jointly study the issues of temporary disability insurance, covered by legislation in 1969, and prepaid health care. The author of the 1971 study that formed the basis of the 1974 legislation cites as the context for prepaid health insurance the repeated federal efforts to produce a compulsory health care act and the passage of Medicare and Medicaid in 1965. In fact, these were the very grounds on which the Chamber of Commerce opposed the bill during its 1973–74 legislative gestation: that it was unnecessary because it would soon become subject to federal preemption. Advocates of the bill saw themselves not so much as bold innovators but as anxious to join what they viewed as an impending national development.[7] It is of equal interest to note that both the author of the original report and its legislative sponsors believed this legislation would eliminate the "gap group," those without insurance coverage of any kind. At the time people without hospital insurance constituted almost 12 percent of the population, while those without physician coverage amounted to more than 17 percent. In promoting the bill, its conference committee manager, Democratic representative Hiroshi Kato would claim that "this bill establishes the concept that every resident of this state has the right to good health care."[8] A decade and a half later John Lewin would say of SHIP that it is but a step toward a more important goal. "We haven't admitted the obvious, that health care should be a right of citizenship—a promise through government."[9]

SHIP

The creation of SHIP in 1989 was, therefore, unique not so much for its presumed universality, since that is precisely what the Prepaid Health Care Act sponsors thought they were achieving in 1974, but rather for its combination of the elements of universality, comprehensive care, and attention to prevention. The latter was, in Lewin's mind, the critical element of the three, for it is here that the larger idea of Hawaii as the health state begins to gain substance. In this view health insurance itself is a lever for social change. The first task is to convince people to choose healthy lifestyles, the second is to sell the economic argument to business that including health values in business makes good economic sense, and the third is to move to a broader social agenda of creating a healthy society. As Lewin wrote in an in-house communication to Department of Health personnel shortly after SHIP's announcement, "Every health professional and citizen in our state may take pride in the fact that Hawaii is about to make history by implementing the most ambitious health insurance program in the United States."[10] Like the Prepaid Health Care Act, the political strength of SHIP lay in the use of existing provider organizations, thereby being institutionally positioned among market forces that could act to control costs. A major selling point of the program was its presumed ability to affect overall utilization patterns, especially the common tendency of noninsured persons to utilize emergency-room facilities in lieu of readily available primary care and other more effective screening mechanisms. (SHIP planners chose to overlook the disproportionate ratio of specialists to primary care physicians in Hawaii, making their case on the tie-ins between public insurance programs and primary care facilities, such as community health centers.) One predicted benefit that sweetened its political palatability among providers was the prospect of reducing the bad debt/uncollectibles pool.

The enabling legislation, which was adopted April 28, 1989, and signed into law in June, provided $4 million for the first sixteen months of operation and $10 million for the second full year. SHIP was seen as a partnership between government, individuals requiring health insurance, and the private sector. Government would subsidize insurance coverage for those unable to pay, insurance companies would provide coverage at rates negotiated by the state, and existing health care providers would deliver direct care.

The gap group addressed by SHIP did not cover the entire uninsured population. It explicitly targeted those who had been uninsured by public or private health care coverage programs but who were at a low enough income level where they could not access current health care coverage. At the time of SHIP's passage, the size of this group was estimated at thirty thousand to thirty-five thousand. In retrospect it is clear that the creation of this gap group had been caused in part by structural changes in the economy that increased the number of workers not covered by the terms of the Prepaid Health Care Act, especially part-time workers. These structural dynamics are equally prevalent within the economy of the continental United States and have contributed significantly to the gap group throughout the nation. The particular contribution of Prepaid had been to reduce the original gap group to an estimated 5 percent of the population by providing coverage for all fully employed individuals. A 1988 survey found this post-Prepaid gap group to be composed primarily of the unemployed (30 percent of the uninsured), dependents (particularly children) of low-income workers, part-time workers, off-Oahu residents, immigrants, seasonal workers, and students.

SHIP established a sliding fee schedule with those individuals whose incomes fall below the federal poverty level paying nothing. Modest premium payments occur thereafter, with adults at income levels between 251 percent and 300 percent of the federal poverty standard paying the entire cost of insurance. To be eligible for SHIP the applicant would need to prove ineligibility for Medicare, Medicaid, CHAMPUS, and VA benefits.[11]

SHIP was viewed as a temporary program, "a hand up" for those in need, most of whom it was assumed would become eligible through employment for coverage under the Prepaid Health Care Act. It was also designed as a health care program, rather than merely a vehicle to provide "sickness" care. The major preventive and primary care provisions permitted health appraisals, of which well-baby care and age-appropriate health screening would be typical, and a package of basic primary care items, such as twelve physician visits a year with a $5 co-payment per visit, laboratory and X-ray services, and immunizations. More costly items were deemphasized within the program and where possible shifted over to Medicaid if spend-downs rendered the individual Medicaid eligible. Hospitalization was limited to five days with a limit of $2,500. Two days were allowed for maternity care. Exclusions included elective surgery and high-cost tertiary care. Costly care and procedures, such as neonatal intensive care, end-stage renal disease care, open-heart surgery, where possible were shifted to Medicaid.[12]

SHIP lasted from its introduction in 1990 until its almost twenty thousand members were subsumed into QUEST in August 1994. In the end the value of SHIP lay as much in the ground it prepared for QUEST as in the coverage provided this portion of the gap group. Before turning to an examination of QUEST, a brief word is due the Blue Ribbon Panel on Health Care, as its story tells much about the recent fate of health care innovation in Hawaii.

The Blue Ribbon Panel

Concern for a general lack of integration among the various components and key participants in Hawaii's overall health care environment produced Act 291, Session Laws of Hawaii, 1990, establishing the Governor's Blue Ribbon Panel on Health Care. The panel was instructed to develop a more comprehensive understanding of the health care system through widespread community consultation, and to develop recommendations facilitative of more effective cost control and application of health care. While acknowledging the key role played by the Prepaid Health Care Act and the combination of coverage established by SHIP, Medicaid, the Community Health Nursing Program, and the certificate-of-need process, legislators underscored those problems not yet addressed by state legislation. These included the burgeoning elderly population, a growing shortage of certain health care professionals, acute and long-term care bed shortages, dramatically increasing health care costs, and cost shifting from "undersupported" public patients to private insurance plans. Two important items were excluded from this agenda of concerns: the persistent problems of native Hawaiian health, and deficient mental health care programs.

In the news release announcing the composition of the Blue Ribbon Panel on December 7, 1990, the governor stressed that the panel "represents a cross section of Hawaii's economic and social leaders including representatives of business, insurance providers, unions, academia, consumers, government agencies, and health care providers."[13] The actual appointment of the twenty-three members proved a delicate political maneuver for the governor's office as it struggled to balance the reality of existing vested interests with the prospect that the panel might actually break new ground.

The panel met almost biweekly for more than fifteen months. In July 1992 it reported out thirty-six recommendations directed at controlling costs in five areas: administrative costs, medical malpractice, consumer expectations, health care resources, and cost shifting. These five were chosen after months of hearing the views of a wide sector of the health care community, and were significant in part for what they did not include. Long-term care, certainly a major factor in the overall cost environment, was not addressed because the Governor's Office on Aging was concurrently preparing its own recommendations. The panel's authorizing legislation identified some specific areas for attention, including insurance rate regulation, health care facility costs, and common purchasing agreements, as areas for panel attention. The first two were rejected after considerable discussion as more the result of cost factors than their effect. Joint purchase is already a routine administrative practice for many medical facilities. In extending the panel's original one-year authorization the legislature suggested that mental health issues were also a matter of concern, but the final report made no mention of mental health issues.

The panel designated eight of its thirty-six recommendations as "key change" proposals. These called for:

1. Reform of administrative procedures, including electronic claims processing, automated record keeping, and a universal claims form.
2. Reform of the regulatory system to lessen the costs of regulatory compliance.
3. Reform of insurance access by developing a revised community rating.
4. Developing a no-fault medical malpractice system.
5. Addressing shortages in health care human services, primarily through better strategic planning.
6. Working to modify consumer expectations for the health care system through more efficient and effective utilization practices, the establishment of a universal basic benefit package, and more effective use of primary care as first access to the system.
7. Eliminating cost shifting by fully funding public support programs that cover all public benefit packages.[14]

The eighth key-change recommendation grew out of the panel's concern that its work result in actual changes in the current system. It called for the creation of an "entity" to implement the panel's recommendations. This was a broad, sweeping recommendation extending beyond the panel's legislative mandate. The "consortium" called for in the recommendation explicitly combined private- and public-sector players in an extensive range of activities, including the gathering, analysis, and dissemination of systemwide data (to make better judgments about cost issues), the implementation of panel recommendations, the creation and monitoring of a basic benefits package, and periodic legislative recommendations on other health care matters that it deemed important.

The success of the Blue Ribbon Panel was its ability to bring together virtually all the important players in Hawaiian health care and have them agree on a set of central recommendations for improving the system by seeking cost control mechanisms. The weakness of the panel was its inability to win effective implementation for its recommendations. The panel had been a legislative creation and while Jack Lewin was a member, the Department of Health never fully committed to the panel as its vehicle for addressing common problems. Indeed, during the panel's existence, Lewin brought into being two parallel organizations that competed for attention and political support. One was the Governor's Subcabinet Task Force for Health Care Reform, made up of members from eleven state departments or agencies. Chaired by Lewin and staffed by his deputy, the task force was given the job of drafting legislation that would complete the Waihee administration's health package, a set of proposals designed to create a "seamless" health care system that would meet all existing publicly supported needs, including reforming Medicaid under managed care to get a better grasp on costs, insurance reform focused on the creation of true community rating, ensuring that individuals do not experience noncoverage waiting periods, and cost containment. The centerpiece of this legislation was a proposed health care commission that would oversee these activities, including the creation and management of a basic benefits package. Lewin had addressed the Blue Ribbon Panel with his "seamless" proposals, but their full significance appeared lost on many private sector participants.[15]

The second group, termed within the Department of Health as "the gang of six," was Lewin's "kitchen cabinet" on health care reform matters. Consisting of Lewin and the respective heads of HMSA, Kaiser, the Health Care Association of Hawaii (the interest group association for hospitals), the Hawaii Medical Association, and the Hawaii Nurses Association, they linked the most important players in the health care community, who Lewin hoped could lobby for the administration's package in the 1993 legislature. This hope was eventually to be confounded by national electoral politics.

The Election of 1992

John Waihee had served on the health task force of the U.S. Governor's Conference with health reform advocates Booth Gardner (D-Wash.) and Bill Clinton (D-Ark.). Along the way, like many others, Waihee had become a "friend of Bill's," with whom he shared a belief that health care was very likely the coming political issue of the 1990s. His closeness to the prospective Democratic presidential nominee was no doubt also enhanced by the happy circumstance of being governor of arguably the most dependable Democratic electorate in the United States. And, as a governor who himself had fashioned "the health state," Waihee had much to contribute to the ideas of the health task force, as did Health Director Lewin, who was not only a regular consultant to the task force but during the 1991–92 period also served as president of the State and Territorial Health Officials, a group much involved with the nitty-gritty of reform efforts at the state level.

Hawaii appeared early in candidate Clinton's speeches as an example of "health care that worked," and especially as a real-life instance of an employer-mandate state that had not suffered the disastrous consequences attributed to the type by its opponents. Throughout the 1992 campaign Lewin in particular was out of state campaigning for health care reform and Clinton's election, frequently on national television. With the actual election of Clinton a positive giddiness swept over the Hawaii health care scene, as the attributed closeness of Waihee and Clinton, and Lewin's campaign efforts, seemed they would be rewarded with appointment to high administrative positions. In the end, Waihee was not offered a high-level domestic administrative position, although he was offered the ambassadorship to Indonesia at the end of his own second term in 1994, only to decline the pleasure of seeking ratification as a staunch liberal before the Foreign Relations Committee chaired by Senator Jesse Helms. Lewin reportedly was offered at least one position of significant rank, albeit not as elevated and significant as he had hoped for. But his purpose lay elsewhere. First, he hoped to be a major player in the Clinton health care task force. When that did not happen, he decided that the real way to promote Hawaii as the health state was through his own direct efforts: he would run for governor.

The timing of these events paralleled the outcomes of the Blue Ribbon Panel in a disastrous manner. Just when Lewin's personal leadership was crucial for combining the interests of his own administrative task force and the panel, he was absent from the state on almost a continuous basis. A feeble effort was made to embody the work of the "entity" into a watered down commission that would be established within the state Health Planning and Development Agency, but that idea was stillborn. No serious follow-up on the Blue Ribbon Panel's recommendations was attempted by the Department of Health. And although the 1992 national election brought joy to Hawaii, its state counterpart produced an unfortunate outcome. The aftermath of the election produced the leadership struggle in the House of Representatives that cost Jim Shon his seat as chair of the Health Committee. While Shon was never a pushover for the administration on health care matters, he and the senior leadership of the Department of Health did share basically similar values and a long history of cooperation and collaboration. Indeed, one of Lewin's top assistants had been Shon's legislative assistant for two terms. Shon was replaced by a junior and inexperienced legislator who over the next two years would demonstrate that she was not a major player in health care. The combination of Lewin's withdrawal of direct leadership and Shon's demise significantly slowed the momentum of reform efforts. While these events were playing out, Waihee himself was suffering the normal loss of momentum of a lame duck administration, the constraints of a depressed economy on legislative initiatives, and a climate of cronyism and minor scandals that had come to symbolize his administration.

Waihee sought to end his term with a major health care innovation. President Clinton's warmth toward health care reform at the state level encouraged Hawaii to seek a Section 1115 Medicaid waiver to address what had become persistent cost overruns in its Medicaid program. Between 1989 and 1993 state Medicaid costs increased 80.1 percent while the population served increased only 36.1 percent. With the tightening budgets of the emergent Hawaii recession, more than tinkering with Medicaid was required. And, to put a more politically palatable face on it, Medicaid reform was consistent with much of the ideology of the Blue Ribbon Panel, especially in its concern to eliminate cost shifting. Whatever the outcome of national health care reform, it was thought, Hawaii could not lose by moving on Medicaid reform. It could once again be ahead of the curve. It was 1974 all over again.

Hawaii QUEST

Hawaii QUEST (Quality of care, Universal access, Efficient utilization, Stable costs, Transformation) is a capitated, managed care system that serves most of the former Medicaid recipients and all of SHIP's. In its 1993 waiver request to the Health Care Financing Administration, the state projected a $435 million saving over six years by moving from the public-sector administration of both programs to private-sector administration. Significantly, in 1993 the average Medicaid client cost the state nearly $2,300 a year, compared with comparable private-sector coverage of $1,400 per client. Unlike SHIP, which had been developed within the Department of Health with close legislative cooperation, Hawaii QUEST was the product of external consultants working with the Department of Human Services, which administers Medicaid. Only modest input was sought from the Department of Health, the legislature, or the community. By the time Hawaii QUEST was brought to the legislature for ratification in the spring of 1994, it was essentially a done deal presenting that body with the hollow choice of going along with the program's essential features or playing spoiler without good cause.[16]

SHIP's innovative nature lay in state support for a gap-group-oriented program aimed in the direction of achieving near universal health care coverage for the state's population. Compared with SHIP, Hawaii QUEST is a major modification of how publicly supported health programs are administered and delivered. It approximates the "seamless" nature of public health care insurance coverage proposed by Lewin and others. Hawaii QUEST combines recipients of Medicaid (General Assistance and Aid to Families with Dependent Children) and SHIP into a large purchasing pool that is then bid to private health plans who provide a common benefit package at a capitated rate. Hawaii QUEST continues the Hawaii practice of providing a "rich" benefit package for Medicaid recipients, with former SHIP recipients gaining increased benefits, including increased numbers of physician visits and hospital stays. The plan was meant not to incur costs greater than those of the fee-for-service system that it replaced. The program gained $647 million in new federal funding over five years to support service delivery, and 90 percent of costs for a new Managed Care Information System.

Hawaii QUEST shifts publicly funded health care insurance from an entitlement structure to an insurance-based system. The emphasis on cost control is placed within the conventional structure of managed care plans in the existing health care market. As noted when discussing SHIP and the Prepaid Health Care Act, the medical insurance marketplace in Hawaii is dominated by HMSA and Kaiser. The first contracts awarded by the Department of Human Services in April 1994 went to five providers, of which HMSA was by far the largest. April 1995 enrollment data revealed that eighty thousand people were HMSA subscribers, twenty-seven thousand with the Queen's plan offered by Queen's Medical Center, eighteen thousand in Aloha Care, a network of physicians linked to the John A. Burns School of Medicine at the University of Hawaii, seventy-six hundred in Kaiser, and twenty-seven hundred in Straub, a smaller HMO with a hospital on Oahu. Subsequent enrollment has sustained those relative proportions. All five plans are available on Oahu, while individuals on other islands can choose from at least two plans. Two dental plans were awarded contracts (DentaCare and HMSA), and in November 1994 a contract was set for a behavioral health plan through HMSA-Biodyne. Standard Medicaid coverage on a fee-for-service basis continued for those receiving benefits under the aged, blind, and disabled categories. This population was intended to be covered under QUEST II, scheduled for implementation in 1997.

Hawaii QUEST proved to be wildly successful. The initial waiver request anticipated ninety thousand Medicaid and SHIP enrollees. By summer 1995 enrollment had topped 150,000 and officials knew they had made a serious miscalculation by not having required a means test for program eligibility. Early analysis of enrollment data indicated that sizable numbers of students had enrolled for Hawaii QUEST, as had many self-employed individuals for whom it was a highly desirable alternative to the purchase of nongroup insurance coverage on the open market. Program rules were rewritten effective July 1995 to make the program available only to those qualifying under the standard of countable assets equal to that required by SSI. Hawaii QUEST officials began efforts to have "overqualified" participants leave the program. Costs, of course, soared as the number of capitated individuals increased far above projected levels.

In June 1996 a new program, QUEST-net, was initiated as a "way-station" program for those who have been declared ineligible either for Hawaii QUEST or the continuing fee-for-service Medicaid program for the aged, blind, and disabled. Eligibility is limited to U.S. citizens or legal resident aliens who are residents of the state, who do not have health coverage, have income less than 300 percent of the federal poverty level, and have assets not exceeding $5,000 for individuals, $7,000 for a family of two, and $7,000 plus $500 per family member for a family of three or more. The plan provides limited medical coverage through a participating managed care program. Benefits include ten inpatient hospital days for medically necessary care, surgery, psychiatric care, and substance abuse treatment, twelve outpatient medical visits, six mental health visits, and limited prescription drugs. Emergency dental services are provided through enrollment in a participating dental plan. QUEST-net will be capped at forty thousand members.[17] QUEST-net operates not unlike a pared-down SHIP program for those who have left Hawaii QUEST.

Hawaii QUEST now provides health care for one of every seven Hawaii residents. What were initially viewed as dislocations in individual coverage caused by one-time implementation problems have developed into what amount to access problems for the most poor of QUEST subscribers who often experience transportation and administrative difficulties in obtaining care. These difficulties often include issues of culture and language, which in a very diverse multiethnic community like Hawaii can easily become barriers to care. Recent efforts to reduce Hawaii QUEST's enrollment, have created a significant burden for the community health centers whose own federal and state funding has been eroded over the past three years. At the Kalihi-Palama Health Center, which serves a lower-income and largely immigrant community, the share of uninsured patients in their caseload has jumped from 25 percent to 48 percent over the past four months.[18] Beth Giesting, executive director of the Hawaii State Primary Health Care Association, now sees Hawaii QUEST as a program with significant potential that it has failed to achieve.

The error of underestimating the number of persons who would seek coverage under the program was compounded by the belief that individuals removed from the program's rolls could have their needs met by the community health centers. As Giesting has put it, "health center funding has been hard-hit over the past two years. Before QUEST, the State Health Insurance Program had a fund to defray the costs of serving the uninsured. SHIP is gone and so is the fund." She concludes, "QUEST diverted resources from quality programs without providing offsetting benefits. It's time to create a new program."[19] In the face of such criticisms officials point to the state budget crisis as having exacerbated inevitable start-up problems, and to the relief that should come from QUEST-net for many who have been forced from Hawaii QUEST rolls.[20] Hawaii QUEST, unlike SHIP, generally does not pay for preventive services.

Health Care Reform and Gubernatorial Politics

In 1993 John Lewin resigned as director of the Department of Health and announced that he would run for governor of the state. In Hawaii, governors are constitutionally limited to two terms, and like many states, Hawaii has a long-standing tradition that the lieutenant governor becomes the leading candidate to succeed the incumbent. As a de facto one-party state, this presumption of succession is, if anything, even greater. Lewin chose to challenge Lieutenant Governor Cayetano, who had served for eight years following many terms in the legislature. After a slow start, Cayetano demonstrated that he could garner the support of traditional Democratic Party big-money contributors and the party's electoral apparatus, which has proved formidable. Lewin built his campaign on grassroots support, fashioning himself as an "outsider" to the existing Democratic Party machine that had been much damaged by charges of cronyism and corruption—the legacy of which he attributed (without real cause) to Cayetano. His primary campaign appeal was as the health care reformer par excellence, a person who had both currency and access to the national administration, a cocreator of the health state, and as one who saw health as far more than mere access to medical insurance. Lewin's vision of the health state included notions of revived community participation, community empowerment, and a general legitimization of the principle that health promotion is a positive and necessary requirement of overall social well-being.

With very little campaign money, Lewin received over 40 percent of the primary vote, but lost to Cayetano, who went on to narrowly win the general election against two opponents, former Republican congresswoman Patricia Sakai and long-time mayor of Honolulu Frank Fasi. Subsequent events have demonstrated that far more was at stake in this election than was apparent during the campaign. Cayetano entered office to discover that the budget situation caused by rapidly declining state revenues was far worse than he had anticipated. Literally his first act as governor was to announce a budget crisis and begin a process of cutback measures. These have targeted a significant number of state agencies and departments for reductions or elimination, reduced the eligibility and funding for numerous state assistance programs, including General Assistance, withdrawn almost 30 percent of state funding from the University of Hawaii (which includes the community colleges, a supplier of health-sector workers), and reduced the state workforce. In his second State of the State message, in January 1996, Cayetano laid out a theory of government that combined a commitment to crisis budget management with the entirety of David Osborne and Ted Gaebler's well-known text, *Reinventing Government*. Like George Ariyoshi before him, Cayetano has proved a fiscally conservative Democrat; going beyond Ariyoshi, he has also demonstrated that his notion of modern government includes a significant reduction of the policy space occupied by the public sector, and a retreat from the social welfare liberalism for which Hawaii has been known. More than any recent Democratic political actor of note, he has conducted himself in office as a committed neoconservative.

Lewin would have, arguably, proved a very different governor, especially in health care matters. Cayetano's view of health care has three basic dimensions: as a potential tourist industry specialization, as a public expenditure that must be limited, and as a public policy area that must be deregulated. On the latter count, for example, one of the agencies he initially targeted for elimination was the State Health Planning and Development Agency (SHPDA). The legislature demurred from this plan and created a task force to review the agency. Cayetano and his current director of health, Dr. Larry Mieke, the former medical director of Hawaii QUEST, were unsympathetic to the review, which was completed in the fall of 1996, and gave only token support to a reform measure in the legislature that would have acknowledged market-oriented reforms but retained the agency. Cayetano, as noted above, has been a long-time advocate of drawing "headliner" medical facilities to Hawaii, such as the Mayo Clinic, which would have a strong appeal to an Asian market. SHPDA and its certificate of need processes, designed to limit costs by controlling market capacity, would place a potential barrier before such a plan—ergo Cayetano's desire to see the agency eliminated.[21]

Lewin's notions of further health care reform for Hawaii would also have focused on market-oriented transformations, but with some key differences. Lewin wanted Hawaii to become a leader in managed care versions of publicly financed programs while simultaneously creating a climate for quality improvement based on public outcome measures for health care providers. His historic commitment to publicly funded programs for care, such as General Assistance, was predicated on a recognition that in Hawaii, all persons receiving that care are physician-certified for some form of disability, whereas the current administration has permitted the budget crisis to serve as a pretext for cutting General Assistance as just another welfare program needing reform. Further, Lewin's focus on health promotion in the broader sense has been de-emphasized within the Department of Health since his departure, which has been reorganized to eliminate divisions dedicated to this purpose—moves that, again, have been justified as budget cutting strategies.

The Lessons of Hawaii

Overall, the tide in health care reform in Hawaii appears to have turned from an effort to place the state at the forefront of innovations designed to provide universal coverage while ensuring a measure of effective cost control, to more generalized and conventional programs directed toward inducing cost control through market-oriented reforms. During the period that the Waihee administration was courting national favor in the health care debate it became fashionable, locally, to speak of the "lessons" in Hawaii health care for the rest of the nation. Lewin emphasized four such lessons.

Lesson 1: Primary care works to contain health care costs. Hawaii's health indicators show the following (even taking into account the poorer health status of Native Hawaiians and other Polynesian peoples): lowest infant mortality in the United States (tied with Vermont); lowest rates of premature mortality in the nation for heart disease (one-third less than the national average), cancer (one-fourth less than the national average), and lung disease (one-half the national average); low hospital use (one-third less than the national average); and low emergency-room use rates (one-third less than the national average). These outcomes may be explained by individuals' access to effective care at reasonable costs, and by the fact that Hawaii's doctors historically have emphasized outpatient care. What makes health care work in Hawaii, John Lewin has argued, is doing "standard stuff" correctly: "Early detection of potentially life threatening conditions results in low premature mortality and low hospitalization. Our people are healthier not because of unique genetics, healthy climate or high tech medicine, but because they have access to primary care."

Lesson 2: Mandated employer coverage can be an effective tool for universal access. The argument here is that mandated employer coverage levels the playing field for all and yet can be structured to provide significant choice of coverage and payment options (meaning that under some circumstances employees can be required to pay portions of the cost).

Lesson 3: Strong insurance reforms must accompany an employer mandate. The key reform is the creation of a community rating, a necessary prerequisite to affordable insurance rates. Hawaii, in part because of the existence of its two nonprofit carriers and the guaranteed market provided by Prepaid, has enjoyed a voluntary rating that has helped to keep rates low.

Lesson 4: Costs can be controlled. Hawaii's costs are significantly less than the rest of the United States, about 12 percent of state domestic product compared with 14 percent nationally. Again, near universal access has been the key as the availability of early, inexpensive treatment tends to eliminate later, more expensive care. When all (or nearly all) have access to care, options are then open to insurance companies to pursue strategies that can further control costs.[22]

The events of the past five years have begun to cloud these "lessons from Hawaii," at least when measured in terms of aggregate cost control. The data are mixed and the phenomena are in flux. For example, analysis of Health Care Financing Administration data on costs in Hawaii through 1991 indicates that during the decade of the 1980s physician and hospital costs in Hawaii moved toward convergence with national rates, with physician costs declining from above normal and hospital costs rising from below normal.[23] These data temper the generalizations offered by Lewin and suggest that Hawaii's edge in cost control may be slipping vis-à-vis national experiences. To the extent some edge remains, the advantage appears to be in part because Hawaii has relatively greater primary care access (a legacy of the historic plantation economy that developed clinics in plantation communities). Hawaii also has fewer hospital beds per capita than many other states, and on average shorter lengths of stay. The retrenchment of hospital facilities in the face of declining health care revenues and a more competitive marketplace has probably been less significant than in sister states. These are all relative measures. In general they suggest that Hawaii is coming to look more like other states in its health care provider profile than it did a decade ago when differences, largely due to the effects of the Prepaid Health Care Act, were larger.

Another question is whether the overall effect of health reform legislation has reduced medical expenditures in Hawaii. The data to date are difficult to interpret. First, Hawaii QUEST was made necessary by the extraordinary growth of fee-for-service Medicaid in the late 1980s and early 1990s. The inception of that program moved most previously qualified Medicaid recipients into Hawaii QUEST and, as we have seen, high program enrollment has dissipated the projected savings accruing from the shift to managed care, some $60 million in the first full year of program operation. Those who remained, some thirty thousand individuals in the aged, blind, and disabled categories, continue to employ fee-for-service care at rates significantly above budgeted levels. For example, Susan Chandler, the head of the Department of Human Services, announced in May 1996 that the department had no more funds to pay providers for Medicaid services in fiscal 1996, and in fact owed some $60 million in payments at the end of April.[24] The state is eager to cover these three categories by managed care in 1997 because officials believe there is no effective way to control fee-for-service spending. At this level of generalization, the movement toward managed care in capitated programs reduces public expenditure.

The second piece of data concerns the utilization of managed care programs by those eligible for publicly funded support. A comparison of managed care capitation rates with fee-for-service rates points to the success of these structures for containing public funding. The influx of Hawaii QUEST subscribers before the establishment of strict eligibility criteria suggests that state efforts to achieve universality prior to this program had left large pockets of uninsured persons in the population. Efforts to determine the size of this "residual gap group" have periodically produced confusing and conflicting estimates. The unexpected success of the program surprised officials who had worked in this policy arena for many years. Because the large number of subscribers to Hawaii QUEST increased the aggregate level of state spending on this category of health care expenditures, sought-after savings will only be available by reducing per capita expenditures in managed care environments.

Third, like many other places Hawaii is experiencing a shakedown in its medical services establishment. Over two thousand nurses became unemployed in the eighteen months between January 1995 and mid-1996. Even as Hawaii's hospital establishment has been lean by the standards of many sister states, it has nonetheless demonstrated that it can and will contract quickly as a result of "feeding the system" less money—a clear intention of managed care as a policy tool. The effect that this will have on outcomes, a universal concern in all managed care growth environments, remains to be determined. Physicians in Hawaii, as elsewhere, continue to decry the deterioration of doctor/patient relationships that accompanies managed care.[25] Hawaii is now in the process of developing a statewide data system (situated within the private sector and financed by providers) that will permit future longitudinal examination of this question. The reduction of cost shifting, a major goal of Medicaid reform in Hawaii, has been significantly affected by the payment structure of Hawaii QUEST.

Finally, the cost of health care reform is differentially borne within the community. The community health care centers have been negatively affected by Hawaii QUEST, as portions of their clientele have been redirected to other providers and their state and federal funding is reduced. Some long time players in the field of health care reform in Hawaii believe that too much ground may have been lost in attempting to assure gap-group care. Andrew Levin, chair of the Senate Health Committee, has said recently, "it seems we made a decision to save money and serve fewer people," in response to the finding that Hawaii had slipped to sixth among the states in the universality of care.[26] House Health Committee chair Len Pepper, who continues to be frustrated with Medicaid cost overruns, anticipates continuing budgetary problems with the fee-for-service aspects of the program. Hawaii QUEST satisfies few players in the health care environment.

1997 will be critical for Hawaii as it seeks to shake off the budget shortfall caused by its weakened economy. Should that occur—and economic signs have improved throughout the past twelve months—the Cayetano administration must assess its commitment to the principle of universality in the face of stubborn financial problems that persist in the financing of long-term care and providing services for the aged, blind, and disabled. David Wilsford has recently suggested that European nations appear to be struggling with the same set of problems observed in Hawaii in recent years: a weakened economy producing fewer government revenues to fund health care programs organized around principles of universality. In many of these nations conservative leaders have proposed a shrinking of the state and a reduced commitment to social welfare programs in general. In virtually every situation, moves toward privatization and market competition are paired with managed care in the reform policy package.[27] Hawaii, which for many years more nearly resembled a European social democratic health care construction than those employed by its sister American states may—perhaps inadvertently—be once again leading the way to an emergent solution to this policy problem. In this case, however, it is a retreat from a commitment to universal care.

Notes

I would like to thank Robert Grossman, former legislative assistant to James Shon and subsequently special assistant to John Lewin, for his contributions to the original draft of this paper. Lynn Anne Mulrooney provided valuable assistance with the revised version, for which I am deeply appreciative.

1. The overall death rate of Native Hawaiians is 34 percent higher than that of the total U.S. population. This group also experiences distinctly higher rates for heart diseases, cancer, cerebrovascular disease, and diabetes mellitus. Eldon Wegner, "A Framework for Assessing Health Needs," *Social Process in Hawaii* 32 (1989): 32–54. Actual life expectancies for all ethnic groups combined are 76.6 years for males and 82.7 years for females. By contrast, Hawaiian males have a life expectancy of 71 years and females 76.6 years. State of Hawaii, Department of Health, *Vital Statistics Supplement, 1993* (Office of Health Status Monitoring, May 1995), 27.

2. Mele A. Look and Kathryn L. Braun, *A Mortality Study of the Hawaiian People 1910–1990* (Honolulu: Queen's Health Systems, 1995), 2, 7.

3. "Medicare Is Running Out of Money," *Honolulu Advertiser,* April 11, 1994, A–8.

4. In 1996 HMSA served approximately 700,000 members, while Kaiser served 190,000. Dr. Fred Fortin, HMSA vice president for community relations and legislative affairs, interview by author, July 9, 1996.

5. Emily Friedman, *The Aloha Way: Health Care Structure and Finance in Hawaii* (Honolulu: Hawaii Medical Service Foundation, 1993), 57.

6. Ibid.

7. Stefan A. Riesenfeld, *Prepaid Health Care in Hawaii* (Honolulu: University of Hawaii Legislative Reference Bureau, Report No. 2, 1971), 9. Note Riesenfeld's reasoning: "The newest development in the field of compulsory health insurance is the President's announcement of his Family Health Insurance Plan for children. . . . Legislative proposals are promised for January 1971. . . . Finally, it should be noted that the general desirability of prepayment plan protection against medical cost was again strongly stressed in the June 1970 recommendations of the United States Department of Health, Education and Welfare, Task Force on Medicaid and Related Programs."

8. State of Hawaii, *House Journal,* 1974, 500.

9. John Lewin, interview by author, October 29, 1990.

10. John Lewin, "From Vision to Reality: Insurance Plan Establishes Hawaii as the Health State," Department of Health, *Hawaii Health Messenger* 52, no. 2 (1989), 1.

11. Ibid.

12. Center for Health Research, Kaiser Permanente, and the School of Public Health, University of Hawaii, *The State Insurance Program of Hawaii: From Legislative Priority to Reality,* vol. 1, 1991, 5–15.

13. News release from the Executive Chambers of the Governor, December 7, 1990, 1.

14. *Report of the Governor's Blue Ribbon Panel on Health Care,* Honolulu, Blue Ribbon Panel, September 1992, 12–13. [Editor's Note: Neubauer served as a facilitator for the panel in its last five months, authoring most of its report.]

15. For a more complete discussion of Blue Ribbon Panel politics, see D. Neubauer, "Hawaii: A Pioneer in Health System Reform," *Health Affairs* 12 (summer 1993): 31–39.

16. A fuller discussion of QUEST is provided in Annette Gardner and Deane Neubauer, "Hawaii's Health QUEST," *Health Affairs* 14 (spring 1995): 300–304.

17. State of Hawaii, Department of Human Services, Med-QUEST Division, Notice of Public Hearing, no date.

18. Angela Miller, "Health Plan Hasn't Gone as Proposed," *Honolulu Advertiser,* June 9, 1996, A-25.

19. Beth Giesting, "QUEST: A Check-up, It Takes Funds from Programs That Worked," *Honolulu Advertiser,* June 9, 1996, B-3.

20. Winifred Odo, "QUEST: A Check-up, Health Plan Doing Its Job Despite Problems," *Honolulu Advertiser,* June 9, 1996, B-3.

21. Some disclosure may be appropriate at this point. This writer served as the chair of the legislatively mandated task force review of SHPDA. Its report, recommending a revised agency with a mandatory evaluation and sunset provision, was presented to the governor in late December 1995. The administration did not support the recommendations, and continued in its efforts to eliminate the agency. The legislature supported the agency in its current form with reduced funding.

22. John C. Lewin and Peter Sybinsky, "Hawaii's Employer Mandate and Its Contribution to Universal Access," *Journal of the American Medical Association* 269, (May 19, 1993): 2538–43. Sybinsky was Lewin's long-time deputy and became health director when Lewin ran for governor.

23. D. Neubauer, "Health Care Costs in Hawaii," in *The Unfinished Health Agenda: Lessons from Hawaii,* ed. R. Grossman and J. Shon (Honolulu: Hawaii Primary Care Association, 1994): 53–74.

24. Helen Altonn, "Medicaid: State Will Start Fiscal Year with Health Care Debt," *Honolulu Star Bulletin,* May 30, 1996, A-1, A-9.

25. Fred C. Holschuh, "QUEST: A Check-up, Patient-Doctor Relationship Needs Protection," *Honolulu Advertiser,* June 9, 1996, B-3.

26. Helen Altonn, "Hawaii Losing Its Top 'Health State' Ranking," *Honolulu Star-Bulletin,* June 13, 1996, A-7.

27. David Wilsford, "States Facing Interests: Struggles over Health Care Policy in Advanced Industrial Democracies," *Journal of Health Politics, Policy and Law* 20, no. 3, (fall 1995): 571–613.

8

The Little State That Could—Couldn't: Vermont Stumbles on the Road to Reform

Howard M. Leichter

Many national media and health policy observers deemed it "inconceivable that Vermont would pass no health system plan" in 1994.[1] Vermonters shared and encouraged this view. In July 1993 a state medical society official told a gathering of health policy experts that "if we can't do this in Vermont, it can't be done."[2] And, on the eve of the 1994 legislative session the Speaker of the Vermont House of Representatives said: "This tiny and different state is on the brink of decision, and the rest of America awaits our action with curiosity and amazement."[3]

Vermont policymakers could be forgiven their hubris and hyperbole; they were still on a political high from the much publicized, if overly romanticized, health reform legislation (Act 160) they had forged in 1992. Among other things, that law promised that the 1994 general assembly would complete the journey begun two years earlier and guarantee to all Vermonters "access to quality health services at costs which are affordable." State leaders were convinced that their little state would become the first in the nation to achieve the goal of universal access and cost containment. To the amazement of many, however, the 1994 Vermont General Assembly adjourned, after its longest session in decades, without taking any action on health care reform.

It is tempting, in view of the high expectations and exposure attending Vermont's reform effort, to ask, "What went wrong ?" It is sobering when the answer comes back from some in the state: "Nothing went wrong." In fact, in the minds of several legislators, on both the political left and right, the Vermont legislature accomplished something quite notable in 1994—it stopped "bad" legislation. This perspective provides insight into one of the most important "lessons from Vermont": the political center—that is, those willing to accept an incremental approach to health care reform—was neither well enough defined nor well enough organized to carry the burden of reform. This, in turn, gave the left and the right a license not to legislate. Vermont lawmakers would return to the reform process again in 1995 but adopt a much more modest plan than the one reformers had envisioned in 1992. This chapter traces Vermont's long history of health care reform.

The Road to Health Care Reform

The antecedents of the Vermont Health Reform Act can be traced at least as far back as 1979, when the state enacted a certificate-of-need (CON) law requiring hospitals and other health care institutions to apply to the Health Department for review and approval of new capital expenditures and the introduction of new health services. In 1987 this responsibility was moved to an independent, quasi-judicial CON board, and in 1990 the process was expanded to review some physician office services. It is indicative of the generally positive relationship that has existed between the state and health care providers that, contrary to the experiences in other states, CON receives high praise in Vermont. This relationship was taken a step further in 1983 with the creation of a Hospital Data Council. The five-member council was responsible for conducting annual budget reviews of Vermont's eighteen nonprofit hospitals and making cost control recommendations. In addition, it collected and analyzed financial and utilization data provided by the hospitals. The council was abolished in 1996 and its functions, along with the CON process, were transferred to a newly expanded Department of Insurance, Banking, Securities, and Health Care Administration.

Vermont's first foray into dealing with its uninsured population came in 1987 when the legislature created the Vermont Health Insurance Plan (VHIP). The legislation set up a VHIP board comprising of representatives of low income people, business groups, and the provider industry. The board was charged with studying ways to extend health insurance to the uninsured. The following year it recommended a play-or-pay option for Vermont businesses, and a state subsidy to finance a basic package of health services for the state's uninsured population. Neither the Vermont General

Assembly nor Governor Madeline Kunin (D) was willing to support a significant increase in state spending on health care at that time. The 1988 legislature did, however, extend access to uninsured children up to age seven, and women whose family incomes were above the Medicaid eligibility level but below 225 percent of poverty. This became the Prenatal and Children's Health Program (or "Dr. Dynasaur," as it is popularly known), a highly successful and popular state effort.

Three years later Vermont took yet another step down the road to reform. In March 1991 Governor Richard Snelling (R) created the Vermont Blue Ribbon Commission on Health. The commission was "to explore and design a comprehensive group of proposals" that would, among other things, ensure "access to adequate health care for all Vermonters."[4] In its final report to the governor on the eve of the 1992 legislative session, the commission proposed "that universal health care should be available to all Vermont residents."

Finally, the backdrop to the 1992 reform also included a significant legislative victory during the 1991 session when the Vermont General Assembly approved a law (Act 52) requiring insurance companies to use community rating and guaranteed acceptance of clients in writing policies for the small-group health insurance market. Act 52 became law with the support of Governor Snelling, despite insurance company warnings that many carriers would cease writing small-group policies in Vermont if the bill were enacted.

The importance of Act 52 cannot be overstated. Legislators realized that they could take on one of the most powerful forces in the health field—and win. As one lobbyist for the insurance industry explained it: "Something happened in 1991. In the first place, the legislature found they could actually enact a bill with community rating. After all this labor, they'd given birth to this thing. They pinched themselves and found out the sun still came up in the morning, and it could be done."[5]

In August 1991 Governor Snelling died and was succeeded in office by the Democratic lieutenant governor, Howard Dean, M.D., an internist who, until he became governor, continued to practice medicine. It is important to underscore the importance of Howard Dean's becoming governor on the timing, tempo, and tenor of the reform effort. When *Governor* Dean speaks, the views of *Dr.* Dean are never entirely obscured. Dr. Dean, for example, shares the distaste of his colleagues for federal micromanagement of medical practices, especially through the much-hated Medicare program. "I hate micromanagement," says Howard Dean. "My biggest fear has been . . . that the federal government would impose Medicare for everybody, and that would be national health care. And, in that case I think you would see the end of decent health care in this country. I didn't want to see that in Vermont."[6]

Howard Dean, then, brought a unique level of knowledge and a physician's perspective to the reform process. Like John Kitzhaber in Oregon, he helped assuage the concerns of the provider community, a group deeply concerned about its ability to participate in the reform process.

The Vermont Health Reform Act: The Legislative Process

Two things were clear as the state's political leadership prepared for the 1992 legislative session: there was broad and deep support for health care reform, and the option with the most visibility was Senate Bill 127 (S.B. 127), a bill that would provide universal access to a comprehensive package of health care benefits through a single-payer insurance system. S.B. 127 was the creation of two progressive (i.e., left leaning) state senators, Cheryl Rivers and Sally Conrad, who during the previous summer had traveled the state stimulating and cultivating popular support for their single-payer plan—and raising the anxiety level of several key players in the game.

In this effort, Rivers and Conrad were joined by two liberal Vermont political heavyweights. The first was the state branch of the National Educational Association, Vermont-NEA, with nearly eight thousand members and one of the best lobbying organizations in the state. The second force behind the single-payer campaign was Vermont's maverick, and politically astute, congressman, Bernie Sanders (I). Sanders used his considerable political organization and skills on behalf of the single-payer idea, appearing on several occasions with Rivers at meetings and rallies in support of S.B. 127.

Coalition Building

Some who opposed S.B. 127 did so on ideological grounds: it involved too much government intervention. Others, like Howard Dean and Jeanne Keller, president of the Vermont Employers Alliance, felt the bill was a fiscal and policy leap in the dark. The Vermont State Medical Society had yet another reason to oppose the bill. In both its original (1991) and revised (January 1992) form, S.B. 127 specifically excluded health care providers from participation in the proposed health care authority. The medical society, and its member physicians, found this both troubling and offensive. As one Vermont State Medical Society official explained it, the deliberate and pointed exclusion of providers was interpreted as a message to physicians saying, "You will not participate in this. You are the bad guys. You are the ones to be regulated. We will set your reimbursement, and if you don't like it, that's just too bad."[7]

For a variety of reasons, then, S.B. 127 became the magnet that impelled an opposing coalition including the business community, hospital association, medical society, Blue Cross/Blue Shield, Governor Dean, the Democratic Speaker of the House, and the Republican House majority leader. As one player explained, "It was fairly easy in some ways for us to build the necessary coalition if we could find something to bind it together. There needed to be a common goal, and the common goal really was [defeat of] S.B. 127."[8]

In December 1991 the Democratic House Speaker Ralph Wright announced his intention to pursue health reform in the upcoming session. A month earlier Wright and Governor Dean had agreed to join forces in this effort. Since the state had a $57.2 million deficit, both the Speaker and the governor agreed that such reform would have to be gradual and not require a significant investment of new money.

Very early in the process, after some hesitation, the Republican leadership, which had created its own task force on reform, decided to sign on to the Dean-Wright plan. Despite partisan considerations, the Wright bill, H.B. 733, shared enough in common with the Blue Ribbon Commission report—which had been created by a Republican governor and chaired by a former Republican state senator—to provide common ground for significant substantive agreement. The bill had one other important virtue; it was not a single-payer plan. The Wright bill was introduced in the House in January 1992 and in almost unprecedented fashion was cosponsored by the Speaker, the Republican majority and assistant majority leaders, and two assistant Democratic minority leaders.

As originally drafted, the bill provided for the establishment of a three-member health care authority that would, among other things: design a health care data base, adopt annual health care expenditure targets, establish a statewide health care resource management plan, conduct hospital budget reviews, administer the certificate-of-need program, design a common benefits program that would constitute a minimum standard for health insurance plans offered in Vermont, design and implement a unified system of purchasing medical supplies and equipment, and "serve as the administrator and single negotiator with hospitals and providers for common benefits provided through the plan."

H.B. 733 contained two other significant proposals. The first built upon the insurance reform of the previous legislature, and proposed expanding community rating to the nongroup (i.e., individual) insurance market. To some, including the governor, this provision would offer the most important immediate benefit of the act. It would also prove to be one of the most contentious issues. Nongroup community rating would make affordable health insurance more accessible to some Vermonters (older people, and those with preexisting medical conditions), but more costly to others (younger, healthier people).

A second issue that would prove contentious was malpractice reform, a matter of considerable importance to two powerful lobbies, physicians and attorneys. The legislative finding introducing the tort reform section reflected the main concerns of both physicians and plaintiffs: the system is slow, costly, inaccessible to many, and seemingly unconnected to quality assurance in medical practice. Finally, the bill addressed the extreme administrative fragmentation of the state's current health care system by bringing various preexisting state agencies under the jurisdiction of the new health authority.

Legislative Politics

Problems began for H.B. 733 when jurisdictional and personal conflicts emerged between the Health and Welfare Committee, to which the bill was originally assigned, and the Commerce Committee. The chairman of the Commerce Committee was Paul Harrington (R), a highly regarded legislator with considerable experience in insurance reform—it was his committee that had crafted Act 52 the previous year. Harrington believed that H.B. 733 was poorly drafted and wanted his committee to have a more active role in revising the bill than would be the case if the Health and Welfare Committee retained dominant jurisdiction. An agreement was worked out whereby the Health and Welfare Committee released the bill to Commerce, where it would receive full scrutiny. Harrington, along with the chairperson of Health and Welfare, redrafted the bill.

With a redraft in its possession and greater autonomy over its content, the Commerce Committee proceeded to address all aspects of the bill. The result was several weeks of sometimes strained exchanges between the two committees (three additional committees, Judiciary, Appropriations, and Government Operations, looked at the bill as well) as each held public hearings and brought different perspectives to the task.

Meanwhile, lurking in the shadows was the single-payer lobby. Fortunately a solution to what might well have been an ugly political battle between the single-payer forces and the coalition behind H.B. 733 presented itself just five weeks into the legislative session. At Paul Harrington's suggestion, Speaker Wright offered Senators Conrad and Rivers a deal: they would abandon S.B. 127, allow H.B. 733 through Senate Health and Welfare, and not insist upon a specific funding mechanism for any reform bill (Rivers's bill proposed a payroll tax). In return the Speaker would offer certain concessions, including a requirement in the law that the health care authority report back to the legislature with *two* universal health plans, one a single-payer, the other a regulated multipayer, and accelerate this report from 1995, as proposed by the governor, to 1994, and postponement of medical malpractice reform until universal access to health care was achieved. Single-payer advocates believed that the proper emphasis of reform was the consumer, not physicians; hence, the providers should receive no benefits from reform before the consumers did. Rivers and Conrad agreed immediately to the terms of the compromise. A single-payer system was dead in Vermont, at least for the immediate future; and the prospects of H.B. 733 were indeed looking up.

With the deal, a major impediment to passage of H.B. 733 was removed— or so it seemed. Although the single-payer plan was dead, at least for this session, Sally Conrad and Cheryl Rivers were still very much alive. Their main concession was to concede the political battlefield to H.B. 733; they did not abandon their right to try to change that bill once it got to the Senate.

On February 21, about six weeks after it began work on the bill, the House Health and Welfare Committee voted unanimously to recommend H.B. 733 to the full House. The major provisions of the committee bill, which for the most part were adopted by the full House, included creation of a Health Care Authority; development of two plans for universal access to health care; mechanisms for cost control, including hospital budget reviews, a health care management plan, global budgeting, utilization review procedures, and uniform health insurance forms and claims procedures; a health insurance purchasing pool; community rating of the nongroup market; and medical malpractice reform. The House approved the measure a week later by a vote of 119 to 17.

H.B. 733 now entered the much less friendly arena of the Vermont Senate where the progressives enjoyed greater strength and the bill would be taken up by Senator Conrad's Health and Welfare Committee. Depending on who tells it, the five-member Senate Health and Welfare Committee, with two progressive Democrats (Conrad and Rivers) and one staunchly conservative Republican, either "eviscerated" the bill or "improved" it.[9] The critical moment in the process came on March 10 when the committee voted 3 to 2 to strip H.B. 733 of the insurance purchasing pool, community rating, and medical malpractice reform. The result was explosive. As Cheryl Rivers described it, "Once we took those sections out of the bill, all hell broke loose."[10]

Conrad and Rivers had several objections to H.B. 733. First, it did not immediately address the needs of the state's sixty thousand or so uninsured people. Second, they were concerned that community rating would drive insurers from the state, leaving thousands of Vermonters without coverage or alternative carriers. This concern was a bit more than theoretical since insurance companies were threatening precisely that. Third, insurers warned that many Vermonters faced "rate shock" when community rating went into effect. This would happen to younger and healthier Vermonters who would subsidize the decreased premiums that older, sicker folks would be paying under the community rating and guaranteed acceptance provisions of the legislation. Many in the legislature, including the two senators, were hearing from constituents who were being informed of this danger by their insurance companies.

Ultimately the governor's staff and the two senators worked out a compromise with three major provisions:

- The creation of an insurance "safety net" to protect individuals who would lose their insurance because their insurer has pulled out of the Vermont market;
- To avoid "rate shock," the commissioner of banking, insurance, and securities would set maximum annual premium percentage rate increases. Under no circumstances could the commissioner approve a rate increase greater than 20 percent in any year;
- Health care benefits under the "Dr. Dynasaur" program for non-Medicaid-eligible children and pregnant women would be extended up to age eighteen from its current limit of age six. In addition, current co-payments in the program would be eliminated.

The next obstacle to H.B. 733 was in the Senate Judiciary Committee, where the state's bar and trial lawyers associations successfully lobbied to prohibit admission of the malpractice arbitration board's findings in a jury trial. The lawyers argued that jurors should not be exposed to any nonjudicial decisions that might influence their judgment. At this point the Vermont State Medical Society threatened to withdraw its support if the committee's decision was not reversed. Nevertheless, the Judiciary Committee approved the change and sent it on to the full Senate. The Dean administration and the Speaker were clearly troubled by the possible defection of the medical society.

The bill's next test came in the full Senate. Insurance companies, which had unsuccessfully fought to remove the community rating provision, marshaled their forces for one last assault. The industry strategy was to emphasize the harm that community rating would cause many, especially younger, Vermonters. Lobbyists from both the Health Insurance Association of America (HIAA) and individual insurance companies appeared before legislative committees to argue that community rating would dramatically increase the premiums of younger policyholders. The industry left little doubt what it would do if community rating were approved: "there is a high probability that many of the carriers that are in Vermont now will not be in Vermont [next year] to sell policies."[11] The insurance industry had, however, few friends in the Senate and that body easily defeated an effort to remove community rating. Next, the senators overrode their Judiciary Committee colleagues and voted to admit an arbitration panel's decision as evidence in a malpractice suit jury trial. On April 13 the Senate passed H.B. 733 by a vote of 23 to 4.

It remained now for the House and Senate to iron out the nearly thirty, mostly minor, differences between the two measures, which they did. The conference report went back to each house where it was approved overwhelmingly. The legislative and administrative structures were now in place for Vermont to take the next major step toward achieving universal access to affordable health care.

The Way It Was Supposed to Be

Act 160 seemed the ideal road map for completing the journey. The newly created Vermont Health Care Authority (VHCA or the Authority) was authorized to implement various reforms, including nongroup insurance community rating, and effectively expand Medicaid access to more children from low-income families through the state's "Dr. Dynasaur" program. In addition, the VHCA was to inventory the state's health resources, develop a uniform benefits plan and a global budget, and prepare two universal access plans, one a single-payer system, the other a regulated multipayer system.

By the time the Vermont General Assembly convened in January 1994 much of the work needed to reform the state's health care system would be completed and the politicians could then make the necessary political choices. That was the vision, but that did not turn out to be the reality. By the time the legislature convened, the VHCA had become the subject of controversy that both adumbrated and contributed to the difficult legislative task ahead. A growing chorus of critics was declaring that the Health Care Authority was "a massive political failure."[12]

The Vermont Health Care Authority: A "Political Disaster"

The VHCA began operation in August 1992, and one can trace many of its problems back to Act 160 itself. Both critics and supporters acknowledge that the law bequeathed to the VHCA an overly ambiguous, ambitious, and politically perilous mandate. As one board member said, given the legislative charge to the VHCA under Act 160 the "process didn't work and in hindsight it probably never could have worked."[13] There was, to begin, both perceptual and statutory ambiguity about the precise political location and responsibility of the Authority. Part of the difficulty was that the agency had both regulatory (e.g., certificate of need, hospital budget approval) and policy development responsibilities. Although not unprecedented, this duality of functions created uncertainty about whether the VHCA was primarily a state regulatory agency, a data gathering and analysis group, or a policy-making arm of the governor's office.

This ambiguity remained and became an institutional liability, particularly with regard to the Authority's role in proposing the two universal access plans. As one of the agency's most persistent critics, the head of the Vermont State Medical Society argues that the VHCA failed in its responsibility to build political consensus around the universal access plans.[14] Others, including members of the governor's staff, believe that Act 160 never gave the VHCA the responsibility of political or policy advocacy.[15] Yet Paul Harrington, now a VHCA board member, admits that in hindsight the Authority should have been given more of a political role in the sense of advocating a particular plan. According to Harrington, developing two separate plans without taking a position on either one was "unwise": "It is hard enough for people to understand one plan and to garner support for a plan. To come forward with two plans without being able to say this one would make more sense for Vermonters than the other really made our work more a theoretical exercise than a process that would assist the General Assembly."[16] Whether the Authority's mandate was ambiguous, faulty, or merely misinterpreted, the result was that different actors had divergent and often irreconcilable expectations of the agency.

Some of the organization's problems were, however, of its own making. One such problem was the VHCA's failure to assuage the fears of various stakeholders that they might not have "a place at the bargaining table." Many key players came to believe that they had been excluded from, or at the very least slighted in, the reform process. For example, various citizen advocacy groups complained that the panels established by the VHCA were dominated by business, insurance, and health provider interests to the virtual exclusion and detriment of the general public. A member of the Vermont Consumers' Campaign for Health charged, for example, that the VHCA "a few months into its process has basically eliminated the public." By one estimate only 21 of the 102 people serving on the five major advisory committees to the VHCA were "unaffiliated consumers or representatives from consumer groups," a number that was much too low as far as critics were concerned.[17]

The Authority Alienates the Provider Lobby

Providers as well as consumers of health care shared the view that they were being neglected by the VHCA. Thus, alternative health care practitioners, including chiropractors, naturopaths, acupuncturists, lactation consultants, and massage therapists, as well as nonphysician providers such as alcohol and substance abuse professionals and nursing home operators, complained that they and those who use their services were inadequately represented in the reform process. More important to the fate of reform, however, was the sense of exclusion felt by traditional medical care providers. Indeed, nowhere were the procedural and public relations failures of the VHCA more evident, and nowhere did they prove more detrimental to the reform process than with this group. Both the Vermont State Medical Society (VSMS) and the Vermont Hospital Association (VHA) had been central players in the passage of Act 160, and both expected to occupy center stage once again. Yet by the fall of 1993 these two groups were off in the wings of reform.

Of the two provider organizations, the state medical society was the more alienated. Although the physicians' group certainly took exception to some of the VHCA's substantive proposals, it was over the failure to grant formal bargaining status to the VSMS that relations deteriorated. Since the time of the debate over Act 160 the physician community had been obsessed with securing a place at the bargaining table. The medical society's support for Act 160 was in no small part tied to a provision of the law that allowed the VHCA to create "health care provider bargaining groups" to negotiate two issues of vital concern to physicians, namely, the health care budget and provider reimbursement.

The VSMS expected to be recognized as an official bargaining group once the VHCA adopted the necessary rules. But by April 1993, eight months after the Authority was formed, the administrative rules had still not been written. According to Karen Meyer, executive director of the medical society, "We were told at that time that they didn't have time to do it."[18] As a result, Meyer said, physicians were "bitterly disappointed." Once a favored participant in the reform process, the VSMS saw its role considerably diminished and its enthusiasm for reform commensurably dampened.

Although provider community alienation was an unforeseen blow to reform, the strained relationship between the VHCA and the single-payer lobby was a bit more predictable—and only slightly less hobbling to the enterprise. Single-payer advocates had, by and large, been reluctant supporters of Act 160. To the extent they held out hope for favorable action by the VHCA, it was because Act 160 required the Authority to provide the legislature with both a regulated multipayer plan and a single-payer plan.

Such hope was relatively short-lived. By the summer of 1993 singlepayer advocates were accusing the VHCA of failing to develop a "true" single-payer model. The view that the Authority had slighted the singlepayer option was shared by leaders of the state's Democratic Party. In mid-November delegates to a state party meeting approved a resolution criticizing the Authority for not developing a "genuine" single-payer model.

Not to be slighted, the political right also weighed in on the issue of the VHCA's unfaithfulness to Act 160. Republican leaders charged that "the Authority has substituted its own invention for the clearly stated legislative intent of the General Assembly."[19] Of particular concern here was the VHCA's proposal to create purchasing alliances, which Republicans felt would lead to the elimination of private insurance companies.

Thus, the Vermont Health Care Authority, the administrative centerpiece of Act 160 and the engine that would pull the state health care reform train, was under attack from forces on all points of the political compass. Instead of facilitating the process of reform, the VHCA had become one of its obstacles. As a consequence, when policymakers geared up for the 1994 legislative session they inherited a legacy of suspicion and disarray—one lobbyist spoke of the "really quite damaged relationship with state government because of our relationship with the Health Care Authority."[20]

(On July 1, 1996, the VHCA ceased to exist as a freestanding agency. In its 1996 session the General Assembly merged the Authority with the Department of Insurance, Banking, Securities, and Health Care Administration, putting the former agency's functions under the control of a deputy commissioner of health care administration and, ultimately, the department's commissioner.)

The Politicians Take the Reins

On July 24, 1993, a headline in the *Burlington Free Press* announced, "Dean Takes Reins on Vt. Health Care." The governor, the story explained, had decided to develop his own health care plan—months before the Health Care Authority was even scheduled to make public a draft of its universal access plans. Up to this point, Dean and his staff were ambivalent about the role they should play in the VHCA's work. Should they stand back and see how the single-payer versus multipayer debate played out, or should they commit to one model? As the Authority's problems accumulated, and with time growing short to develop his own plan and to build political support for it, the governor decided to offer his particular vision of reform.

In the months leading up to the start of the 1994 legislative session, then, health reform in Vermont traveled on two separate tracks. The VHCA continued with the process dictated by Act 160 by holding public hearings around the state, including an interactive television broadcast on Vermont public television, to collect public comment on their universal access plans prior to submitting their final report to the legislature in November.

Meanwhile the governor, his staff, and key legislators had begun meeting during the summer to prepare for the January legislative session. The pace of this prelegislative activity picked up considerably and dramatically in October when Speaker Wright announced that he was creating a special health care reform committee to draft legislation. The purpose of the committee was to expedite House consideration by avoiding four of the six standing committees that had jurisdiction over health reform legislation. It would also give the Speaker greater control over the process and its outcome. Wright chose Sean Campbell (D), the House majority leader and a close political ally, to chair the committee. Mindful of the need for Republican votes to gain passage in the House, Wright asked the Republican minority leader and three other, moderate, Republicans to serve on the eleven-member committee.

The Governor's Plan

In late November, Howard Dean personally appeared before the special committee to present his own vision of health care reform. In his outline to the committee, the governor called for a regulated, multipayer system with an employer mandate in which employers and employees would each pay 50 percent of the premiums. Many in his own party criticized the 50-50 split, which they feared would encourage employers, most of whom now paid 75 to 80 percent of their employees' premiums, to drop back to 50 percent. In addition, Dean proposed subsidies for small businesses and low-income individuals, as well as an expansion of Medicaid to help cover the unemployed. This latter provision was opposed by the Vermont State Medical Society, whose members dislike Medicaid because of its practice of underreimbursement. The plan would cost $30–38 million and be funded through so-called splinter taxes on gasoline, tobacco, and alcohol. Employers would be encouraged to join a state insurance buying program that would emphasize managed care and, it was hoped, help lower costs. Finally, the state's health care system would operate under a global budget. The governor indicated that he would be flexible on the specifics of any legislative proposal. However, there was one specific point on which he was completely unyielding—what one aide called his "nuclear bomb"—the governor would never accept an increase in the state's income tax to fund health care. Dean was convinced that Vermont's high income tax was already a drag on the state's economy and its capacity to attract new businesses. This position put the governor at odds with single-payer advocates, and liberals in general, who favored progressive funding for health care reform.

Republicans and business leaders reacted positively to the governor's outline. Senator John Carroll, the Republican majority leader, declared the governor's plan "a good start."[21] While Dean's plan seemed to satisfy the political right, at least for the moment, it did nothing to assuage the concerns of the state's strong single-payer lobby. In December, Congressman Sanders issued a report on the cost of a single-payer system that grew out of the task force on single-payer health care that he had created. The task force concluded that it would cost Vermonters $562 million to fund a single-payer system, "$284 million less than the $864 million Vermonters will spend in insurance premiums and out-of-pocket payments in 1994 for the same benefits if there is not reform," and $427 million less than the VHCA's proposed multipayer plan.[22] Dean denounced the task force's findings as misleading and irresponsible.

The prospects of Vermont going to a single-payer health care system in 1994 were remote. Republicans, who controlled the Senate, and Governor Dean ("I would never do a Canadian-style single payer")[23] both opposed the model. Nevertheless, single-payer advocates were a force that could not be ignored; they were the best (nearly the only) organized and most dedicated health reform lobby in the legislature and in the state.

While single-payer advocates were proposing a major overhaul of the state's health care system, the state's Republican leaders were promoting something more modest. The message from the Republican leadership was, we "will move rather cautiously. The last thing we need right now is radical and precipitous reform that will permanently damage 'what works' in Vermont."[24]

"Health Plan du Jour:" The House Does Reform

When the Vermont General Assembly convened on January 2, 1994, a majority of the legislators believed that the state's health care system needed reform. However, a survey of legislators at the time found that none of the plans that had been publicly discussed had the support of more than one out of five members.[25] The divisions and evolving anxiety among Vermont legislators mirrored those of the general population and interested groups. To give just one example, members of the business community, whose support Dean deemed vital to passage of reform, were all over the map on the issue. The fifteen-hundred-member state Chamber of Commerce opposed both employer mandates and a single-payer system; the Vermont Employers Health Alliance, representing over one hundred large and small businesses in the state, favored employer mandates, but opposed single-payer; and the Vermont Retail Association favored a single-payer system. Given the diversity of positions on the issue, cobbling together a legislative majority for any bill would be a daunting task.

First out of the gate was the governor's bill (H.B. 645), which was formally sponsored by Speaker Wright. Unlike in 1992, when the Speaker also sponsored what was to become Act 160, this year the Democratic leadership of Vermont would not speak with one voice on health care reform. In October, Wright announced that he personally favored a single-payer system. Thus, although he formally sponsored H.B. 645, "An Act Relating to Universal Access to Health Care," it was with little enthusiasm.

H.B. 645 was assigned to the special committee, which heard nearly three months of testimony from every conceivable interest group in the state. At the time the conventional wisdom in Vermont (and in the nation) was that a single-payer system, for all its putative virtues, was politically unfeasible. It came, then, as more than a small surprise when, in early February, the chair of the special House committee, Sean Campbell, announced to his colleagues that he had figured out how Vermont could do a payroll- and income-tax-financed system in which one state health alliance would purchase insurance for all Vermonters.

Campbell's announcement caused quite a stir in the statehouse. Senate Republican leaders warned Governor Dean that if he did not "straighten out" Campbell and Wright, health reform would be dead for this session. For his part Dean tried to downplay the significance of the proposal, which he described as nothing more than "a tempest in a teapot."[26]

Events now began to move quickly and somewhat chaotically. As it had done in 1992, the prospect of a single-payer system became the catalyst for a search for a less "radical" plan. One week after Campbell's bombshell, two moderate Republicans on the special committee, Richard Westman, the House minority leader, and Thomas Little, submitted just such a plan. Incredibly enough, even for moderate Republicans, the proposal called for an employer mandate, with a 70-30 employer-employee split, state subsidies for low-income and unemployed individuals, as well as certain small businesses, and a prescription drug benefit for Medicare recipients. The plan would be funded by beer, tobacco, and gasoline taxes, and a 5 percent provider tax. The total cost of the plan, around $75 million, was more than twice Dean's proposal, but considerably less than the estimated $610 million that Campbell's payroll- and income-tax-based scheme would have cost.

On February 18, about two weeks before they were scheduled to vote on a reform bill, the 88 Democrats from the 150-member Vermont House of Representatives caucused to hear a progress report from the majority leader on the special committee's progress. The committee had started with the Dean 50-50 employer mandate, and a $35 million price tag; it had flirted with Campbell's $610 million tax-based system, and as of mid-February was back to a premium-based, 70-30 employer-mandate plan. Meanwhile the single-payer lobby lurked in the shadows. Although no formal vote was taken, the caucus appeared evenly divided between supporters of a single-payer tax-based system and a system based on employer mandates and multiple insurance carriers. House Republicans, on the other hand, could agree on only what they didn't want, namely, a single-payer system.

It was in this atmosphere of political uncertainty that on February 22 the special committee gave preliminary approval to the Westman-Little proposal. Campbell acknowledged that the decision was a bow to political reality. "We have to forward health care this year," he said. "I think that single-payer probably couldn't get through the House."[27] The critical problem now was whether there were enough single-payer Democrats and anti-employer-mandate Republicans willing to hold their noses and vote for a premium-based system. Signals coming from the Democratic left (the single-payer caucus) were not encouraging. Despite this opposition, on March 4 the committee voted, 10-to-1, for a modified version of the Westman-Little proposal, including an employer mandate, and sent it on to the Ways and Means and Appropriations Committees.

Normally one could expect that a bill with 10-to-1 bipartisan committee endorsement would have relatively easy sailing. However, from the moment it left the special committee it was clear that the bill was going to be a tough sell. The great divide in the House and among the public was over financing. The political left favored income and/or payroll taxes; the political right, to the extent that it supported reform at all, would accept only splinter taxes; and the political center, which dominated the special committee, preferred primarily premiums, with additional revenue from splinter taxes.

On March 15 Speaker Wright, after conferring with other House Democrats, dropped the second "bombshell" of the session—he and the Democratic leadership were switching their support to an income- and payroll-tax-based system. The plan called for an 8.8 percent payroll tax and a 3.2 percent income tax that together would raise just over $750 million.

Although strictly speaking not a single-payer system, since it allowed non-profit insurance companies such as Blue Cross/Blue Shield to participate, the plan was close enough with its progressive funding to gain single-payer support. The special committee, which eleven days earlier had voted 10 to 1 in favor of a premium-based system, now voted 8 to 3, with three of the four Republican members in opposition, for the tax-based plan that maintained most of provisions from the original bill.

The shift to tax-based funding was an act of political desperation. Although Speaker Wright counted eighty-one votes for the tax-based system, five more than were needed for passage, everyone understood that there was no way that either Howard Dean or Senate Republicans would ever accept it. House approval of a tax-based system recommended itself for one reason: it would keep reform alive by moving the bill on to the Senate. In one of the more curious moments in an already bizarre session, Dean urged House Democrats to vote for the bill he would veto if it ever reached his desk, simply to get it out of the House.

What occurred next was one of the pivotal moments in the Vermont health care debate. On Thursday, March 17, the *Burlington Free Press* ran a table on its front page showing how much the tax bill of various sample families and individuals would increase under the most recent Democratic plan. It showed, for example, that a middle-class family of four with an adjusted gross income of $60,000 would see its Vermont income tax go from $1,909 to $3,714 per year, a 95 percent increase, while an individual with an annual income of $30,000 would see a 101 percent rise from $898 to $1,801.[28] The impact of the story was dramatic. Legislators heard from angry constituents that if this was the cost of health care reform they wanted no part of it.[29] Meanwhile the governor reiterated his opposition to an income tax. But most ominously for the leadership, many of the eighty-one Democrats who had told the Speaker they would support a tax-based bill were getting skittish about signing on to a $750 million tax increase that would hit the middle class particularly hard, even though the new taxes would replace, and in many instances be lower than, household health insurance premiums.

Legislative leaders now scrambled to find an alternative to both the tax-based system, which the governor, most Republicans, and now the public rejected, and a premium-based system that did not have seventy-six votes in the House. The day the *Free Press* article appeared, the Speaker's office was a hub of activity as key legislators met behind closed doors trying to find a way to keep alive health reform in 1994. What emerged was a plan that would keep most of the structure of the latest version of H.B. 645 and commit the state to providing universal access and cost control in

1996. However, it would postpone, until the 1995 legislative session, decisions on the benefits package (and hence the cost) and, most notably, financing. In the interim the VHCA would prepare a Goldilocks plan—high, medium, and low benefits packages and proposed funding for each. Although the bill retained structural features of its predecessor (e.g., a Vermont Health Alliance as well as private employer purchasing alliances), it was a mere shell of a program. The governor once again urged Democrats to hold their noses and vote to get the bill out of the House. In the end that is precisely what the legislators did. On a vote of 99 to 39, with 76 of the 88 Democrats and 22 of the 55 Republicans supporting it, the House approved, in principle, a promise to provide all Vermonters access to health care beginning January 1, 1996, and to control health care costs through global budgeting and caps on insurance premiums. The bill now moved to the Senate, where the governor hoped it would be revitalized.

The Senate Will Fix It

Initially, at least, it looked as if the Senate might pull it off. The majority leader, John Carroll, asked the Senate president pro tempore to convene a special bipartisan group to identify areas of agreement on reform and to prepare legislation. The message seemed to be that the Senate Republican leadership wanted some kind of health care reform. Although this group met only three or four times before the process reverted back to the normal committee system, Carroll's overture and his decision to work with the Democratic chairwoman of the Senate Health and Welfare Committee, Jan Backus, seemed to bode well for a bipartisan effort.[30]

Carroll and Backus began by identifying points of common agreement between them. Given the spectacle of the House debacle, and the lateness of the session, both had independently concluded that only a modest or incremental, not a comprehensive, reform was possible at this point. The two senators were able to agree on a four-page outline of principles that included the following: an individual mandate providing that uninsured Vermonters would have to purchase health insurance by July 1, 1995; individuals who could not afford to do so would receive an income-based sliding scale subsidy from the state; all employers now providing health insurance would have to continue to do so; state subsidies would be gradually replaced, over a two- or three-year period, by mandatory employer-employee contributions; and the program would be funded by a 5 percent tax on all health goods and services.

Led by Senator Backus, the Health and Welfare Committee set out to turn the four-page outline into a comprehensive bill. Unlike the House committee, which spent nearly five months and held over sixty committee meetings, taking testimony from hundreds of interested parties, the Senate committee would have about six weeks to do its work. Therefore, Senator Backus decided to narrow the focus of her committee meetings and to limit the range of people from whom the committee would take testimony.

But time was not the only enemy of reform in the Senate. First, it was not merely a question of the amount of time remaining in the session, but the timing of the Senate's deliberations. It was now late in the legislative session and health care reform was competing for the time, attention, and political energy of a second major piece of controversial legislation, property tax reform. In addition, with the debacle of the House efforts fresh in their minds, most Vermonters, as measured by comments to legislators, talk shows, and letters to the editor, were at best skeptical of the legislature's capacity to do reform. Finally, although the political dynamics of the 30-member Vermont Senate are quite different from those of the 150-member House, the political divide over health reform was just as wide. If anything, the number of legislators who were willing to do nothing was greater in the Senate than in the House.

The bill that took shape in the Senate Health and Welfare Committee followed the broad outlines agreed to by Carroll and Backus. It proposed extending health insurance benefits to the uninsured by requiring that they purchase insurance from newly created insurance purchasing cooperatives that would offer both an HMO-style managed care option as well as a standard fee-for-service plan. The proposal called for a relatively modest benefit package and would subsidize insurance for low-income individuals. Funding for the subsidies would come from a ten-cent per package increase in the cigarette tax, and a 5 percent tax on health insurance premiums for individuals and businesses. Most important, the bill included a play-or-pay option—employers who were not currently providing health insurance to their employees either had to do so or pay tax-deductible fees, not to exceed 6 percent of their payroll, to help pay the costs of the uninsured. The plan proposed to contain costs by setting nonbinding budget targets and making the managed care option as attractive as possible. The total annual cost of the plan, by 1996, was $53 million.

Despite the relatively modest nature of the proposal—in essence it left alone the health care system for all but the approximately fifty-six thousand uninsured Vermonters—it attracted criticism from several directions. The Vermont Grocers' Association, which had opposed employer mandates, payroll taxes, and cigarette and beer taxes when the bill was on the House side, again raised objections and ran newspaper advertisements in opposition to the Senate bill. Similarly, the influential state Chamber of Commerce opposed the bill as a threat to the state's businesses and economy. The Vermont Consumers' Campaign for Health, a single-payer advocacy group, renewed its call for a single-payer system.

Nevertheless, on May 3, the Senate Health and Welfare Committee narrowly approved the bill, 3 to 2, and forwarded it to the Finance Committee. The close committee vote, with two of the three Republicans voting against the bill, did not bode well for bipartisan support in the Senate. And the next bit of news did not improve its prospects. The day after the committee vote, IBM, the state's largest private employer, announced that the tax on health insurance premiums was unacceptable. In a thinly veiled threat, a company spokesman noted that IBM had a significant investment in Vermont, "but if that kind of tax change were to take effect we would certainly have to look long and hard before making additional investments" in the Vermont facility.[31] Other business interests and groups weighed in against the employer mandate. The position of the business community was reflected in the Republican caucus, in which nine of the sixteen senators indicated that they would support the bill only if the employer mandate was eliminated, and another five said they favored allowing the bill to die in the Finance Committee.

This latter option had haunted reformers from the very beginning of the legislative session. The seven-member Finance Committee consisted of three Democrats, including Cheryl Rivers, who were strongly identified as single-payer advocates, and four Republicans, two of whom, including its chairman, were among the most conservative members of the party and unalterably opposed to mandates. The political "center" of the committee, then, consisted of two Republicans, only one of whom appeared willing to entertain the idea of an employer mandate.

The Senate Finance Committee held two days of perfunctory hearings. Witnesses who spoke in support of the bill complained of being given little opportunity to make an adequate case, and one lobbyist reported that the committee "was incredibly hostile."[32] The problem for the bill's supporters was that the left was as critical of its content as the right. Cheryl Rivers opposed the bill for three main reasons—aside from the fact that it was not a single-payer plan. First, the individual mandate imposed an undue hardship on working-class Vermonters. Second, the 5 percent health premium tax would increase health insurance rates for all Vermonters, without any offsetting cost containment. Finally, although the bill provided that all employers currently providing health insurance could not drop their coverage, it specified that their contribution could not fall below 50 percent of the premiums. This meant, Rivers charged, that some companies could drop their contribution from, say, 75 percent to 50 percent. In the end, she concluded, "Many of us that were concerned about the problem [of health care] felt that the uninsured Vermonters would be better off with the status quo than under the mandatory health insurance provisions that were contained in the bill that we finally got at the end."[33]

With no center to sustain it, either on the committee or in the full Senate, this latest version of H.B. 645 died on May 11 when the Senate Finance Committee voted unanimously to table the bill. Although the committee was criticized by the governor and the Republican majority leader for not allowing the full Senate a chance to vote on the bill, there was general agreement that it would have made little difference—the votes were not there.

The Next, Small Step

But unlike their federal counterparts, Vermont policymakers could not or would not turn their backs on the fact that health care costs do not moderate, nor does access to health care improve, when lawmakers do nothing. Hence in 1995 Governor Dean introduced, and the state legislature approved, more modest, incremental reform legislation. On April 11, 1995, Dean signed into law the Vermont Health Access Plan (VHAP). The new law has three major provisions.

First, between January 1, 1996, and July 1, 1997, the state will extend Medicaid coverage to an additional sixteen thousand low-income Vermonters who are currently ineligible for the program, despite having incomes below the federal poverty level ($7,470 for an individual or $15,150 for a family of four). State officials estimate that by extending insurance to this group, its uninsured population would drop to 8.3 percent (from about 11 percent), compared with a 1996 national average of 14 to 15 percent. The benefits under the new VHAP program are limited to routine office visits, diagnostic tests and X-rays, immunizations, outpatient mental health, chemical dependency and family planning services, and in-office minor surgery. In addition, the program pays for 40 percent of prescription drug costs, but does not cover hospital inpatient services or dental, ophthalmological, and nursing home care services.

Second, in an effort to control Medicaid costs, these new participants ultimately will have to enroll in capitated managed care programs, although initially they will be in traditional fee-for-services programs. In addition, on July 1, 1996 the state began moving about sixty-six thousand of its existing eight-two thousand Medicaid patients into capitated managed care programs as well.

Third, the state now pays the prescription drug benefit for low-income Medicare recipients, which Medicare does not otherwise provide. Implementation of the program required a Medicaid waiver from the Clinton administration, which the state received in August, 1995.

The state is financing the Medicaid expansion and the prescription drug benefit by more than doubling its cigarette tax (from twenty cents to forty-four cents per pack), increasing the tax on other tobacco products, extending a 4 percent tax on gross hospital inpatient revenues, and increasing the tax on nursing homes. In addition, there is an enrollment fee of up to $20 every six months, and co-payments ranging from $2 for a physician visit to $25 for an emergency-room visit.

In a telling reminder of just how difficult health care reform can be, both politically and administratively, the VHAP program has teetered on the brink of extinction since its enactment. First, in August 1995 the state solicited bids to enroll the first wave of new participants in the Medicaid managed care program that had been scheduled to begin on January 1, 1996. Unfortunately the state received just two bids, only one of which it was able to get a rate agreement on. Since the law required that there be at least two carriers competing for the Medicaid business, the state was unable to begin the program in a managed care environment. In December 1995 state health officials prepared to solicit bids again, but decided to begin an interim fee-for-service program for the uninsured until satisfactory carriers were found for the program. State officials ultimately received acceptable bids and were confident that they would be able to move most new Medicaid (i.e., VHAP) recipients into managed care programs.

At least as serious as the problem of finding adequate managed care plans to deal with the expanded Medicaid population was that of maintaining political support for the expansion. In 1996 the Republican-controlled Senate voted, 17 to 13, to freeze enrollment in the new plan, which would have meant that VHAP would not have covered all sixteen thousand Vermonters who were eligible for the plan. Ultimately a compromise was worked out with the House whereby the enrollments were continued. Nevertheless, according to one Republican state senator who supports VHAP, the program remains vulnerable. Speaking of her senate colleagues, Senator Helen Riehle said: "There were [sic] some people [in the legislature] who are looking at the possibility of canning the whole program."[34] Clearly health care reform in Vermont is a work in progress.

Despite the fact that health care reform in Vermont has fallen short of the ambitious goals set in 1992, it is important to remember what has been accomplished. Every child up to age seventeen, every pregnant woman, and all other Vermonters with incomes below the federal poverty level are guaranteed access to health care through Medicaid; there is a health insurance safety net for people in the group market but who lose their jobs and are not subsequently covered by another group plan; health insurance companies which sell policies in Vermont may not use such risk classification criteria as age, gender, geographic setting, prior medical condition, or type of job; there are uniform health insurance claims, controls on hospital costs, and systemwide health expenditure targets; and the state is systematically collecting and presenting health care and cost trends in its Health Resources Management Plan. When one compares the accomplishments of the federal government and Vermont it would be somewhat churlish to belittle the state's efforts.

Nonetheless students of health care reform remain interested in why truly comprehensive reform remains so elusive, even under the apparently favorable political conditions that existed in Vermont in the early 1990s. What lessons, then, does the Vermont experience offer?

Lessons from Vermont

It is always a bit dicey to generalize from one state's policy experience to that of others. This is especially perilous when the state is Vermont, with 560,000 mostly white, rural, comparatively healthy people, served by a part-time, citizen legislature. Nevertheless the Vermont story reveals and reflects many of the same obstacles that face other states as they try to grapple with the chronic problems of high costs and incomplete access to health care. There were both proximate and long-term obstacles to comprehensive reform in Vermont that are relevant to the genus "health care reform."

Vermonters will explain the failure of the highly anticipated 1994 reform in one or more of the following ways: (1) there was a lack of leadership from the governor, during both the prelegislative (i.e., VHCA deliberations) and legislative periods; (2) the 1994 legislative session witnessed, in terms of money spent and effort exerted, an unprecedented level of lobbying, especially from groups opposed to health care reform; (3) unlike in 1992, when both branches of government were controlled by the Democrats, the partisan split in the Vermont General Assembly produced an unusual degree of partisan and personal conflict in 1994; (4) between the political left (who wanted an as yet unenactable single-payer system) and the political right (who wanted little if anything) there was not enough of a center to pass a bill; (5) the Vermont Health Care Authority poisoned the well of reform by its failure to develop a process with which the key players could be comfortable and, therefore, accomplices to reform; (6) the legislature simply tried to do too much at once—health care reform itself was a two-session issue, and when major property tax reform was piled on top of it, the system collapsed; (7) the contemporaneous national debate over health care reform undermined some of the urgency for a state solution.

Taken together these explanations provide the necessary, but not sufficient, cause of the failure of reform in Vermont in 1994 and subsequent reluctance to enact even more modest health care system changes. To this equation one must add the factor that connects these discrete explanations— namely, the failure on the part of the governor, the legislators, and nongovernmental advocates of reform to convince Vermonters of the need for comprehensive change in the way they receive and pay for health care, and of the capacity of government to accomplish this change. This, I would suggest, is the major lesson from Vermont.

The difficulties facing state and federal lawmakers in this regard are indeed formidable. One must remember three critical existential realities of American health care reform in the 1990s: (1) the vast majority (85 to 90 percent) of Vermonters, and Americans in general, have health insurance; (2) 80 percent of Vermonters (and a comparable percentage of Americans) indicate that they are satisfied with the health care they receive; and (3) dissatisfaction with government is at an all-time high— about 80 percent of Vermonters believe that the 1994 general assembly did a "fair" to "poor" job, a figure comparable to that of citizen evaluation of the U.S. Congress.[35]

No one in the state made a credible case, especially to middle-class Vermonters, about why they should abandon what they had, flaws and all, for something they knew nothing about and that seemed to benefit only the uninsured. Looking at the national scene, David Rothman sees the failure to "co-opt the middle-class" as the underlying explanation for the failure to pass national health care reform. He argues that this point underscores "a moral failure, a demonstration of a level of indifference to the well-being of others that stands as an indictment of the intrinsic character of American society."[36] This is a view shared by Howard Dean: "The biggest factor [explaining the defeat of reform] was a climate of fear among the public that reform was going to cost a lot of money. I don't think, when it came to the bottom line, many people cared about the uninsured."[37]

The task of educating Vermonters about the need for reform was, indeed, a daunting one. To begin, in both micro- and macroeconomic terms there was no longer the sense of urgency that seemed to have fueled statewide or indeed national public demand and support in previous years. In 1992, when Vermont Act 160 was passed, George Bush was president, health care costs were soaring, and the number of Vermonters without health insurance had doubled in just three years. Bill Clinton's election recast, in the minds of some, the issue from one that had to be solved at the state level, to one that the national government would or should take care of—a rather quaint notion given the subsequent unfolding of events in Washington.

In addition, and ironically, health care reform in Vermont in 1994 was partly a victim of its own earlier successes. In 1989 the state had mandated guaranteed acceptance and community rating for small-group health insurance, and Act 160 extended this to the individual insurance market. These reforms, along with an improving (albeit very slowly) Vermont economy resulted in a leveling off of the rapid growth (from thirty thousand to sixty thousand people) in the uninsured population the state had experienced between 1989 and 1991. The number of uninsured has held steady since 1993 at about 11 percent of the population while increasing nationally. Part of the reason for this is the increase in the number of children from low-income families who were receiving health care under the state's Dr. Dynasaur program as a result of Act 160: between July 1, 1992, and January 1, 1993, the number of children covered increased from 1,500 to nearly 6,200, although in some cases this represented a shift from one publicly funded program to another. By July 1996 there were 13,400 children enrolled in the program. Implementation of the 1995 Vermont Health Access Plan will help reduce the uninsured population further, although the program got off to a slow start, with only about twenty-five hundred people enrolled by July 1996 out of a possible population of sixteen thousand. The slow start was attributed to uncertain support of the 1996 legislature for the program and the decision by officials to delay a major public information campaign until the plan's status was more certain. This campaign began in the fall of 1996 and state officials anticipate enrollment will pick up.

Finally, the sense of urgency to reform the health care system that gripped Vermonters in 1992 moderated in part because health care costs have moderated in the state. Some of this moderation was prophylactic in anticipation of mandatory hospital budget caps, while some were the result of the overall decline in inflation. Whatever the reason, in fiscal year 1993 Vermont's fifteen nonprofit hospitals increased their budgets an average of 7.7 percent (the lowest increase in five years). This was followed by a 5.1 percent increase in 1994 and 3.5 percent in 1995. State newspapers and newsmakers lauded Vermont hospitals for cutting back bureaucracy, improving efficiency, and freezing patient costs. In sum, an improved overall economy and an improved health care economy tempered both the need, and the perception of the need, for reform among Vermonters.

However, the cooling of the public's ardor for health care reform was both cause and consequence of the events that unfolded in 1994 and continue today. Popular disenchantment was not exclusively the consequence of the changing personal economic calculus of individual Vermonters. Vermonters were soured on reform in no small part because they, not unlike Americans during the 1993–94 national debate, lost faith in the capacity of government to get health care reform right. As I have described above, the seeds of this disillusionment were sown by the performance of the VHCA, which, despite mandated efforts to engage the public in the reform process, was never able "to get people fired up."[38]

In the final analysis, it was always up to the state political leadership to build a legislative and interest-group coalition around reform, and then sell it to Vermonters, and especially the middle class. That this was never successfully done is in part because there was no organized support for reform from which policy leaders could draw political strength. Reformers were never as clear, coherent, confident, and steadfast about what they stood for as opponents were about what they were against. Without public support behind it, no vision of health care reform could withstand the onslaught of opposition from the scores of groups with largely limited, parochial interests to protect. This is especially a problem in a state like Vermont, with its citizen legislature where a lobbyist can stand in the well of the House of Representatives and speak on a cellular telephone to a client flying over Colorado, while state legislators have no personal offices, no personal telephones, and no personal staff.[39]

For state—or indeed national—comprehensive reform to succeed in the future, it will be necessary for the political leadership to present a focused, consistent message to the public, and one that explains why reform is in the interest of all Vermonters, not merely the uninsured. It will be up to the state's political leadership to assuage the public's anxiety about government's capacity to do reform in a way that will not endanger what Vermonters like about the health care system.

Notes

Portions of this article originally appeared in Howard M. Leichter, "Health Care Reform in Vermont: A Work in Progress," *Health Affairs* 12 (summer 1993): 71–81, and Howard M. Leichter, "Health Care Reform in Vermont: The Next Chapter," *Health Affairs* 13 (winter 1994): 78–103. The material is reprinted by permission of Project HOPE. The People-to-People Health Foundation. Health Affairs, 7500 Old Georgetown Road, Suite 600, Bethesda, Md. 20814.

1. "Health Care: If Even There . . . ," *Economist,* May 21, 1994, 29. See also Alexandra Marks, "Vermont Aims to Pioneer Health Care Reform," *Christian Science Monitor,* September 21, 1993, 2.

2. Karen Meyer, executive director, Vermont State Medical Society, interview by author, August 3, 1993. Hereafter, Meyer interview, 1993.

3. Ralph Wright, "Commentary," *Rutland Herald,* January 4, 1994, 12.

4. *Final Report of The Vermont Blue Ribbon Commission on Health,* January 1992, 2.

5. Richard Saudek, lobbyist for the Health Insurance Association of America, interview by author, July 24, 1992.

6. Governor Howard Dean, interview by author, July 21, 1992.

7. Nancy Eldridge, director of governmental relations, Vermont State Medical Society, interview by author, July 23, 1992.

8. Norman Wright, interview by author, July 21, 1992.

9. Bryan Pfeiffer, "House-Senate Split on Health Care Widens," *Rutland Herald,* March 23, 1992.

10. Cheryl Rivers, interview by author, July 22, 1992.

11. Mark Litow, testimony to House Commerce Committee, January 24, 1992.

12. Editorial, "Health Care Reform: Who'll Do the Job," *Burlington Free Press,* January 9, 1994, 4E.

13. Paul Harrington, interview by author, June 6, 1994. Hereafter, Harrington interview, 1994.

14. Karen Meyer, interview by author, June 1, 1994. Hereafter, Meyer interview, 1994.

15. Anya Rader, deputy chief of staff to Governor Howard Dean, interview by author, June 1, 1994.

16. Harrington interview, 1994.

17. Bryan Pfeiffer, "Health Care Reform Hard to Do, Even Harder to Explain," *Rutland Sunday Herald,* June 13, 1993, 1C.

18. Meyer interview, 1993.

19. R. Sneyd, "Health Plan Attack Is Bipartisan," *Burlington Free Press,* October 23, 1993, 1B.

20. Meyer interview, 1994.

21. Bryan Pfeiffer, "Governor's Plan Attracts Businesses, Conservatives," *Rutland Herald,* November 24, 1993, 5.

22. "Report of Congressman Sanders's Task Force on Single-Payer," mimeo from the Office of Congressman Sanders, December 6, 1993.

23. Quoted in Richard Barlow, "Dean Wants Health Compromise," *White River Junction Valley News,* December 11, 1993, A8.

24. John Bloomer, president pro tempore, Vermont Senate, "Commentary," *Rutland Herald,* January 4, 1994, 12.

25. Candace Page, "Choosing Health Care Reform," *Burlington Free Press,* January 2, 1994, 1A.

26. Jack Hoffman, "Governor Says He'll Stay Above the Fray," *Rutland Herald,* February 3, 1994, 24.

27. Mark Lewis, "Single Payer System Booted," *Burlington Free Press,* February 23, 1994, 1B.

28. Mark Lewis, "Health Reform Plan Hits Tax Bill Hard," *Burlington Free Press,* March 17, 1994, 1A.

29. Ross Sneyd, "House Compromise Would Delay Parts of Health Care Bill," *Rutland Herald,* March 18, 1994, 11.

30. It is one of the peculiarities of the Vermont General Assembly that members of the minority party can serve as chairpersons of legislative committees. In this case Jan Backus, who had experience on the Senate Health and Welfare Committee during enactment of Act 160, was appointed chair by the Senate Republicans despite her somewhat liberal inclinations.

31. Bryan Pfeiffer, "IBM Displeased With Health Tax," *Rutland Herald,* May 5, 1994, 6.

32. Jeanne Keller, president, Vermont Employers Health Alliance, interview by author, June 3, 1994.

33. Cheryl Rivers, interview by author, June 1, 1994.

34. "Vermont Still Seeking Medicaid Managed Care Providers," *State Initiatives,* March/April 1996, 8.

35. Jack Hoffman, "Lawmakers Fare Poorly in Poll of Voters," *Rutland Herald,* June 28, 1994, 1. The disapproval rating for members of Congress in June 1992 was 77 percent. "Organization of the Congress: Final Report," (Washington, D.C.: Government Printing Office, 1993), 185.

36. David Rothman, "A Century of Failure: Class Barriers to Reform," in *The Politics of Health Care Reform,* ed. James A. Morone and Gary S. Belkin (Durham, N.C.: Duke University Press, 1994), 13.

37. Janice Somerville, "Vermont Failure Clouds State Reform Picture," *American Medical News,* July 4, 1994, 1.

38. Bryan Pfeiffer, reporter for the *Rutland Herald,* interview by author, June 2, 1994.

39. This example was provided to me by Representative Ann Siebert.

9

Health Care Reform in Minnesota: A Journey, Not a Destination

Howard M. Leichter

Minnesota has long been considered at "the forefront of state-based health reform."[1] This assessment is based upon the state's record since 1992 of addressing a wide range of reform issues including cost containment, expanded access, insurance reform, improvement of rural health, and health data collection initiatives. Indeed, by 1994 Minnesota's lawmakers were ready to announce that it was their goal to achieve universal access to health care by July 1, 1997.

One year later, however, much had changed: The Democratic majority in the state legislature had shrunk, four of the so-called Gang of Seven who had spearheaded the reform were no longer in the state legislature, the Clinton initiative had failed, a requested ERISA exemption was not forthcoming, and there was a Republican-controlled Congress in Washington. As a result the 1995 state legislature backed away from its one-year-old commitment to universal access, instead proclaiming as its goal reducing the number of uninsured Minnesotans to fewer than 4 percent of the population by January 1, 2000. In addition, the legislature dropped a previous individual mandate requiring that all Minnesotans purchase health insurance by July 1, 1997, eliminated a provision that would have regulated doctors' rates in the fee-for-service market in the state, and halted any further private insurance policy reforms. In fact, so dramatically had the politics of reform changed in the state that the Minnesota Republican Party adopted a plank in its 1996 platform calling for the repeal of MinnesotaCare, the state's program of subsidized health insurance for low-income people.

Despite these political and legislative setbacks, Minnesota remains an important model of health care reform. The story that follows highlights the passage of MinnesotaCare in 1992, the state's promising attempt to contain costs and expand access to the state's low-income but Medicaid-ineligible population. State lawmakers have revisited and revised MinnesotaCare each year since 1992 as they sought to accommodate the fiscal and political realities within the state and the nation.[2] The Minnesota case is an important reminder that health care reform is, in the words of one local observer, "a journey and not a destination."[3]

Background to Reform

In the fall of 1991 Minnesota politics was a microcosm of national politics. The state was running a huge budget deficit; it had a Republican governor who was suffering the highest disapproval rating (55 percent) of any Minnesota governor in nearly a half century; the Democrats controlled both houses of the legislature but without a veto-proof majority; and public opinion polls indicated that a majority of Minnesotans were concerned about health care costs.[4] Despite strong public support for reform, however, on June 3, 1991, Governor Arne Carlson (R) vetoed the Health Care Access Bill, which would have completely revamped the state's health insurance system and moved Minnesota toward universal access to health care. Although the governor did not face reelection in 1992, the entire state legislature did. Pundits were muttering gridlock, citizens were expressing dissatisfaction with state government, and an unprecedented number of legislators were contemplating retirement.

Ten months later, Governor Carlson and four Democratic and three Republican state legislators, dubbed the Gang of Seven, along with the state's House and Senate leadership, stood arm-in-arm to announce to the press that they had reached an agreement on a bipartisan plan to reform the state's health care system. The bill, House File (H.F.) 2800, originally called HealthRight but subsequently renamed MinnesotaCare, promised to contain costs and expand access to health care, modify private health insurance practices, and put Minnesota at the very forefront of reform in the nation. How and why the state's political leadership moved from acrimony to accommodation provides a fascinating glimpse into the changing landscape of state health care politics in America. Before turning to that story, it would be useful to first outline the provisions of the Minnesota reform.

MinnesotaCare: Provisions of the Law

Containing Costs

At the heart of the Minnesota reform is cost containment. Indeed, it is a measure of the times in general, and the political dynamics of Minnesota in particular, that Article I of the law deals with cost containment while the issue of access is taken up sixty pages and three articles later in the law. At the time of the 1992 debate, Minnesota, like every other state in the nation, was experiencing a rapid escalation in health care costs. Total public spending on medical assistance had increased 41.4 percent from 1985 to 1990 (from $992.7 million to $1.403 billion), and private-sector costs, too, were becoming a burden to Minnesotans. In 1991 Minnesota ranked ninth in the nation in terms of average health payments per family, with an average family expenditure of $7,252, up from $2,936 in 1980. The Minnesota Health Care Access Commission found, "*The current health care system is unaffordable for many Minnesotans.* One in three uninsured Minnesotans have unpaid medical bills, averaging $826. One in five individually insured Minnesotans have unpaid medical bills, averaging $1,207."[5]

It is not surprising, then, that the legislative finding introducing Article I described the "devastating effect on the health and cost of living in Minnesota" due to the "staggering growth in health care costs." It went on, however, to link cost control "to the maintenance of the many factors contributing to the quality of life in Minnesota: our environment, education system, safe communities, affordable housing, provision of food, economic vitality, purchasing power, and stable population."[6] MinnesotaCare sought to contain health care costs through a combination of marketplace competition and state regulation, although the original 1992 law relied heavily upon a regulatory approach to cost containment. At the forefront of this effort is a twenty-five-member Health Care Cost Containment Commission that, along with the state's health care commissioner, attempts to control costs through the following activities. First, it oversees a provision of MinnesotaCare that has set a target for slowing overall health care cost inflation, for payers, hospitals, and providers, by 10 percent per year. Thus, for example, health care growth limits were 9.4 percent in 1993, 6.2 percent in 1994, and were expected to drop below 5 percent in 1995. Under the law providers may not increase their revenues beyond an annually prescribed growth limit. Those who do so theoretically must pay an "assessment" to the Health Care Access Fund, although there has been no attempt or intention to enforce this provision of the law.

Second, the commission created six regions in the state to help foster planning and coordination of health care delivery to monitor and manage cost controls. Third, the commissioner of health retrospectively reviews major technology purchases in excess of $500,000 to determine their necessity, as well as monitoring the effectiveness and outcomes of various treatment methods (i.e., so-called practice parameters). Finally, the 1995 legislature approved moving all of those receiving subsidized health insurance under MinnesotaCare into managed care programs. State officials expect that this process will be mostly completed by the beginning of 1997.

In addition to a regulatory approach to cost containment, Minnesota has also proposed relying on marketplace competition. Central to this strategy was the proposed creation in 1993 of a system of statewide Integrated Service Networks (ISNs) "that provide the full range of acute and preventive care to a defined enrolled population for a pre-determined, [annual] capitated premium. They may be formed by HMOs, insurers, hospitals, providers, local governments, purchasers, or by a combination thereof."[7] ISNs, which are similar to HMOs, would compete on the basis of price and quality for both the public and private health care markets in the state. The 1993 law directed the commissioner of health to recommend to the legislature the necessary statutory language and administrative rules to establish and encourage the creation of the provider networks. In 1995 the commissioner reported to the legislature that in the department's judgment ISNs were not necessary because the marketplace was naturally moving toward managed care, and recommended repealing the ISN provision. In 1996 the legislature suspended the legislative mandate to the health department to write the rules for the ISNs. In effect, however, the state has gradually been revising the rules governing HMOs in a way that will have the consequence of moving an increasing proportion of Minnesotans into managed care. According to one state legislator, "In reality what we are doing is we're changing the HMO laws so that they are like what we wanted for ISNs."[8]

Thus, although ISNs are a dead issue, the idea of containing costs through the use of competition among managed care providers remains a central, albeit not legislatively mandated, feature of the Minnesota reform. In fact, the state is already far ahead of the nation in terms of embracing HMO-style managed care, with about one-fourth of all Minnesotans enrolled in these programs, compared with a national average of about 19 percent. If one adds other forms of managed care, such as preferred provider organizations

(PPOs), the number of Minnesotans in this provider environment increases to nearly one-half of the population.

Expanding Access for the Uninsured

For most of the current decade, approximately 9 percent of Minnesota's population has been without health insurance. The majority of the uninsured earn too much to qualify for Medicaid but not enough to purchase private insurance, or do not work for businesses that offer employer-sponsored insurance. MinnesotaCare addresses the needs of this population. Beginning in October 1992 family members of children enrolled in the state's Children's Health Plan (CHP) became eligible for subsidized health insurance. Established in 1988, CHP had been providing health care to children in families with incomes up to 185 percent of the federal poverty level. MinnesotaCare extended CHP coverage to the families of these children and extended eligibility to those whose incomes fall below 275 percent of the federal poverty level (for a family of four in 1995, 275 percent equals $41,464), as well as to single adults and individuals without children with incomes to 135 percent of poverty level (for one person in 1995, 135 percent equals $10,092). In addition to the income requirements, to be eligible a person must not have had any health insurance for at least four months and had not been able to get employer-paid health insurance for the previous eighteen months. Benefits under the plan include both inpatient (up to a maximum of $10,000) and outpatient care. Approximately ninety-three thousand low-income Minnesotans who are ineligible for Medicaid receive subsidized health insurance under MinnesotaCare, the majority of whom are in prepaid, managed care plans. (There are about four hundred thousand Minnesotans, or 8.9 percent of the population—compared with a national average of about 15 percent—who are uninsured. As noted above, the legislature has set as its goal reducing that number to 4 percent by the year 2000.)

MinnesotaCare also addresses the cost and accessibility of private health insurance for the nonpoor. The 1991 Health Care Access Commission had found that thousands of Minnesotans had "individual insurance marred by high premium costs, high deductibles and stringent insurance underwriting policies which can result in policy denials, cancellations or pre-existing condition exclusions." Although many reformers favored individual and small-group-market community rating, strong Republican opposition prevented discussion of the issue. Hence, the law only went as far as eliminating gender-based rating from the entire insurance market, and established limits on different rates that insurers can charge for occupation and age. Insurers are, however, prohibited from denying coverage (i.e., guaranteed issue) or renewing coverage (i.e., guaranteed renewal) to small businesses with fewer than fifty employees because of the risks associated with a particular occupation or the health status of employees. This provision does not extend to the individual insurance market or to large and/or self-insured companies.

In addition, the law mandates that insurers offer health care coverage to persons with preexisting medical conditions after a waiting period of no longer than twelve months, even when an employee changes jobs (i.e., portability of coverage). Finally, the law makes the purchase of health insurance more affordable to employers (as well as nonemployment-based groups within a common geographic area) either by allowing them to form geographic- and occupation-based health insurance purchasing pools, or to purchase employee insurance through the Minnesota Employees Insurance Program (MEIP), a state-sponsored voluntary purchasing alliance. As of January 1995 about two hundred companies, with an average of eight workers, were enrolled in MEIP.[9] In both cases the goal is to enable employees and employers to get the more favorable insurance rates associated with large-group purchasing. Finally, on February 1, 1993, the legislature approved standardized health care insurance forms for all companies doing business in the state.

Although Minnesota has an international reputation for health care excellence, resources are not evenly distributed throughout the state. Rural Minnesota has a higher percentage of uninsured people than the rest of the state, and it has been faced with hospital closures and a loss of health care providers. MinnesotaCare addressed rural health care problems by creating an Office of Rural Health and Primary Care to improve health care planning and access. In addition, funds were made available to forgive state-funded loans to doctors, nurses, and other midlevel practitioners who serve in rural areas, increase the number of primary care residents at the University of Minnesota who will train in rural parts of the state, and help financially troubled rural hospitals.

Paying the Bill

No portion of the Minnesota plan generated more political conflict among legislators and interest groups than the funding proposal. Since I will discuss this issue below, I need only note here that the main battle was between advocates of an income tax surcharge (supported by health care providers, the hospital association, and certain key Democratic legislators, but vociferously opposed by Governor Carlson), and a 2 percent tax on gross revenues of providers and hospitals. Ultimately the provider tax, with a "passthrough" provision allowing physicians and hospitals to transfer the cost to health insurance plans, was approved.[10] In addition to the provider tax, MinnesotaCare is partially funded by various premiums and co-payments, such as a $3 co-payment for prescription drugs for adults, and a 10 percent co-payment for inpatient hospital care with an out-of-pocket maximum of $2,000 per individual and $3,000 per family. There are no co-payments for any services for children and pregnant women. Monthly premiums are based on a sliding fee scale depending upon income, and range from 1.5 percent for the lowest-income earners to 8.8 percent of gross family income for the highest; a family of four with a gross monthly income of $1,000 paid $18 per month in 1996. Finally, a five-cent per package cigarette tax was used for start-up costs and then transferred to the state's general fund.

Because the 1992 law and the accompanying legislative battle remains at the core of the Minnesota reform story, the rest of this chapter is devoted to chronicling that tale.

Prelude to Reform

As noted above, MinnesotaCare is the direct descendant of the 1987 Children's Health Plan. Initially CHP provided physician services for non-Medicaid-eligible, low-income pregnant women, and children under six years of age. The program was funded by an annual fee of $35 for pregnant women and $25 for children, and a one-cent per package cigarette tax. CHP, which was expanded in January 1991 to include all children through age eighteen, was one of the most successful and popular programs in the state. As such, it provided a good administrative and political base upon which to build MinnesotaCare.

In 1989 the Minnesota legislature created a twenty-five-member Health Care Access Commission to undertake a review of health care access problems in the state and to "develop and recommend to the legislature a plan to provide access to health care for all state residents."[11] The work and report of the commission provided the genetic material for MinnesotaCare. Two members of the Gang of Seven, Senator Linda Berglin (D) and Representative Paul Ogren (D), were commission members, and the commission's extensive research provided much of the empirical basis for MinnesotaCare.

The commission's proposals were broad and ambitious in scope. Briefly, the commission recommended that the state guarantee access to basic health care to all Minnesotans, subsidize the purchase of insurance for low-income (up to 275 percent of the poverty level) people, require insurance companies to use community rating, set statewide limits on health care spending, create reforms to control the administrative costs of insurers and providers, and consolidate the state's health care programs by creating a new Department of Health Care Access to improve administrative efficiency and service and to reduce costs.[12]

The commission's recommendations were incorporated into a Democratic-sponsored bill, Minnesota's Health Care Plan or House File 2. The bill sparked an unprecedented lobbying effort, involving a coalition of thirty groups called Minnesotans for Affordable Health Care (or simply, the Affordables). Supporters of H.F. 2 included health care providers, including the Minnesota Medical Association, farmers' groups, religious organizations, labor unions, and social advocacy groups. Spearheaded by the Affordables, these groups sent out thousands of postcards and petitions, held rallies across the state, lobbied every state legislator, and covered the state with lawn signs, buttons, bumper stickers, and billboards proclaiming "Health Care for **ALL** Now!" The bill did not, however, have Governor Carlson's support—or that of the insurance and business communities—and on June 3 the governor vetoed H.F. 2, charging that it was "budget-busting," contained no cost control mechanism, would increase insurance premiums for small-group employers and young people, and, perhaps most important, contained no long-term funding source.[13]

Significantly enough, it was the absence of a funding mechanism that probably held together the coalition in support of H.F. 2. As long as no one—providers, employers, workers—was being asked to make any financial sacrifices, diverse support was easier to sustain. Following the veto the governor invited legislative leaders to work with his administration, and other interested parties, to develop "an affordable solution to the health care access problem." "Our collective charge will be first to fashion a responsible proposal that serves all of Minnesota's citizens well, a proposal that Minnesota taxpayers can afford," Carlson expounded.

Attention next turned to the prospects of a veto override. Supporters advocated the effort when the legislature returned, but the prospects were not promising. The bill had passed by eight votes fewer in the House than were needed for an override, although it was likely to succeed in the Senate. As legislative supporters contemplated their next step, a chance meeting of minds and personalities occurred that determined the next stage in this journey.

The Policymaking Process

Anyone interested in health policy reform will find the process of policymaking in Minnesota at least as interesting and instructive as the substance of the reform. Even the participants in the process look back on the experience with a sense of amazement as well as accomplishment. Although the process followed in Minnesota may not be replicable elsewhere in all of its byzantine facets, it certainly offers one possible strategic approach to orchestrating consensus building, sustaining political will, and inoculating participants from the interest-group virus.

The Gang of Seven

Remember that by the fall of 1991 Minnesota politics hardly appeared conducive to a bipartisan approach to health care reform. Despite Governor Carlson's veto of H.F. 2, there were important political factors that dictated a reconciliation among the various players: the public wanted health care reform, the governor needed a political boost to revive his sagging popularity, and in 1992 the entire Minnesota legislature was up for reelection. As a Republican member of the Gang of Seven put it, "We realized that we needed each other; they had the votes and we had the veto."[14] Political reality thus became the midwife of reform.

Conception occurred in the summer of 1991 when Representative Paul Ogren, a liberal Democrat, and Representative Dave Gruenes, a conservative Republican, met at a Chamber of Commerce luncheon where both were to speak on health care reform and discovered substantial areas of mutual agreement. After the luncheon meeting Ogren and Gruenes continued to meet and talk about general principles and problems. Both agreed that expanded access and cost control were interrelated and should be central to any reform. As they went along they decided to bring additional House and Senate colleagues into the discussions. In the end, the group consisted of seven legislatively well-placed and experienced lawmakers, including the chairs or subcommittee chairs of the critical Health and Human Resources and Appropriations Committees, as well as key party leaders, each of whom was apparently committed to accommodation rather than partisan posturing. Indeed, there was an explicit agreement that they would try to avoid the partisan one-upmanship endemic in the typical legislative session. Neither of the political parties, nor any individual, would take credit for the end product. And, perhaps most important, each agreed that once the group concurred upon a bill, they would stand together in defending every part of it, even those provisions they might individually have opposed. Lobbyists would not be able to use a "divide and conquer" strategy.

Let the Games Begin

The Gang of Seven began to meet formally in the latter part of November 1991. Participants and their staff agreed not to speak with the media, lobbyists, or other legislators, except in the most general terms, about what was going on in the meetings. The group identified general issues and concepts that all agreed were essential to reform: cost control, expanding access for the uninsured, especially children, malpractice reform, rural health care problems, and creation of a health care access commission. In addition to operating by consensus and secrecy, there was another important procedural decision that helped facilitate political accommodation and avoidance of political intramurals: Governor Carlson agreed to stay out of the process until a bill was ready.

Despite all these precautions, in early March the entire amicable and consensual process threatened to unravel. The main problem involved the cost-control provisions of the final draft. Everyone had agreed, conceptually, on the need to control costs. When the specifics were spelled out, however, the Republicans were quite surprised at the scope and methods of the process. What they saw was a substantial new state bureaucracy, enforcing global budgeting right down into the individual health care provider's office. In addition, the draft contained a certificate-of-need provision that might halt, not merely slow, introduction of new technology. The whole process was far more regulatory than any respectable Republican could possibly be comfortable with, and they began to have second thoughts.

While disharmony was breaking out among the gang members, there was unhappiness in another quarter. The governor's staff had obtained a "bootlegged" copy of the draft, and they were "appalled" at what they saw for many of the same reasons that were giving pause to the Republican negotiators, namely, too much bureaucracy and state regulation.

Following a tense week of negotiations involving the Gang of Seven and the governor's office, an agreement was reached in the early morning hours of March 10, 1992, and outlined in a document called "Health Reform for Minnesota: A Proposal by the Bipartisan Health Care Working Group." In essence the agreement closely resembled the final MinnesotaCare law described above; a new insurance plan for the uninsured, modified community rating of health insurance policies, various measures to control costs, creation of an office of rural health to implement reforms to improve health care services in rural areas, and funding through cigarette and provider taxes.

MinnesotaCare on the Fast Track

The story of MinnesotaCare's first week in the legislative arena is the stuff of which legends are made. The negotiators had five working days to get the bill through six policy committees (i.e., nonrevenue/appropriations committees) in at least one chamber, to meet a deadline set by the legislative leadership. To expedite the process the gang introduced three separately numbered but identical versions of the bill in each chamber, thus allowing simultaneous consideration. In addition, the legislative leadership in both houses and in both parties agreed, with the governor's support, not to accept any amendments to the bill in the policy committees. Four days after it was introduced, the bill passed its sixth and final House policy committee. One lobbyist, reflecting angrily on this period, recalls testifying before two or three House committees and not being asked a single question.[15] The bill moved equally expeditiously through the Senate policy committees.

The Opposition Emerges

Once out of the policy committees, however, and with the elimination of any pressing deadline, MinnesotaCare ran into trouble. It must be remembered that interest groups knew little of the bill's content before its official unveiling. This, combined with the unprecedented speed with which it traveled through the policy committees, provided them with little time or information to understand and respond to the proposal. By the end of that first week, however, certain key stakeholders were sufficiently educated about the bill and its implications to know that they did not like it. Thus, by the third week in March opposition accelerated and the process slowed down. What followed was "an awesome lobbying campaign," according to Paul Ogren. "There were literally over a quarter of a million letters and faxes sent in to legislators, driven by insurance agents, by the medical association, by the hospital association. The ferocity of the opposition really can't be exaggerated."[16] Foremost among the emerging opponents were elements of the provider industry, particularly the Minnesota medical and hospital associations.

During the weekend following the tumultuous first week of MinnesotaCare's debut, the Minnesota Medical Association (MMA) leadership voted unanimously to oppose the bill. The association objected to the spending limits on health care and limits on the acquisition and use of new technology and procedures, the prohibition of balanced billing for Medicare patients (i.e., charging patients the difference between what Medicare would reimburse and what doctors actually charged), mandatory participation in medical assistance programs, and restrictions on provider ability to refer patients to services in which they had a financial interest.

But particularly troubling to the MMA was the proposed 2 percent provider tax, which the association characterized as a "sick tax" that penalized people for going to the doctor. The physicians' association believed that program funding should be more broadly based so that everyone contributed to its support. Backers of the provider tax argued that revenues should be drawn from current health care expenditures and thus serve, in part, as a cost-control mechanism. Furthermore, Republicans believed that there was more than enough money in the health care system to extend access to the uninsured and the provider tax was the best way of redistributing that money. Finally, the governor was absolutely opposed to any increase in what was already one of the highest state income taxes in the country.

The MMA began an aggressive lobbying effort against MinnesotaCare that included solicitation of patient signatures on petitions opposing the law, and a day of protest in which 450 physicians descended upon the state capitol to lobby lawmakers. Legislators reported being "fed up" with what they thought to be the arrogant, self-serving behavior of the physicians.[17]

The physicians were joined by the Minnesota Hospital Association (MHA), although the association's opposition was not nearly as unconditional. According to the chief lobbyist for the association, the MHA could have supported the bill if the legislature eliminated the mandatory Medicare assignment, modified, or better still, eliminated any certificate-of-need type of provision, and replaced the provider tax with a broad-based tax.[18]

Aside from these specific points, there was another issue lurking just beneath the surface that, according to John Kingrey of the hospital association, may have been the association's most fundamental concern. "I think our priority [concern] is the government involvement in the running of health care, and what we saw as the potential for a single-payer system ultimately being accepted."[19] This fear was shared by others, but especially those in the health insurance industry, another group that vehemently opposed the bill. Reacting to the reform proposal, the president of the Agents Coalition for Health Care Reform wrote to his members, "as the fine print was flushed [sic] out, it became clear that the intent of this legislation was no longer to fine tune a private sector health care industry but rather to replace the current system with a single-payer system, much like Canada."[20]

Provider opposition to the reform bill was strongest and most vocal in rural communities. This was especially so in the case of rural hospital administrators who saw their very existence threatened. The basis of this concern was twofold. First, the bill would exacerbate the already difficult task of recruiting and retaining physicians in rural areas. As one rural hospital administrator explained it, the bill's provision to establish practice parameters "would affect Minnesota in general, but it's already very difficult in rural areas to recruit physicians. Some doctors are going to look at those practice standards and feel the state is taking away their autonomy."[21]

The proposed reform threatened rural hospitals in another way. The 2 percent tax might push financially troubled rural hospitals over the brink. It was in large part for this reason that the Minnesota Farm Bureau Federation, the state's largest farm organization, representing about thirty-five thousand farm families, opposed the bill.

Not all members of the provider community opposed MinnesotaCare. Most notably, support came from the Minnesota Council of HMOs, representing ten HMOs with over one million members. In addition, an ad hoc coalition of providers was formed in support of MinnesotaCare and included the Minnesota chapter of the American Academy of Pediatrics, along with state associations representing nurses, psychologists, chiropractors, public health workers, mental health professionals, and the community health clinics. PASS, or the Providers' Alliance to Show Support, joined with over seventy other labor, educational, social advocacy, religious, and philanthropic organizations lobbying on behalf of the bill. Despite this enormous show of support, opposition from both the provider community and rural interests threatened the near fairy tale existence of the bill.

The first significant dose of reality came on April 8 when the full House Appropriations Committee eliminated most of the new technology controls from the bill. The following day the House Tax Committee, on a 17-to-15 vote, dealt the bill a near fatal blow by dropping the provider tax and replacing it with an income tax surcharge. This latter defeat was significant not merely because it undercut one of the major provisions of the bill, but also because it threatened the bipartisan coalition that had forged MinnesotaCare.

Republican negotiators were incensed at both the provider lobby and their fellow Democratic House negotiator, Paul Ogren. Ogren chaired the House Tax Committee and although he actually voted against the surtax, Republicans accused him of betrayal for not successfully resisting pressure from physicians and hospitals. One of the main dangers of the change was that Governor Carlson was unalterably opposed to an income tax increase. Curtis Johnson, one of the governor's emissaries to the gang, declared the Tax Committee's action "a vote to kill the bill."[22]

In addition to the squabbling over the tax and technology votes, there was another bit of disquieting news. The head of the reports and statistics division of the Human Services Department reported that the plan to cover the uninsured would cost, by 1997, not the originally estimated $200 million per biennium, but rather $540 million, and could reach $1 billion by the end of the decade. The new estimate had two immediate consequences. First, the Health Policy Coalition, a group of more than two dozen prominent business organizations, withdrew its support for MinnesotaCare. Second, the House Tax Committee voted to scale back enrollment and reduce state subsidies to the plan for the uninsured. The prospects for universal access were beginning to dim.

Meanwhile, the bill was having a somewhat less troubled trip through the Senate. After having gone unscathed in the policy committees, and the Taxes and Tax Law Committee, the bill went to the Finance Committee. Finance, much like its counterpart in the House, removed the technology controls and eliminated a one-year moratorium on new equipment and capital purchases that was intended to prevent a mad rush of purchases before the controls were put in place. Mindful of the new cost estimates, the committee changed the waiting period for eligibility from four months without insurance to one year. The bill passed the Finance Committee, 18 to 10, and was sent to the full Senate, where it was approved, 48 to 18.

On April 11 the House voted, 76 to 58, to approve MinnesotaCare, with sixty-nine Democrats and just seven Republicans in favor, and forty-nine Republicans and nine Democrats opposed. Despite an attempt by Paul Ogren to get the House to overturn his own Tax Committee's decision, the House rejected the health provider tax on a 91-to-42 vote. The bill would now go to a ten-member House-Senate conference committee to resolve the differences; all the members of the Gang of Seven were on the conference committee.

The Bill Goes to Conference

Despite some technical differences, the critical sticking points in the conference involved the financing (provider tax versus income tax surcharge) and eligibility provisions. Nevertheless, an agreement was hammered out over two exhausting days because virtually all the conferees recognized that this was not a bill that anyone in the legislature could walk away from; some decision, up or down, had to be made.

The financing mechanism was certainly the most difficult obstacle to overcome. The conferees found themselves between a rock and a hard place: accept the income tax surcharge and face an almost certain veto by the governor, or accept the provider tax and face possible defeat in the House, where that option had been overwhelmingly defeated (91 to 42) just a few days earlier. In a sense, of course, there really was no choice. The Gang of Seven, who were a majority of the conferees, were committed to supporting their original agreement; that meant a provider tax.

Ultimately, then, the Senate version, with the provider tax, prevailed. In order to make the tax more palatable to the House, the conference committee adopted a variety of strategies. First, the conferees agreed that the health care commission would review the provider tax after one year to determine if it was the appropriate vehicle for funding the program (it remains in place today). Second, the conferees sought to assuage the concerns, particularly strong among House members, about the potentially mammoth costs of the program, through more effective cost-control mechanisms. They scaled back the program in terms of benefits, most notably with a $10,000 limit on inpatient hospital services. (According to legislative staff estimates, about 85 percent of hospital admissions incurred expenditures under $10,000.)[23]

The conferees further decided to limit eligibility in the MinnesotaCare insurance plan. One of the main reasons for the recent upwardly revised cost of the program was the prediction that many of those in the individual insurance market would leave that market and enter the less costly state-subsidized program. The conference substantially reduced this possibility by requiring that people be uninsured for four months and without employer-provided insurance for eighteen months before entering the state-subsidized plan. In addition, the conferees imposed a six-month state residency requirement for coverage, thus discouraging people from coming to Minnesota just to enter the program.

Three further changes appeared to be aimed at physicians, perhaps in hopes of reducing their opposition: a five-year phase-in of the mandatory Medicare assignment, elimination of a felony penalty for the conflict-of-interest restriction on physician referrals to services in which they have a financial stake, substituting a $1,000 fine, and elimination of a certificate-of-need approval provision, substituting one that requires providers to inform the Department of Health when they make major purchases.

MinnesotaCare Becomes Law

The compromise bill now went back to both houses, where typically conference committee reports are approved routinely. This, however, was not a routine case. Remember that only five days earlier the House had rejected a provider tax by an overwhelming 91-to-42 margin. The compromise reached the House floor on April 15 where an emotional debate ensued, the roll was called—and a problem emerged. The number of those voting "yes" stopped at sixty-two, six short of the sixty-eight-vote majority needed for passage. At this point the House Speaker stopped the vote board clock to allow the leadership of both parties to round up the necessary majority. The Speaker called Governor Carlson and asked him to send aides over to the House chamber and to telephone Republican members on the floor, which the governor did. Finally, after sixty-five minutes the board was reopened and eight additional votes were registered in favor of the bill; the House passed MinnesotaCare on a vote of 70 to 64. Seventeen Republicans, ten more than had voted for the original House version, and fifty-three Democrats, sixteen fewer than had supported the original bill, voted in favor of it. And herein lies one of the last pieces of political controversy surrounding MinnesotaCare.

Republicans are convinced, and some Democrats have admitted, that the Democrats had the votes to pass the bill without additional Republican support. There were between ten and twenty more Democratic votes that the party leadership could have gotten if it had wanted them. The Democratic leaders, however, wanted to give some of their rural members a chance to avoid their constituents' ire by voting against the bill—over 85 percent of those who voted against MinnesotaCare came from rural parts of the state. To do this, they needed some Republican votes. Hence the Speaker's call to the governor.

Shortly after the House action, the Senate, in much less dramatic fashion, overwhelmingly approved MinnesotaCare, 49 to 18, after only brief debate.

Conclusion

There is by now something remarkably reminiscent about the progression of reform in Minnesota. Much like in Oregon and Vermont, a much her-alded, major policy departure ran aground on the shoals of state and national political reality. The result was revision, in some instances retreat, and ultimately a scaling back of the substance and promise of reform. Minnesota reformers, like their colleagues in Oregon and Vermont, began in the late 1980s and early 1990s with an ambitious vision of transforming their health care system and a sense that history and politics were on their side. Surely the time was ripe for a major reform of the American health care system. Progressive states, like Minnesota, would lead the way and, so most observers believed after the 1992 presidential election, the federal government would help complete the journey. But the federal government did no such thing. In fact, the failure of the Clinton plan itself became a major obstacle to advancing reform in Minnesota and elsewhere. Not only did states like Minnesota not get the federal help they needed to expand access and control costs, but the very notion of health care reform was tarnished by the spectacle of the 1993–94 national debate. This, combined with a national shift to the political right, and an overall improving economy, has robbed health care reform of the sense of political and economic immediacy and urgency that it had at the beginning of this decade.

The question that remains is: what are the relevance of and lessons to be derived from the Minnesota experience? Let me begin with a point that I made earlier in this book: the problems with the nation's health care system have not gone away simply because the federal government has done nothing about them. It is true that increases in the cost of health care have moderated, especially in Minnesota, in part because overall inflation has been reduced, and in part (again, particularly in Minnesota) because more people are moving into managed care.

Yet many problems remain. There are, for example, fewer people today covered by employer-based insurance than there were when health reform first appeared on the national policy agenda in the late 1980s. In Minnesota, for example, those covered by employer-based insurance fell from 65.7 percent in 1987 to 60.6 percent in 1992.[24] In addition, in many states women, people with preexisting medical conditions, or those who get new jobs or work in hazardous industries pay more for and have a more difficult time getting health insurance than other groups. Similarly, people in rural areas have poorer access to hospitals, physicians, and the most modern medical technology than their urban and suburban counterparts.

The MinnesotaCare reform has not solved all of these problems, but the state has made significant progress on these and others. It is illegal to charge women more for health insurance than men, and the differential rates for people in different age groups or occupations are limited by law; people with preexisting medical conditions cannot be denied health insurance for longer than a twelve-month waiting period, and can take their insurance to another job; small businesses cannot be denied access to basic health insurance for their employees and now have the opportunity to join insurance purchasing pools that enhance their bargaining and purchasing capacity; health care costs have moderated dramatically, and rural areas are receiving assistance to attract and keep health providers. And, perhaps most visible and important, nearly one hundred thousand low-income Minnesotans, most of whom would not have been able to purchase health insurance on their own, now have state-subsidized health insurance and the peace of mind that goes with such coverage. This may not be all that reformers hoped for, but it is far more than the federal government was able to achieve.

Where does Minnesota go from here? As noted earlier, the 1995 legislature eliminated or scaled back a number of MinnesotaCare's provisions, and the 1996 state Republican Party convention called for its outright repeal. Is reform, in one of the most progressive states in the nation, in jeopardy? Probably not. It is unlikely, to be sure, that much more progress can be made in Minnesota, or in any other state, in the absence of a statewide and/or national shift to the political left of the magnitude that occurred on the right in 1994—or in a dramatic reversal of fortunes for health care reform at the national level. On the other hand, I think it is equally unlikely that the state will abandon the core of what it now has. The reason for this—and I believe that this will be one of the health policy lessons emerging from the states in the 1990s—is that there is a constituency of one hundred thousand people, living in virtually every state legislative district, who now rely on MinnesotaCare for their health insurance, and many more for whom access to private insurance has been made more affordable because of the law. It will be politically, and morally, difficult to turn back the clock on these and others who have benefited from the reform.

I would like to close with an observation about the process of reform, and particularly the much criticized cabal-like approach of the Gang of Seven. The question here is: was the extraordinary secrecy surrounding the process really necessary, or could reform have proceeded more openly? This is a question of more than passing interest given the controversy over, and putative harm done by, the secretive deliberations of the Clinton administration's national task force on health care. The question is also relevant for would-be reformers in other states. For Minnesota's negotiators the answer is clear: "Could the process have been more open? Perhaps. Would we have been successful? I rather doubt it," was how one of them put it.[25] The private negotiations of the Gang of Seven inoculated them from the viral interparty and legislative-executive conflict that had caused the stalemate over H.F. 2. "Who said what to who, who said what about what, was to be kept private," said another negotiator. "This is what led us to be able to find out what we agreed on. It would've been impossible in a formal [open] context."[26] The decision by the governor to stay informed but out of the process until a proposed package was ready, and the implicit decision by the negotiators that this was not going to become a partisan issue, gave reform a chance. During the negotiations these seven legislators developed an esprit de corps and a sense of ownership over the emerging package. This was fostered by perhaps the group's most prescient procedural decision, namely, that once they reached an agreement on a particular provision they would all stand by that decision, regardless of their own or their party's position. For the most part, the social contract into which these seven legislators entered held up remarkably well.

There is another point that needs to be reiterated about the nature of the group that helps explain its success—and distinguishes it from the Clinton task force. Each of the seven was a legislator who held some position of formal authority and brought to the process exceptional experience in the health care policy process, along with a legislative insider's understanding of the issue. This gave the negotiators both the strategic advantage of controlling the process at various critical junctures, and the tactical advantage of knowing a good deal more about the issue than their colleagues. Although the critical negotiations took place outside the normal legislative process, the participants enjoyed the legitimacy and understanding that go with the role of elected official. Furthermore, although health care was not a traditionally Republican issue, the months of private negotiations leading up to MinnesotaCare helped bring the Republican negotiators up to speed and prepared them for dealing with their colleagues.

The decision to isolate health reform from routine partisan and intragovernmental bickering enhanced the prospects for its success. This approach, however, had mixed results with regard to interest-group politics, and perhaps the ultimate outcome of the process. For the Gang of Seven members, one of the virtues of their approach was that they would be insulated from pressure-group politics. They would decide who would know what and from whom to solicit information. The negotiators could take this approach in part because they were not dependent upon interest groups for information. Health reform had been such a well-plowed field in recent years that the group had about as much information on the various issues and problems as it ever was going to have. Thus, the negotiators did not need the lobbyists, as they so often do, for information. This freed them from the influence peddling that is the implicit quid pro quo in legislature-lobbyist information exchanges.

By not having to rely on lobbyists, or even to keep them informed, the gang had, of course, another tactical advantage. As one negotiator said, "we did take them by surprise," when the bill was finally made public.[27] It took lobbyists nearly a week to launch a counteroffensive, and by then the bill had cleared every House policy committee and some Senate committees as well. And, it did so without any significant changes. One lobbyist—a former state legislator—who was both sympathetic to the cause of reform and critical of the process admitted, "If this thing had been done by the normal process, you [the interviewer] wouldn't be here. There wouldn't have been a thing done. . . . I think in terms of good government . . . it's a real dangerous way to do business, but it was the only way this thing was going to happen."[28]

Yet there was a long-term cost associated with the process as well. Representatives of the provider groups, and particularly the Minnesota Medical Association, used such terms as "knifed in the back," "like Eastern Europe before the fall of communism," and "left out" to describe the process and their treatment. As a result, there may be less support for the reform today than there might otherwise have been if more groups had been brought into the process earlier. On the other hand, had the process been more open, there may not have been any reform at all.

Notes

Portions of this article originally appeared in Howard M. Leichter, "Minnesota: The Trip from Acrimony to Accommodation," *Health Affairs* 12 (summer 1993): 48–58. The material is reprinted by permission of Project HOPE. The People-to-People Health Foundation. Health Affairs, 7500 Old Georgetown Road, Suite 600, Bethesda, Md. 20814

1. Intergovernmental Health Policy Project, "Health Care Reform: Fifty State Profiles" (Washington, D.C.: George Washington University, July 1994).

2. It should be noted here that the original 1992 law was called HealthRight, but because of a copyright dispute the name was changed to MinnesotaCare. To avoid confusion, I will use this latter term throughout the chapter. Confusion cannot be completely avoided because the term MinnesotaCare is used, officially, to designate two aspects of the reform, namely, the state-subsidized health insurance program for low-income Minnesotans, and the overall package of reform measures. I will try to make clear to which I am referring in the text.

3. The phrase comes from Allan N. Johnson, "Health Reform is a Journey, Not a Destination," *Minneapolis Star Tribune,* January 21, 1995, 15A.

4. Although I will use the terms "Democrat" and "Republican" in this paper, the actual titles of the two parties in Minnesota are the Democratic-Farmer-Labor Party (DFL), and the Independent Republican Party (IR).

5. Minnesota Health Care Access Commission, *Final Report to the Legislature* (January 1991), 4. Emphasis supplied as in original.

6. State of Minnesota, HealthRight Law, Chapter 549, Article I, Section 1.

7. Minnesota Department of Health, *MinnesotaCare: A Comprehensive Summary of Health Care Reform in Minnesota, 1992–1995* (St. Paul: Minnesota Department of Health, September 1995), 6.

8. Representative Lee Greenfield, telephone interview by author, June 5, 1996.

9. See Dan Wascoe, Jr., "A State of Flux: Universal Health Insurance in Minnesota by 1997," *Business and Health* 13 (February 1995): 43.

10. In 1995 the provider tax survived a court challenge by several self-insured companies claiming the tax was a violation of the 1974 federal Employee Retirement Income Security Act (ERISA).

11. Minnesota Health Care Access Commission, *Final Report,* 2.

12. Ibid., 5–6.

13. Veto Message of Governor Arne Carlson, June 3, 1991.

14. Representative Dave Gruenes, interview by author, August 13, 1992. Hereafter, Gruenes interview.

15. John Kingrey, senior vice president of the Minnesota Hospital Association, interview by author, August 14, 1992. Hereafter, Kingrey interview.

16. Representative Paul Ogren, interview by author, August 10, 1992.

17. Donna Halvorsen, "Doctors at Capitol Tell Health-Care Bill Fears," *Minneapolis Star Tribune,* April 1, 1992.

18. Kingrey interview.

19. Ibid.

20. James A. Walker, chairman, Agents Coalition for Health Care Reform, "Legislative Alert," March 24, 1992.

21. Al Zdon, "Health Industry Rallies against Bill," *Hibbing* (Minn.) *Daily Tribune,* March 18, 1992.

22. Donna Halvorsen, "Tax Change Threatens to Sink HealthRight Measure," *Minneapolis Star Tribune,* April 9, 1992.

23. Dennis Lien, "Health Care Conferees Drop Income Tax Proposal," *St. Paul Pioneer Press,* April 16, 1992.

24. Minnesota Department of Health, *MinnesotaCare,* 2.

25. Gruenes interview.

26. Lee Greenfield, interview by author, August 10, 1992.

27. Linda Berglin, interview by author, August 11, 1992.

28. John Clawson, executive director, Community Clinic Consortium, interview by author, August 12, 1992.

10

Health Care Reform in Kansas: A Policy Before Its Time

Raymond G. Davis and Barbara E. Langner

Kansans have traditionally approached major policy issues with care, caution, and in a process of open consultation. Health care reform policy, Kansas policymakers found, required more. They discovered that a timely and expansive approach was required to engage the state's chronic health care policy problems. Reform became a priority issue in Kansas, as elsewhere, because the state faced the dual problems of increasing costs and decreasing access but had little ability to resolve these problems with conventional, incremental policies. Reform also rose to a higher priority as a consequence of President Clinton's election and his proposed national health care reform. Kansas and other states were forced to consider how they were going to respond to the national proposal.

The Kansas approach to health care reform, which emerged from recommendations of previous commissions and task forces, was the creation of a single, semiautonomous commission charged with drafting a comprehensive reform proposal. The result was the Commission on the Future of Health Care, Inc., or 403 Commission, which was created in 1991 and reported its recommendations to the legislature and governor in 1994. The commission had broad scope and authority, but what helped make it viable was the leadership of Dr. William Roy, a physician who had served in the Congress from 1971 to 1975 and was an expert on health policy issues.[1]

Problems of Cost and Access

At the end of the 1980s, health care reform was an idea whose time had come to the country and to Kansas. Kansas, like many other states, had been forced to consider comprehensive changes in the way health care was paid for and delivered as a result of increasing difficulty in financing the Medicaid program, coupled with the impression among legislators that there were growing access problems.[2] State general fund monies devoted to medical assistance more than doubled from 1980 to 1990—from $81 million to $188 million. Even with that level of spending, the number of uninsured individuals continued to rise. Perhaps as important, in 1990 the supplemental appropriation request to cover the unanticipated growth in the medical assistance program reached 22 percent of the original appropriation as the result of a series of federal mandates.[3] The mandates ranged from changes in the age of children to be covered in Medicaid-eligible families to changes in the oversight and compliance required of states in certifying nursing home eligibility for reimbursement. At issue at the time was whether the federal government was going to take the initiative to reform the "Medicaid problem." It seemed likely that President Bush would be reelected and it was thus unlikely that a federal solution to health care cost and access problems would emerge.

A Search for Options

Elected state leaders were uneasy about state government undertaking comprehensive health care reform because the problems driving change were not clear. When legislators focused on problems of access and cost, they found a politically volatile and complex issue. Kansas legislators could not fully comprehend the problem or, consequently, explain it to their constituents. For many legislators, reform started with access and cost and burgeoned into recommendations for changing the entire health care system. Incremental approaches to reform promised marginal relief at best but would fail to address the underlying causes of increased cost and decreased access.

Marginality

The authority and capacity of the state to engage the problems of cost and access were also restricted. As policy solutions were considered for particular health care problems, the state frequently found that it had only marginal authority to address the problem. In the beginning, discussions about reform focused on the increasing number of Kansans who were uninsured or under-insured, as well as on the unrelenting increases in cost, as health care consumed an ever larger portion of the state's resources. Kansas, like other states discussed in this volume, was constrained in what it could do in the area of public and private insurance reform by federal Medicaid and ERISA legislation. Additional barriers were created by the enormous influence that health care providers and insurers exert when faced with changes in reimbursement or eligibility.

Kansas had well-qualified and capable legislative and executive staff to assist in policymaking; however, the state lacked the policy research capability to delve into a policy issue as complex and comprehensive as health care reform. In addition, the state government rejected playing an active role in defining the options for significant policy decisions. The state also had not invested in data gathering and analysis to deal with comprehensive reform.

Searching for Answers

During the 1980s Kansas policymakers employed a dual approach in addressing health care issues, initially dealing with narrow problems (for example, extending liability coverage under the Kansas Tort Claims Fund to physicians who volunteer at indigent care clinics) through incremental policy initiatives and later forming study panels to deal with broader issues. Beginning in 1986, Kansas undertook a more comprehensive approach to exploring options that would address how to limit state government costs, coordinate executive and legislative initiatives, and control cost increases and/or limit the range of services.

Commissions

From 1986 through the early 1990s, the executive and administrative branches of the state government established various commissions charged with the tasks of examining the underlying cost and access issues and formulating recommendations. Most of the commissions' recommendations were never implemented, a failure of linking findings with action illustrated in Table 10.1.

In addition to the issues of cost and access, the state also addressed problems in its public health system. The Kansas Public Health Association, in cooperation with the state Department of Health and Environment and the Association of Local Health Officials, conducted a thorough review of the state public health system. These groups concluded, as had the national Institute of Medicine, that the public health system was in disarray.

Table 10.1

Commission Actions

Commission	Recommendation	Action
Commission on Access to Services for the Medically Indigent and the Homeless	All Kansans should have access to health services and the state should improve its health data and research	No action
Commission on Health Care	Creation of a state health authority	No action
Task Force on Social and Rehabilitation Services	Improvement of services available to children	Action on only minor sections

The report suggested that substantial changes needed to be made in how state and local governments financed public health, and suggested that the capacity of health departments in terms of human resources, physical plants, and treatment authority was inadequate. No action, however, was taken on the report.

The legislature's first major step toward structuring itself to engage its health care cost and access problems was made in 1990. In that year, the legislative Commission on Access to Services for the Medically Indigent and the Homeless recommended the creation of a bipartisan standing Joint Committee on Health Care Decisions for the 1990s. The membership of the Joint Committee came from standing committees that had jurisdiction over health-related issues. Thus, for the first time the legislature had a committee with a global perspective and the experience and authority to draft comprehensive health policy legislation.

Incremental Policy Solutions

Many of the incremental policy initiatives adopted by Kansas policymakers during the 1980s and early 1990s focused on specific barriers to access, especially those created by current health insurance practices and the inadequate supply of rural health care providers. The problems of rural Kansas were threefold: how to assure that a health care delivery system continues in rural areas, to enhance the variety of rural medical and health care services, and to recruit and retain health care providers in rural Kansas. The problem of recruitment and retention was exacerbated during the 1980s and 1990s by the financial strain on rural hospitals and the decline of rural economies.

There have been several federal and state attempts to develop more coherence in the rural health care system in Kansas. The federal government supported rural systems through the Essential Access Community Hospital-Rural Primary Care Hospital (EACH-RPCH) Program, foundations created the Kansas Health Foundation's Integrated Community Health Development program, hospitals and other providers created various systems, and small hospitals and providers attempted to build systems from the bottom up. Rural health issues first appeared on the state policy agenda as a result of efforts by the Kansas Hospital Association and an initiative funded by the Kansas Health Foundation—called the Integrated Community Health Development (ICHD) program—to offer assistance to local communities that wished to integrate their local hospitals into a broader health care system. The twin issues of how to maintain a rural health care system as well as offer incentives for providers to locate in rural areas were part of the state's habit of defining problems narrowly rather than dealing with underlying causes.

Another incremental approach to the state's problems was through modification of insurance laws. Between 1990 and 1992 the state enacted a series of insurance reforms, including making insurance more portable, limiting the exclusion of enrollees with preexisting conditions, regulating rate increases for different insured groups, and extending access to health insurance for small businesses. Yet insurance reform alone could not solve state access and cost problems.

The conventional approach of piecemeal, incremental reform was inadequate to the task. Kansas legislative leaders knew that health care problems were imposing in their complexity, scale, and importance. Hence the creation of the independent Kansas Commission of the Future of Health Care, Inc. The commission elected a chairman who had a vision of how to deal with the problems and the ability to bring a majority of the commission to a plan.

Caution Turns Bold—The 403 Commission

The Joint Committee on Health Care Decisions for the 1990s operated at a time when national health care reforms seemed a remote possibility, and a half-dozen states that couldn't wait for a federal solution were creating innovative approaches to the underlying problems. At its monthly meetings, the committee explored in depth the health care reform initiatives adopted or under consideration by other state legislatures.

The Inception

Energized by those discussions about states that were proactively dealing with health care cost and access issues, a core group of legislators became committed to reforming Kansas health care. The group identified the processes used in other states that seemed influential in moving health care reform from the idea stage to enacted legislation. The result, in 1991, was S.B. 403, which included proposals for comprehensive reform, adequate financing, creation of a small but representative group of citizens who were insulated from political pressure, an adequate time period to create a viable plan, sustained communication between the group and policymakers, who ultimately would have the responsibility for enacting the recommendations, and engagement of the public in the construction of the health care reform plan. The bill was approved by the governor on May 23, 1991, after a unanimous vote in the Senate (May 4, 1991) and by a vote of 105 to 20 in the House (May 2, 1991). All twenty votes against the bill were cast by Republicans.

S.B. 403 created an eleven-member commission—the Kansas Commission on the Future of Health Care—with representatives from provider, labor, and other outside groups appointed for three-year terms. The legislative charge given the commission was fourfold:

1. Develop a long-range health care policy plan, including both short- and long-term strategies.
2. Identify the social values of Kansans.
3. Provide a forum for Kansans to participate in the development of health policy.
4. Report periodically, but not less than semiannually, to the governor and the Joint Committee on Health Care Decisions for the 1990s.

The statute stipulated that the governor would select one board member from nominees from each of the following: the Kansas Hospital Association, the Kansas Medical Society, the Kansas State Nursing Association, the Kansas Chamber of Commerce, the Kansas AFL-CIO, and the Kansas Association of Osteopathic Medicine. The governor would also appoint a board member trained in health care ethics. The remaining board members were appointed by the majority and minority leaders of the Kansas House and Senate.

Shortly after S.B. 403 became law in May 1991, legislative leaders, representatives of the nominating organizations, and the governor met to develop a process for determining commission membership. This preplanning was intended to yield a commission representing the diversity of the state as well as having the necessary expertise. This approach was novel in coordinating the appointments across parties and branches, and signaled a realization that the tasks assigned to the commission would require consensus if public and legislative ownership of this reform were to be achieved.

Slow Start-Up

It was not until mid-September that ten of the eleven appointees were announced, and the next month the last appointee was named. Late in October, the president of the Senate convened the first meeting of the group, voicing the hope that the group would come to the legislature with a plan to restructure the health care system, identify the prevailing grassroots social values, and recommend a public-private financing mechanism to move the system forward.

Even after the commission was created, circumstances kept it from devoting its full energies to the ambitious assignment. During the 1991 legislative session the Kansas legislature passed both authorizing and appropriation legislation without Governor Joan Finney's involvement. The governor, a Democrat, approved the legislation creating the commission but not the funding because of her pledge to veto any new spending. Thus, before the 1992 legislative session began the commission was forced to spend a considerable amount of time lobbying the governor and legislature for adequate funding, and crafting a fund-raising campaign to acquire private sector financial contributions. More than 150 private foundations, corporations, and special interest groups were approached in this campaign. Eight groups responded positively—one foundation and seven professional organizations interested in the commission's deliberations made contributions totaling $80,000.

During the next (1992) legislative session, the legislature and the governor "strongly supported the goals of the commission but directed the commission to continue to aggressively seek financial support from foundation grants and other private sources, and recognized, however, that private financing was unlikely to materialize until the state indicates a financial commitment to the commission."[4] Private fund-raising activities were only moderately successful although considerable in-kind donations were obtained from a variety of sources, including the media, which helped the commission achieve its legislative charges.

Planning Activities

The commission used a multistage community-interaction strategy to provide a forum for Kansans to participate in the development of health policy and to elicit information about Kansans' social values. In three types of statewide public meetings (Critical Issues Health Forums, Kansas Health Values Forums, and Citizen Input Meetings), information was collected from Kansas citizens and used to develop the Kansas Specific Health Care Reform Plan.

Critical Issues Health Forums were the commission's first entry into local communities, held through the fall of 1992. These forums provided public education about health care issues and stimulated public participation in the development of health policy. The project was initiated with a three-week statewide collaborative media information campaign in print, television, and radio. Following this media blitz, twenty-five town meetings were held across the state utilizing a structured format developed by the Public Agenda Foundation. Citizens attending town meetings had the opportunity to weigh the advantages and disadvantages of the three most commonly discussed approaches to health care reform: minor changes in the existing system, national health insurance, and employer-mandated health insurance. More than forty-five hundred Kansans responded to questionnaires about values distributed in newspapers and at the town meetings. The majority of respondents supported universal access to comprehensive health care and vehemently opposed limits being placed on choice of providers. Given the three policy options, 34 percent of Kansas respondents preferred a national health insurance program, 33 percent favored an expanded version of the current system, and only 19 percent preferred employer-mandated insurance coverage.[5]

The next statewide community meetings were the Kansas Health Values Forums held in the spring of 1993, which were patterned on the Georgia Health Decisions model. The purpose of these forums was to discover the values and principles that Kansans believed should underlie the health care system. At the twenty-five values forums participants responded to two exercises. The first asked them to prioritize resource allocations using seven case scenarios. Consistently, participants gave a high priority to ranking resource allocations that targeted prevention, yielded favorable cost-benefit health outcomes, have proven effectiveness, improved the quality of life, increased the years of productivity, or aimed at early intervention. The second exercise identified twenty attributes of a health care system frequently deemed important, and participants were asked to rank the most desirable of these attributes in an ideal health care system. Almost universally, participants identified affordable health care for all, assured quality of care, choice of doctor, quality of life, and right to decide, as the most desirable attributes of any health care system.[6]

Paradoxes in the citizen input at these two sets of town meetings highlighted the difficulty of developing reforms that would be embraced by the

Table 10.2

Inclusion Criteria Derived from Public Forums

Universal coverage
Comprehensive benefits
Equitable financing
Incentives for efficiency and effectiveness
Cost containment
Consumer choice of provider
Administrative simplicity
Flexibility
General acceptability to providers and consumers
Fiscal responsibility

public. Participants emphasized that access to health care for all Kansans was essential, for example, but substantial numbers asserted that they did not want to be told that they had to carry or buy health care insurance.

The commission used the input from forums to develop criteria for inclusion of specific policy options in the comprehensive health care reform plan. Agreement among commissioners on the essential ingredients of any long-range health care policy plan provided a mechanism to judge competing policy options. The commission's adoption of universal access as a major criterion of reform predetermined that the plan would be a comprehensive reform model; other critical issues identified by the commission are shown in Table 10.2.

The Changing Political Climate

The political climate had changed greatly by the time the commission began to develop the comprehensive health care reform plan during the summer and fall of 1993. Several factors had an impact on the state agenda, including events at the national level. Harris Wofford's election to the Senate from Pennsylvania in 1992 signaled a rise to prominence of health care reform on the national policy agenda. Kansas, however, treated the Wofford election as an isolated event rather than marking a trend. Clinton, on the other hand, interpreted the Wofford election as signaling the public's support for health care reform, and after the presidential election placed reform on the top of his policy agenda. After Clinton took office, the Kansas policy calculus changed as the president's health reform initiative began to overwhelm the commission's agenda. The state now had to be concerned about its authority to address problems and to anticipate that federal reforms would create greater responsibilities for and obligations on the state. As a result, the commission adopted the position that its reform plan should complement federal reform activity.

The Plan

The Kansas Commission on the Future of Health Care presented its plan to the legislature and governor in January 1994. The plan addressed what the commission thought were the fundamental problems with the health care system status quo:

- Many Kansans were uninsured (a minimum of 13 percent), and those with health insurance coverage had benefit packages heavily skewed toward sick care services.
- Consumer choice in provider selection was rapidly eroding; selection was made by employers and insurers.
- Interference in the critical health care decision-making process from third party payers was decreasing opportunity for provider and patient input.
- Perverse financial incentives were rewarding providers for delivering greater volumes of services.
- A significant portion of health care dollars was not being spent to purchase health care services.[7]

The Commission's Recommendations

The commission created a comprehensive reform plan that attempted to deal with those fundamental flaws. The Kansas Specific Health Care Plan included a set of complementary policy options that would preserve valued elements of the current system but would remove the perverse incentive structure fueling escalating costs. All legal Kansas residents would have access to health care services, including health promotion and disease prevention interventions. Individuals would enroll to receive services from a health service network or a fee-for-service provider of their choice. Health service networks would be organized by the providers and would each determine the amenities they would offer enrollees, the method of provider payment, the extent to which managed care strategies would be integrated, and the availability of nonbenefit-package services within the network. Competition between networks would be based on those factors, quality of services, makeup of the provider panel, and enrollee satisfaction, rather than on price.

The Health Care Purchaser for All Kansans, a five-person, governor-

Figure 10.1 **Kansas Specific Health Care Plan**

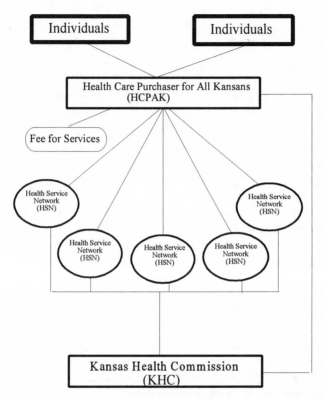

appointed commission, would be responsible for collecting premiums from enrollees and making payments to health service networks and fee-for-service providers. The establishment of a single entity responsible for financing and administration would greatly decrease administrative costs and increase the proportion of health care dollars spent for direct health care services. The Health Care Purchaser for All Kansans would also perform ombudsman duties.

The Kansas Specific Health Care Plan, diagrammed in Figure 10.1, maintained the ability of consumers to choose their provider and eliminated interference by third-party payers in the medical decision-making process, two attributes highly valued by Kansans. The development of seamless delivery systems (health service networks) maximized system efficiency and the utilization of capitation as the primary payment mode encouraged providers to make wiser resource utilization decisions. In the commission's plan the insurance industry was removed from its pivotal role in defining health care, and the primacy of the relationship between patient and provider was restored. In the words of the *Wichita Eagle,* the plan "proposes to retain the best elements of the current medical system: choice for patients, competition and high-caliber medical services. But it also proposes to eliminate its flaws: lack of coverage for thousands of Kansans, costly duplicative paperwork and misallocation of medical resources."[8]

The commission recognized the formidable fiscal and political constraints surrounding legislative endorsement of its comprehensive health care reform plan. It recommended a phased-in approach that would enable the legislature to study the commission's recommendations and prepare to implement the reform plan. It requested the legislature to establish the Kansas Health Commission, which would undertake the critical preliminary tasks needed to implement the plan. An incremental strategy was chosen for two primary reasons: it bought time to educate and influence policymakers about the merit of this comprehensive approach, and financing would be more feasible if the plan was phased in.

Leadership, Brokerage, and Experts

The political landscape in Kansas changed dramatically following the 1992 elections, when the Republicans regained control of the state House of Representatives. In 1994, the conservative wing of the Republican Party took control of the House by deposing the incumbent Speaker. This signaled an ideological rather than a political turn. In 1991, when S.B. 403 was passed with endorsement of the leadership of both House and Senate, power was evenly balanced between the two houses—the Democrats controlled the House and the Republicans were in power in the Senate.[9] After the 1994 election, the Republicans firmly controlled both houses of the legislature, with the House taking a decidedly conservative bent. The Democrats continued to control the governor's office. The governor, however, prided herself on having a limited agenda that included few social issues, none of which related to health care.

Although commission members worked well together, they lacked bipartisan political heavyweights who could broker the recommendations through the legislature and the governor's office. Bill Roy, a former Democratic congressman, was more influential among Democrats than Republicans. When the Democrats lost control of the House in 1992, not only was the Democratic voice muted but the more heavily conservative Republican majority was hostile to any expansion of the role of government. In addition, no prominent political leader, Democratic or Republican, championed health care reform. Governor Finney (1991–95) exhibited little interest in health care reform and showed even less interest in the value of policy research and information. No Republican in a leadership position advocated health policy reform either before or after the Commission on the Future of Health Care made its report. The major provider and insurance groups stood on the sidelines during reform deliberations; these groups did not want to appear to be obstructionist to a legislative commission. Moreover, when the commission's direction became apparent, they became less interested in trying to publicly influence its recommendations and more interested in privately influencing the reception that it would receive among legislative leaders.

During the deliberations of the commission, the Senate Public Health and Welfare Committee, with support from the Kansas Health Foundation, sought the advice of a number of national health care experts. Seminars were held in the state and were open to any legislator interested in attending. The presentations were academic introductions to the problems and may have convinced some legislators that the problems and proposed solutions were complex and politically risky. Legislators found it difficult to see the relevance of many of the presentations. The presentations, they thought, tended to have a Washington "inside the beltway" focus.

The eleven members of the commission were of diverse ideological and political persuasions. This diversity proved to be a strength because it reflected the opinions of Kansas citizens, thus providing the commission with a preview of the likely response of the population to particular policy options. The members, who met monthly for lengthy sessions, repeatedly discussed, debated, voted on, and often revisited all elements of the plan. In December 1993 nine commissioners voted to approve the plan, and two commissioners signed a minority report emphasizing their opposition to governmental intrusion in the delivery of health care. The minority report, signed by the one prominent Republican on the commission, was a preview of the later reception the "Roy Report" would get from the Republican leadership. Roy had a plan but he did not have a consensus.

By 1994, the legislative environment that had created the commission in 1991 had changed in two important respects. The legislature changed from being equally divided between the two parties to a partisan environment with both houses controlled by the Republicans. In addition, the imperative of national reform was rapidly vanishing from the national political agenda. The 1994 Kansas legislature no longer had a compelling reason to act. The opportunity window for consideration of health reform in Kansas had been open for a short period of time and then closed, and in any case probably was open only for a proposal that was far less ambitious. The legislature and governor never explicitly rejected the commission's proposal; rather, they refused to give it consideration. The proposal never even received a public hearing.

Popguns and Problems—The Ground Shifts

Health care reform reached the policy-making agenda in Kansas but receded quickly because of complications that muddled the next step—the specification of alternatives from which a policy choice could be made. Kansas's early attempts at health care reform (pre-1991) were linked to problems of access, as well as cost and alternative choices. Once the process turned to choices that might engage access and cost, the policy-making prospects became both complex and blurred.

In this complex environment, suddenly the focus of the legislature and the commission changed as a result of the Clinton initiative to impose a federal health care reform framework. The Kansas legislature changed from proactive to reactive. When the Clinton plan failed, the rationale for Kansas reform disappeared. Earlier, the state was trying to propose ways to address complex policy problems in an incremental fashion. Later, with the commission, the state was trying to address the issues of access and cost as well as respond to the Clinton initiative through a more comprehensive structure. If Clinton's proposal passed and the states were obligated to comply, Kansas faced great uncertainties about the effectiveness of proposed solutions and its response. The 403 Commission was the state's planning response.

A series of impediments hindered the success of the 403 Commission:

- Perceptions about Bill Roy: The legislative reaction to the proposed reform plan of the 403 Commission was influenced by the impression that the ideas in it were solely the work of Bill Roy. The bill that was introduced incorporated the commission's recommendations, but it was dubbed "the Roy Bill" by legislative staff. Roy, an active Democrat who had been honored by the Democratic Party at a dinner while on the commission, was seen by Republicans purely in partisan terms.
- The Governor's resistance: Governor Joan Finney, who was in office at the creation of the 403 Commission, was a veteran political campaigner but a novice at governance. Neither she nor anyone on her staff had a background in health policy. After signing the legislation creating the 403 Commission, she vetoed a $50,000 appropriation to support its operation. This appropriation had been carefully negotiated between legislative leaders to leverage private funds for the support of the commission. The governor did not appear to be aware of the legislative negotiations and was more concerned about new legislative appropriations during her first year in office.

- The Clinton eclipse: As the work of the 403 Commission evolved, the Clinton administration was formulating its health reform proposal. By early 1993, the Clinton proposal had been presented to the public in a series of national forums. As attacks began to mount on the complexity and ambitiousness of the reform, the proposal advanced by Dr. Roy and the majority of the commission came under similar criticism—too much, too soon, too risky. As the Clinton proposal ebbed from the national agenda, the imperative for reform in Kansas waned as well.
- The Health and Environment proposal: The secretary of the state Department of Health and Environment provided a way for the legislature to avoid engaging the 403 Commission proposal by presenting his own alternative. The secretary, an appointee of the governor but seemingly acting on his own, proposed using the state employees' insurance system as a base that would be expandable to a coalition of employers in the state with little market power to buy affordable health care for their employees. The secretary presented a Band-Aid proposal; the commission had suggested major surgery. The secretary's proposal, however, allowed the legislature to focus on a less comprehensive yet politically safer proposal.
- Shifting ground: Kansas legislators and others had difficulty adopting a comprehensive approach to health care reform. They were more comfortable with a more modest policy-making process. The 403 Commission proposed a comprehensive, ambitious approach, but the legislature, the governor, providers, insurers, other health-related organizations, and the public were unprepared for such scope. The legislature rejected it out of hand. It was too much for Kansas.[10]

The Dilemma

Both the Kansas legislative and executive branches learned to be cautious from the experiences of the late 1980s and early 1990s. The state's leadership, much like its national counterparts, mastered one of the inexorable lessons of American politics—to get too far ahead of public opinion and events generates considerable risk. In Kansas, the dual issues of cost/access and anticipated national reform offered significant risk to state policymakers. In this dynamic environment, caution was advised. As a consequence, Kansas opted to allow marketplace reform of the health care system and to not impede changes ongoing in the market affecting health care, including

Medicaid managed care in Kansas and elsewhere. There is little evidence, however, that a market approach to reform will truly address the problems of cost and access. Nevertheless, this approach does have the advantage of shifting political risk from elected officials to the private sector.

Although initiating reform before Clinton's election, Kansas learned again the influence of the federal government on state policy options. The Clinton plan at first preempted action in Kansas and later, with its demise, left Kansas without momentum for reform. The Clinton plan "stole the wind" from any state initiative, particularly from the recommendations of the 403 Commission.

Kansas also discovered that in proposing a solution to the state's health care cost and access problems, caution was double-edged. From 1982 to 1990, the state was cautious in addressing reform through a series of executive and legislative task forces with limited power. This approach was unsuccessful. In 1991, the state attempted a much bolder approach, and it was equally unsuccessful. The simultaneous problems of increasing costs, decreasing access, and improving the appropriateness and quality of health care delivery are issues that require a comprehensive approach, yet comprehensiveness invites opposition and uncertainty. The 403 Commission offered an unconventional approach to generating policy recommendations. The commission was a private corporation, appointed for three-year terms, with a cross section of members appointed by legislative leaders and the governor, and it had the promise of public-private funding. The commission's initial recommendations to the legislature at first suggested an incremental approach but in reality its approach was comprehensive. The cautiousness of the Kansas response was predictable, as were the concerns of health care providers and insurers.

The heath care issues that gave rise to the creation of the commission in 1991 are still present today. Kansas continues to have a policy problem that it cannot escape—substantial costs to the state general fund and significant numbers of uninsured—for which market reforms only approximate a solution. The state has no policy-making structure to confront health care problems and propose solutions.

The reform experience in Kansas demonstrates the critical need for leaders who understand the policy issues and who can avoid getting stuck in a policy cul-de-sac. Bill Roy knew the issues and was willing to point in the direction the state should take, but he was a minister without portfolio. He brought to the health reform discussion an exceptional understanding of the issues, the ability to craft a cogent solution, but no formal power base. Equally important, the reform experience documents the need for political leadership from the legislature and governor in order to make any policy recommendation viable. In Kansas, there was no legislative or executive leadership on health reform and the result was predictable—the 403 Commission's comprehensive policy recommendations died without a hearing.

The Kansas experience also points to the need for congruence between the structure a state establishes to explore reform and the dominant values of the state in general, and the legislature and governor in particular. The Kansas health reform story was marked by a substantial change in party dominance in the legislature along with the election of a governor who was not a significant player in policy issues. Together these events had a significant effect on health reform.

The vital lesson learned "by the five states who had the gumption to tackle the 800-pound gorilla of health care reform," was the absolute necessity of mobilizing political will.[11] This failed to occur in Kansas. This political inertia, reinforced by the defeat of the Clinton health reform proposal, removed any incentive for action by the legislature.

Notes

1. During his tenure in Congress, William H. Roy, M.D., J.D., was the author of or played a principal role in several major national health policy laws, including the Health Maintenance Organization Act, the Health Professionals Education Act, the Health Manpower Act, and the National Health Service Corps Act. Roy served on the Health and Environment Subcommittee of the House Energy and Commerce Committee. In 1974, he was narrowly defeated in his senatorial race against Bob Dole, winning 49.1 percent of the vote against Dole's 50.9 percent. After this defeat he returned to Kansas and served on a variety of policy boards in the public and private sectors.

The 403 Commission and Roy's chairmanship were noted as the entry of Kansas among the states that "couldn't wait." Dr. Roy was invited to attend the Milbank Memorial Fund meeting in 1992, before the commission began considering its plan, as a representative of three states "identified as making substantial progress in enacting health care reform legislation." See Commission on the Future of Health Care, minutes (November 2, 1992), 2.

2. Don Wilson, president of the Kansas Hospital Association, testimony to the 403 Commission, December 17, 1991. Wilson commented that a study conducted by the KHA in 1986 had established that 13 percent of Kansans were without health insurance. Even with these data, the commission did not have any accurate *trend* data about access. There was a strong perception among the legislative leadership that access problems were increasing. This was the reason for the creation of the predecessor to the 403 Commission—the commission on Access to Services for the Medically Indigent and the Homeless. The 403 Commission assumed that several insurance reform measures—for example, state exemption of small-employer insurance benefit packages and creation of a catastrophic insurance pool—were not remedying the access problem.

3. Raymond G. Davis, "Public Health Policy: Perplexing Problems and Proximate

Policies," in *Public Policy and the Two States of Kansas,* ed. H. George Frederickson (Lawrence: University Press of Kansas, 1994), 72.

4. Kansas Legislature, House Bill 2720, House Appropriations Subcommittee Recommendations #16 (February 1992), 6.

5. The *Wichita Eagle* and *Topeka Capitol Journal* funded a statewide telephone survey in support of the commission's values project.

6. Commission of the Future of Health Care, *Critical Issues Health Forums: A Town Meeting Project* (February 1993).

7. Commission on the Future of Health Care, *Kansas Health Values Project* (December 1993).

8. David Aubrey, editorial page editor, "Proposed Health Plan Would Work for Kansas," *Wichita Eagle Beacon,* August 3, 1993, 6A.

9. Commission on the Future of Health Care, *Kansas Specific Health Care Plan: Final Report to the Governor and the Joint Committee on Health Care Decisions for the 1990s* (Topeka, January 1994).

10. A preview of the controversial nature of the proposal was the reception that Dr. Roy and the staff of the commission received from the Kansas Life and Health Insurance Guaranty Association meeting in Topeka. Dr. Roy shared a panel with a state congressman and the state insurance commissioner. Roy, who had received a standing ovation from this same group the previous year, was booed by the crowd as he approached the podium.

11. Daniel M. Fox and John Iglehart, eds., *Five States That Could Not Wait* (New York: Milbank Memorial Fund, 1994), 1.

Selected Bibliography

Acs, Gregory, Stephen H. Long, M. Susan Marquis, and Pamela Farley Short. "Self-Insured Employer Health Plans: Prevalence, Profile, Provisions, and Premiums." *Health Affairs* 15, no. 2 (1996): 266–78.

Boeckelman, Keith. "The Influence of States on Federal Policy Adoption." *Policy Studies Journal* 20, no. 3 (1992): 365–75.

Bowman, Ann O'M., and Richard C. Kearney. *The Resurgence of the States.* Englewood Cliffs, N.J.: Prentice-Hall, 1986.

Brown, Lawrence D. "The National Politics of Oregon's Rationing Plan." *Health Affairs* 10 (June 1991): 28–51.

Butler, Patricia A. *Roadblock to Reform: ERISA Implications for State Health Care Initiatives.* Washington, D.C.: National Governors' Association Center for Policy Research, 1994.

Cantor, Joel C., Stephen H. Long, and M. Susan Marquis. "Private Employment-Based Health Insurance in Ten States." *Health Affairs* 14 (summer 1995): 199–211.

Chi, Keon S. "Trends in Executive Reorganization." *Journal of State Government* 65 (April–June 1992): 33–40.

Clark, Jane Perry. *The Rise of a New Federalism: Federal–State Cooperation in the United States.* New York: Columbia University Press, 1938; reprinted, New York: Russell and Russell, 1966.

Conlan, Timothy. *New Federalism: Intergovernmental Reform from Nixon to Reagan.* Washington, D.C.: The Brookings Institution, 1988.

Derthick, Martha. "Crossing Thresholds: Federalism in the 1960s." *Journal of Policy History* 8, no. 1 (1996): 64–80.

Dowell, Emery B., and Thomas R. Oliver. "Small-Employer Health Alliance in California." *Health Affairs* 13 (summer 1994): 350–51.

Elazar, Daniel J. *The American Mosaic: The Impact of Space, Time, and Culture on American Politics.* Boulder, Colo.: Westview Press, 1994.

Enthoven, Alain C. *Theory and Practice of Managed Competition in Health Care Finance.* New York: Elsevier Science Publishers, 1988.

Enthoven, Alain C., and Sara J. Singer. "Market-Based Reform: What to Regulate and by Whom." *Health Affairs* 14 (spring 1995): 105–19.

Erikson, Robert S., Gerald C. Wright, and John P. McIver. *Statehouse Democracy: Public Opinion and Policy in the American States.* New York: Cambridge University Press, 1993.

Fallows, James. "A Triumph of Misinformation." *Atlantic Monthly,* January 1995, 26–37.

Fox, Daniel M. "Negotiating Health Problems." In *The State, Politics and Health: Essays for Rudolf Klein*, ed. P. Day, D. M. Fox, R. Maxwell, and E. Scrivens. Cambridge, Mass.: Blackwell Publishers, 1996, 95–106.

Fox, Daniel M., and John Iglehart, eds. *Five States That Could Not Wait*. New York: Milbank Memorial Fund, 1994.

Fox, Daniel M., and Howard M. Leichter. "Rationing Care in Oregon: The New Accountability." *Health Affairs* 10 (summer 1991): 7–27.

———. "The Ups and Downs of Oregon's Rationing Plan." *Health Affairs* 12 (summer 1993): 66–70.

Fox, Daniel M., and D. C. Schaffer. "Health Policy and ERISA: Interest Groups and Semi-Preemption." *Journal of Health Politics, Policy and Law* 14 (summer 1989): 239–60.

Friedman, Emily. *The Aloha Way: Health Care Structure and Finance in Hawaii*. Honolulu: Hawaii Medical Service Foundation, 1993.

Gardner, Annette, and Deane Neubauer. "Hawaii's Health QUEST." *Health Affairs* 14 (spring 1995): 300–304.

Gardner, John. Introduction to *The Sometime Governments: A Critical Study of the Fifty American Legislatures*, Citizens Conference on State Legislatures. New York: Bantam Books, 1971.

Ginzberg, Eli. "Improving Health Care for the Poor: Lessons from the 1980s." *Journal of the American Medical Association* (February 9, 1994), 465.

Hall, Mark A. "The Political Economics of Health Insurance Market Reform." *Health Affairs* 11 (summer 1992): 108–24.

Hansen, Karen. *Living With Term Limits*. Denver and New York: Milbank Memorial Fund and National Council of State Legislatures, forthcoming, 1997.

Heclo, Hugh. "The Clinton Health Plan: Historical Perspective." *Health Affairs* 14 (spring 1995): 86–98.

Helms, W. David, Anne K. Gauthier, and Daniel M. Campion. "Mending the Flaws in the Small-Group Market." *Health Affairs* 11 (summer 1992): 7–27.

Hill, Kim Quaile. *Democracy in the Fifty States*. Lincoln: University of Nebraska Press, 1994.

Institute for Health Policy Solutions. *State Experience with Community Rating and Related Reforms: A Report for the Kaiser Family Foundation*. Washington, D.C., 1995.

Intergovernmental Health Policy Project. *Fifty State Profiles: Health Care Reform*. Washington, D.C.: George Washington University and the Henry J. Kaiser Family Foundation, October, 1995.

Jewell, Malcolm E. "The Neglected World of State Politics." *Journal of Politics* 44 (August 1982): 638–57.

Johnson, Haynes, and David S. Broder. *The System: The American Way of Politics at the Breaking Point*. Boston: Little, Brown and Company, 1996.

Kaiser Commission on the Future of Medicaid. *Medicaid in Transition*. Washington, D.C.: Kaiser Family Foundation, October 1995.

Kettl, Donald F. "The Maturing of American Federalism." In *The Costs of Federalism*, ed. R. T. Golembrewsky and A. Wildavsky. New Brunswick, N.J.: Transaction Publishers, 1984.

Key, V. O. *American State Government: An Introduction*. New York: Alfred A. Knopf, 1956, reprinted 1963.

Leichter, Howard M. "Health Care Reform in Vermont: The Next Chapter." *Health Affairs* 13 (winter 1994): 78–103.

———. "Health Care Reform in Vermont: A Work in Progress." *Health Affairs* 12 (summer 1993): 71–81.

————. "Minnesota: The Trip from Acrimony to Accommodation." *Health Affairs* 12 (summer 1993): 48–58.

Lewin, John C., and Peter Sybinsky. "Hawaii's Employer Mandate and Its Contribution to Universal Access." *Journal of the American Medical Association* 269, no. 19 (May 19, 1993): 2538–43.

Mashaw, Jerry L., and Theodore R. Marmor. "Can the American State Guarantee Access to Health Care?" In *The State, Politics and Health: Essays for Rudolf Klein,* ed. P. Day, D. M. Fox, R. Maxwell, and E. Scrivens. Cambridge, Mass.: Blackwell Publishers, 1996, 61–76.

McKay, David. *Domestic Policy and Ideology: Presidents and the American State, 1964–1987.* New York: Cambridge University Press, 1989.

McLaughlin, Catherine G., and Wendy K. Zellers. "The Shortcomings of Voluntarism in the Small-Group Insurance Market." *Health Affairs* 11 (summer 1992): 28–40.

Mongan, James. "Anatomy and Physiology of Health Reform." *Health Affairs* 14 (spring 1995): 99–101.

Moon, Marilyn, and John Holahan. "Can States Take the Lead in Health Care Reform?" *Journal of the American Medical Association* 268 (September 23/30, 1992): 1588–94.

Nathan, Richard P. "Federalism—The Great 'Composition.'" In *The New American Political System,* ed. Anthony King, 2d version. Washington, D.C.: American Enterprise Institute, 1990.

Nelson, Harry. *Federalism in Health Reform: Views from the States That Could Not Wait.* New York: Milbank Memorial Fund, 1994.

Neubauer, D. "Hawaii: A Pioneer in Health System Reform." *Health Affairs* 12 (summer 1993): 31–39.

O'Brien, David M. "Federalism as a Metaphor in the Constitutional Politics of Public Administration." *Public Administration Review* 49 (May 1989): 411–49.

Oliver, Thomas R., and Emery B. Dowell. "Interest Groups and the Political Struggle over Expanding Health Insurance in California." *Health Affairs* 13 (spring II 1994): 123–41.

Osborne, David. *Laboratories of Democracy.* Boston: Harvard Business School Press, 1990.

Pound, William. "State Legislative Careers: Twenty-Five Years of Reform." In *Changing Patterns in State Legislative Careers,* ed. Gary F. Moncrief and Joel A. Thompson. Ann Arbor: University of Michigan Press, 1992.

Reeves, Mavis Mann. "The States as Polities: Reformed, Reinvigorated, Resourceful." *Annals of the American Academy of Political and Social Sciences* 509 (May 1990): 83–93.

Reforming States Group. *Information for Accountability in Health Care Purchasing: A Report on Collaboration Between the Private and Public Sectors.* New York: Milbank Memorial Fund and the Reforming States Group, 1996.

Rogal, Deborah, and W. David Helms. "Tracking States' Efforts to Reform Their Health Systems." *Health Affairs* 12 (summer 1993): 27–30.

Rothman, David. "A Century of Failure: Class Barriers to Reform." In *The Politics of Health Care Reform,* ed. James A. Morone and Gary S. Belkin. Durham: Duke University Press, 1994.

————. "A Century of Failure: Health Care Reform in America." *Journal of Health Politics, Policy and Law* 18 (Summer 1993): 271–86.

Rowland, Diane, Barbara Lyons, Alina Salganicoff, and Peter Long. "A Profile of the Uninsured in America." *Health Affairs* 13 (spring II 1994): 283–87.

Sharkansky, Ira. *The Maligned States.* New York: McGraw-Hill, 1978.

Skocpol, Theda. "The Rise and Resounding Demise of the Clinton Plan." *Health Affairs* 14 (spring 1995): 66–85.

Sparer, Michael S. "States in a Reformed Health System: Lessons from Nursing Home Policy," *Health Affairs* 12, no. 1 (1993): 8.

———. *Medicaid and the Limits of State Health Reform.* Philadelphia: Temple University Press, 1996.

———. "States and the Health Care Crisis." *Journal of Health Politics, Policy and Law* 18 (summer 1993): 503–13.

Steinmo, Sven, and Jon Watts. "It's the Institutions, Stupid! Why Comprehensive National Health Insurance Always Fails in America." *Journal of Health Politics, Policy and Law* 20 (summer 1995): 329–72.

Stone, Deborah A. "The Struggle for the Soul of Health Insurance." *Journal of Health Politics, Policy and Law* 18 (summer 1993): 287–317.

———. "Why the States Can't Solve the Health Care Crisis." *American Prospect,* no. 9 (spring 1992).

Sundquist, James. *Making Federalism Work.* Washington, D.C.: The Brookings Institution, 1969.

U.S. Advisory Commission on Intergovernmental Relations. *Federal Regulation of State and Local Governments: The Mixed Record of the 1980s.* Washington, D.C.: Government Printing Office, July 1993.

———. *Federal Statutory Preemption of State and Local Authority: History, Inventory, and Issues.* Washington, D.C.: Government Printing Office, September 1992.

———. *The Question of State Government Capability.* Washington, D.C.: Government Printing Office, January 1985.

U.S. Congress. General Accounting Office. *Access to Health Care: States Respond to Growing Crisis.* GAO/HRD–92–70, 1992.

Wiebe, Robert H. *Self-Rule: A Cultural History of American Democracy,* Chicago: University of Chicago Press, 1995.

Wilsford, David. "States Facing Interests: Struggles over Health Care Policy in Advanced Industrial Democracies." *Journal of Health Politics, Policy and Law* 20, no. 3 (fall 1995): 571–613.

Wise, Charles, and Rosemary O'Leary. "Is Federalism Dead or Alive in the Supreme Court?" *Public Administration Review* 52 (November-December 1992): 559–72.

Zimmerman, Joseph F. *Contemporary American Federalism: The Growth of National Power.* Westport, Conn.: Praeger Publishers, 1992.

———. *Federal Preemption: The Silent Revolution.* Ames, Iowa: Iowa State University Press, 1991.

Index